our address
NUESTRA DIRECCIÓN

MW00572301

STREET *CALLE*

CITY *CIUDAD*

STATE *ESTADO*

ZIP *CODIGO POSTAL*

PHONE NUMBER *NUMERO DE TELEFONO*

emergency contacts
CONTACTOS EN CASO DE EMERGENCIA

1.
NAME *NOMBRE*

RELATIONSHIP *RELACIÓN*

☐ HOME *CASA*
☐ OFFICE *OFICINA*
☐ CELL *CELULAR*

TEL 1

☐ HOME *CASA*
☐ OFFICE *OFICINA*
☐ CELL *CELULAR*

TEL 2

2.
NAME *NOMBRE*

RELATIONSHIP *RELACIÓN*

☐ HOME *CASA*
☐ OFFICE *OFICINA*
☐ CELL *CELULAR*

TEL 1

☐ HOME *CASA*
☐ OFFICE *OFICINA*
☐ CELL *CELULAR*

TEL 2

3.
NAME *NOMBRE*

RELATIONSHIP *RELACIÓN*

☐ HOME *CASA*
☐ OFFICE *OFICINA*
☐ CELL *CELULAR*

TEL 1

☐ HOME *CASA*
☐ OFFICE *OFICINA*
☐ CELL *CELULAR*

TEL 2

health insurance information
INFORMACIÓN DE SEGURO MÉDICO

INSURANCE COMPANY *COMPAÑIA DE SEGURO*

GROUP/POLICY NUMBER *NÚMERO DE GRUPO/ NÚMERO DE POLIZA*

POLICY HOLDER'S NAME *NOMBRE DEL ASEGURADO*

POLICY HOLDER'S ID NO. *NÚMERO DE IDENTIFICACIÓN DEL ASEGURADO*

known allergies
ALERGIAS

NAME *NOMBRE*   ...IS ALLERGIC TO *ES ALERGICO(A) A*

NAME *NOMBRE*   ...IS ALLERGIC TO *ES ALERGICO(A) A*

NAME *NOMBRE*   ...IS ALLERGIC TO *ES ALERGICO(A) A*

NAME *NOMBRE*   ...IS ALLERGIC TO *ES ALERGICO(A) A*

NAME *NOMBRE*   ...IS ALLERGIC TO *ES ALERGICO(A) A*

NAME *NOMBRE*   ...IS ALLERGIC TO *ES ALERGICO(A) A*

ENGLISH / SPANISH

Bilingual Babycare

bridging the communication gap
between parents and caregivers

MIMI TOWLE

PUBLISHED & DISTRIBUTED BY OAM SOLUTIONS, INC.
SAN FRANCISCO, CA   WWW.LILAGUIDE.COM

the lilaguide: bilingual babycare –
english/spanish

Written by: Mimi Towle

Published by:
OAM Solutions, Inc.
139 Saturn Street
San Francisco, CA 94114, USA
Tel: 415.252.1300
orders@lilaguide.com
www.lilaguide.com

After observing countless toddlers babble effortlessly in Spanish at our local park, my husband and I knew we wanted this same 'early language immersion' for our kids. So when it came time to find childcare, we faced a rather unusual challenge in addition to the usual issues such as; personality, cost, and schedules. We wanted someone who would speak Spanish with our children.

The only problem with this plan was that most of the Spanish-speaking sitters we encountered spoke little to no English, and our Spanish was limited to favorite foods and basic greetings. What if our children were in a dangerous situation, and we needed to communicate with their nanny about something important? We certainly didn't want a language barrier to diminish the quality of our children's care. Assuming there would be books or websites we could turn to for help, we took our chances with a wonderful non English-speaking nanny. Much to our surprise, despite the hundreds of English/Spanish translation and childcare books on the market, there wasn't anything that covered both topics.

So we decided to write our own! The book you now hold in your hands is the result of over five years of collaboration with parents in similar 'Spanish immersion' childcare situations.

Whether your childcare needs are part-time, full-time, luxury or necessity, we hope this book will enrich your relationship with your child's nanny or babysitter.

Disfrute! Have fun!

We hope Bilingual Babycare will become a Rosetta stone for parents and their child's caregiver. For the English speaker we have eleven chapters broken down by subject followed by nine chapters for the Spanish speaker. The entire book (except for a few pages written as guidance) is bilingual, and intended to be passed back and forth between parent and caregiver.

Emergency Contact Forms

Perhaps the most useful tools are the charts in the front of the book. We put these as the very first pages for easy access, in case of an emergency. Fill them out immediately, show them to your childcare provider and keep the book in a central location.

Quick Looks

Each chapter starts off with a 'quick look' page listing a handful of common terms used in that chapter. All of these words are translated in the glossary in the back.

Chapters

We have broken down the information consisting of phrases one might need during the course of a day. Some chapters have a few subsections while others only have one. Within the phrases you will see **p##**. This means that in the glossary on that specific page you will find a list of words to choose from to finish that particular phrase.

Glossary

This glossary is designed to help you or your childcare provider find that specific word (or something close enough) to communicate. For example, if you are looking for the word *sidewalk* – check 'Urban Destinations', in the Activities section. Looking for avocado, it's a fruit and can be found in the Food section under fruits (along with tomatoes). The sections are broken down as follows: Baby Basics; a list of baby related words, Everyday Phrases; common words and phrases, People; family member, descriptions and careers, Time, Digits & Days; number related, Nature; flora, fauna and words about the weather, House Words; rooms and cleaning terms, Food; from breakfast to dessert, Activities; Indoor and outdoor fun, Clothes; from getting dressed to laundry terms, Health & Safety; injuries and symptoms, Useful Verbs; some conjugated and infinitive forms.

Navigating these sections should be easy. However everyone's mind works differently, therefore we suggest taking a few minutes to thumb through the following pages to familiarize yourself with what words are available and how to find them in the future.

In some instances we have added the beginning of a typical sentence to help communicate a complete thought. For instance, instead of pointing at your pouting tot and saying "cansado" meaning "tired", we've added "The baby is __. El bebé está __." Simply piece the sentence together and you've got: The baby is tired. Or, take it a step further and add a name.

A–Z Vocabulary

These last few pages of each language section are for quick reference on words found in this book.

Health and Saftey

Throughout the book you will find health and safety phrases, or published information throughout the book. We have verified the accuracy of the information to the best of our abilities with various health and government agencies. Since it is unlikely that your nanny will pick up this book during an earthquake, we suggest that you ask him/her to read through the Englsh – Spanish chapters four and eleven as a review tool. Another step towards peace of mind would be to enroll your nanny or babysitter in a CPR and first aid course.

Getting the Words Right

In Spanish, nouns are either feminine or masculine. Masculine nouns are preceded by the article "el", and feminine nouns are preceded by the article "la". Adjectives usually come after the noun, with the masculine adjectives often ending in 'o' (as in 'bueno') and the feminine ones in 'a' (as in 'buena'). Throughout the book you will see o(a) after certain words, pick the appropriate one according to the gender of the noun.

Another tricky aspect to English – Spanish translations is that Spanish has both formal and informal ways of saying "you". The first two chapters were translated in the formal 'usted', since we can assume you don't know the job candidate yet. From chapter three on, we chose the informal 'tu', since it is considered the more appropriate way to speak to someone you know well.

This book is designed to aide the reader in the translation of words and phrases from English into Spanish and vice versa. It is sold with the understanding that the information contained in the book represents the author and publisher's subjective opinion about the relevance of the phrases and the accuracy of their translations.

The publisher and author shall have neither liability nor responsibility to any person or entity with respect to any loss or damage caused, or alleged to have been caused, directly or indirectly, by the information contained in this book.

If you do not wish to be bound by the above, you may return this book to the publisher for a full refund.

We'd like to thank the many friends who helped us think of, organize and translate the hundreds of phrases and words that make up this book.

The first group of Spanish translators including, Sindy Davila, Leucrecia Coomber and Sally Gallagher, were invaluable, followed by Serra Simbeck, our meticulous and thoughtful Spanish editor, who was able to create consistent and correct translations as well as share her valuable point of view as a mother of three. Finally, Mauricio Simbeck, a native of Mexico City, thank you for reading and re-reading this manuscript for authenticity and accuracy.

Agencies such as the USDA, Food And Safety Institute, American Association of Poison Centers, the United States Geological Services were helpful in providing prevention and safety information.

Additional thanks to the skilled English speaking editors Julia Bourland, and Stephanie Durran and the design help from Satoko Furuta and Liz Fiorentino.

And last, but certainly not least, our families for inspiring the topic and enduring the process of creating this book.

Gracias!

bilingual babycare

English

to

Spanish

1

introduction
introducción

introduction

. . . .

apartment	*el apartamento*
baby	*el bebé*
bus	*el autobús*
bus stop	*la parada del autobús*
car	*el coche*
child	*el niño/la niña*
children	*los niños*
city	*la ciudad*
come in	*pase/adelante*
country	*el país*
daughter	*la hija*
family	*la familia*
good afternoon	*buenas tardes*
good evening	*buenas noches*
good morning	*buenos días*
good-bye	*adiós*
hello	*hola*
house	*la casa*
husband	*el esposo*
interview	*la entrevista*
name	*el nombre*
nanny	*la niñera*
neighbor	*el vecino*
neighborhood	*la vecindad/la colonia*
pet(s)	*la(s) mascota(s)*
please	*por favor*
profession	*la profesión*
son	*el hijo*
state	*el estado*
thank you	*gracias*
train	*el tren*
transportation	*el transporte*
welcome	*bienvenidos*
wife	*la esposa*
work	*el trabajo*

meeting & greeting
el primer encuentro

Hello	*Hola*
Please come in.	*Pase por favor.*
Nice to meet you.	***Mucho gusto.***
My name is __.	*Mi nombre es __.*
This is my...	***Él/Ella es mi...***
– husband.	**– *esposo.***
– wife.	**– *esposa.***
– partner.	**– *pareja.***
– p 92.	**– *p 184.***
His/Her name is __	*Su nombre es __.*
What is your name?	***¿Como se llama usted?***
Thank you for coming.	*Gracias por venir.*
Would you like some...	***¿Le gustaría...***
– water?	**– *agua?***
– juice?	**– *jugo?***
– coffee?	**– *café?***
– tea?	**– *té?***

about our family
acerca de nuestra familia

We have...	***Tenemos...***
– a boy/a girl.	**– *un niño/una niña.***
– two children.	**– *dos niños.***
– three children.	**– *tres niños.***
We have…	*Tenemos…*
– twins.	*– gemelos.*
– triplets.	*– triates.*
Our...	***El nombre de ...***
– son's	**– *nuestro niño***
– daughter's	**– *nuestra niña***
...name is__.	**... *es__.***
He/She is…	*Él/Ella tiene…*
– p 95 years	*– p 187 años.*
– p 95 months	*– p 187 meses.*
…old.	
We have...	***Tenemos...***
– a dog	**– *un perro***
– a cat	**– *un gato***
– p 98	**– *p 190***
...named__.	**... *que se llama__.***

what we do
nuestro trabajo

I am/My spouse is <u>p 94</u>.	***Yo soy/Mi esposo(a) es <u>p 186</u>.***
I don't work and will be in and out of the house.	*Yo no trabajo. Estaré entrando y saliendo de la casa.*
I work/My spouse works... **– at home.** **– at an office.**	***Yo trabajo/Mi esposo(a) trabaja*** ***– en la casa.*** ***– en una oficina.***
I work/My spouse works... – full time. – part time.	*Yo trabajo/Mi esposo(a) trabaja...* *– tiempo completo.* *– medio tiempo.*
I leave/My spouse leaves the house at <u>p 95</u>.	***Yo salgo /Mi esposo(a) sale de la casa a las <u>p 187</u>.***
I come /My spouse comes home at <u>p 95</u>.	*Yo regreso/ Mi esposo(a) regresa a la casa a las <u>p 187</u>.*
I go/my spouse goes to work... **– by car.** **– by bus.** **– by train.**	***Yo voy/Mi esposo(a) va a trabajar...*** ***– en coche.*** ***– en autobús.*** ***– en tren.***

our neighborhood
nuestra vencindad

Our address is __.	***Nuestra dirección es __.***
Our... – upstairs – downstairs – nextdoor ...neighbor's name is__.	*Nuestro vecino de...* *– arriba* *– abajo* *– la casa de junto* *...se llama__.*
– The grocery store **– The park** **– The bustop** **... is located__.**	***– El supermercado*** ***– El parque*** ***– La parada del autobús*** ***...está__.***

2

about the job
acerca del trabajo

about the job

....

afternoon	*la tarde*
car	*el coche*
compensation	*la compensación*
contract	*el contrato*
driver's licence	*la licencia de manejar*
extra hours	*horas extras*
full-time	*tiempo completo*
health insurance	*el seguro médico*
(to) hire	*contratar*
hourly	*por hora*
hours	*las horas*
house cleaning	*la limpieza de casa*
laundry	*el lavado de ropa*
legal resident	*el residente legal*
meal(s)	*la(s) comida(s)*
month	*el mes*
morning	*la mañana*
night	*la noche*
part-time	*medio tiempo*
passport	*el pasaporte*
question(s)	*la(s) pregunta(s)*
salary	*el sueldo*
taxes	*los impuestos*
(to) drive	*manejar*
transportation	*el transporte*
week	*la semana*
weekend	*el fin de semana*
work	*el trabajo*
working visa	*la visa de trabajo*
year	*el año*
monday	*el lunes*
tuesday	*el martes*
wednesday	*el miércoles*
thursday	*el jueves*
friday	*el viernes*
saturday	*el sábado*
sunday	*el domingo*

interviewee background
antecedentes del entrevistado

Where are you from?

¿De dónde es usted?

Do you have children?

¿Tiene hijos?

How old...
– is your child?
– are your children?

¿Cuantos años...
– tiene su hijo?
– tienen sus hijos?

What type of job are you looking for...
– full-time?
– part-time?
– live-in ?
– live-out?

¿Qué tipo de trabajo está buscando...
– de tiempo completo?
– de medio tiempo?
– de vivir en casa?
– de vivir fuera de la casa?

Can you...
– read
– write
...English?

¿Puede...
– leer
– escribir
...en Inglés?

Where do you live?

¿Dónde vive usted?

How long have you lived in this area?

¿Cuánto tiempo tiene viviendo en esta área?

Why did you move to this area?

¿Porqué se mudó a esta área?

Do you have any special requirements, such as...
– taking care of anyone else?
– picking up your kids from school?

¿Tiene alguna necesidad especial, como...
– cuidar a alguien más?
– recoger a sus hijos de la escuela?

How do you feel about working for a stay-at-home mom?

¿Cómo se siente trabajando para una mujer que se dedica a la casa?

Do you have a car?

¿Tiene coche?

Do you have a driver's license?

¿Tiene licencia de manejar?

What do you do in your spare time?

¿Qué le gusta hacer en su tiempo libre?

Are you a smoker?

¿Fuma?

Are you CPR certified?

¿Tiene certificado de RCP?

Will you take a CPR class if I pay for it?

¿Tomaría una clase de RCP si yo la pago?

Do you know how to swim?

¿Sabe nadar?

Are you available for...
– weekends
– evening babysitting
...in addition to your regular job?

¿Está disponible para trabajar...
– los fines de semana
– en las noches
... además de su horario regular de trabajo?

WORK HISTORY

Have you worked as a nanny before?

What were your responsibilities?

Why do you want to work as a nanny?

How long did you work for the last family?

How many children did you care for?

Have you ever cared for twins/triplets?

What types of things do you like to do with the children?

What did you like most about your last position?

What did you like least about your last position?

Why did you leave the last family?

Do you have a list of references, including the last family you worked for?

Is it OK if I call them?

LEGAL

Are you a US citizen?

May I check your legal documents?

May I see your...
 – social security card?
 – driver's license?
 – passport?
 – work visa?

Could you make me a photocopy of these documents?

EXPERIENCIA DE TRABAJO

¿Ha trabajado cuidando niños?

¿Cuáles eran sus responsabilidades?

¿Porqué quiere trabajar cuidando niños?

¿Cuánto tiempo trabajó con la última familia?

¿A cuántos niños cuidaba?

¿Ha trabajado cuidando gemelos/triates?

¿Qué cosas le gusta hacer con los niños?

¿Qué fue lo que más le gustó de su último trabajo?

¿Qué fue lo que menos le gustó de su último trabajo?

¿Porqué dejó de trabajar con la última familia?

¿Tiene una lista de sus referencias de trabajo que incluye la última familia para la cual trabajó?

¿Está bien con usted si les hablo por teléfono?

LA PARTE LEGAL

¿Es usted ciudadano de los Estados Unidos?

¿Puedo verificar sus documentos legales?

¿Puedo ver su...
 – tarjeta de seguro social?
 – licencia de manejar?
 – pasaporte?
 – visa de trabajo?

¿Me podría sacar una copia fotostática de estos documentos?

job description
descripción del trabajo

OUR REQUIREMENTS	NUESTROS REQUISITOS

We are looking for…
– a part-time nanny.
– a babysitter.
– an au pair.
– a full-time nanny.

– a live-in nanny.

Estamos buscando…
– una niñera de medio tiempo.
– una niñera de vez en cuando.
– un "au pair".
– una niñera de tiempo completo.
– una niñera que viva en la casa.

We would like you to…
– read
– go to the park
– play games
…with the children.

Nos gustaría que usted…
– leyera
– fuera al parque
– jugara juegos
…con los niños.

We would like you to help us with…
– light housecleaning.
– laundry.
– shopping.
– preparing meals.
– taking our child to school.
– giving our child a bath.
– getting our child dressed.
– emptying the dishwasher.
– picking our child up from school.

Nos gustaría que usted nos ayudara a…
– limpiar la casa.
– lavar la ropa.
– hacer las compras.
– preparar las comidas.
– llevar el niño a la escuela.
– bañar el niño.
– vestir el niño en la mañana.
– descargar el lavaplatos.
– recoger el niño de la escuela.

We would like you to help clean…

– the baby's room.
– the toys.
– the kitchen when you use it.

Nos gustaría que usted nos ayudara a limpiar…
– el cuarto del bebé.
– los jugetes.
– la cocina, después de que la use.

At the end of the day, please make sure the house is as clean as when you arrived.

Al final del día, por favor asegúrese de que la casa esté tan limpia como la encontró cuando llegó.

We would like him/her to learn Spanish.

Nos gustaría que él/ella aprendiera a hablar español.

I will/We will get back to you…

– in the next few days.
– in a week.
– a couple of weeks.

Me comunico/Nos comunicamos con usted…
– durante los próximos días.
– en una semana.
– en dos semanas.

Do you have any questions?

¿Tiene alguna pregunta?

SHARE CARE	COMPARTIENDO NIÑERAS

Can you care for two children at the same time?

¿Puede cuidar a dos niños al mismo tiempo?

We would like you to care for two children…
– today.
– tomorrow.
– sometimes.
– every day.
– for p 95 hours per day.
– for p 95 days per week.

Queremos que usted cuide a dos niños…
– hoy.
– mañana.
– a veces.
– todos los días.
– p 187 horas al día.
– p 187 días a la semana.

We will pay you $ __ (dollars) for both children.

Le vamos a pagar $ __ (dolares) por cuidar a los dos niños.

If a neighbor comes over to play, we will/will not pay you extra for this child.

Si un vecino viene a la casa a jugar, le pagarémos/no le pagarémos más por ese niño(a).

Please wash all the toys after the children play with them.

Por favor lave todos los juguetes después de que los niños jueguen con ellos.

If one of the children is sick, we will/will not pay you for him/her.

Si uno de los niños se enferma, le pagarémos/no le pagarémos por ese niño(a).

He/She can sleep in…
– his/her crib.
– the portable crib.
– his/her stroller.

Él/Ella puede dormir en…
– su cuna.
– su portacuna.
– su carriola.

Please stay in the house or yard when you have two or more children.

Por favor quédese en la casa o en el jardín cuando esté cuidando a más de un niño.

HOURS & DAYS

HORAS Y DÍAS

We are looking for help…
– every day.
– on p 95.

Estamos buscando ayuda…
– todos los días.
– para p 187.

We are looking for help…
– in the morning.
– in the afternoon.
– in the evening.
– all day.
– from p 95 to p 95.

Estamos buscando ayuda…
– en la mañana.
– en la tarde.
– en la noche.
– todo el día.
– de p 187 a p 187.

Can you start working on __?

¿Puede empezar a trabajar...

LIVE INS

CUANDO VIVE EN LA CASA

We will provide you with…
– a room.
– an apartment.
– a car.
– meals.
– a phone line.
– health insurance.

Le proporcionarémos…
– un cuarto.
– un departamento.
– un coche.
– las comidas.
– una línea de teléfono.
– seguro médico.

We would like you to work …

– exclusively for us.
– p 95 hours a week.
– only on weekdays.

We would prefer that you not work for other families while you are working with us.

Do you have someplace you can stay when you are not working?

Nos gustaría que usted trabajara…
– exclusivamente para nosotros.
– p 187 horas a la semana.
– solamente entre semana.

Preferimos que no trabaje para otras familias mientras esté trabajando con nosotros.

¿Tiene un lugar en donde puede quedarse cuando no esté trabajando?

COMPENSATION

We will pay $ __ …
– per hour.
– per week.
– per month.
– per overnight stay.

We will/will not pay…

– your taxes.
– for vacation.
– for sick days.

COMPENSACIÓN

Nosotros vamos a pagar $___…
– por hora.
– por semana.
– por mes.
– por quedarse en la noche.

Nosotros vamos/no vamos a pagar…
– sus impuestos.
– las vacaciones.
– los días que no trabaje por causa de enfermedad.

This does/does not include national holidays/ religious holidays/ p 97.

We will/won't provide you with…
– a cell phone.
– a car.
– health insurance.
– meals.

Is there anything else that you need?

– The grocery store
– The park
– The bustop
… is located __.

Esto incluye/no incluye los días festivos nacionales/los días festivos religiosos/ p 189.

Le darémos/No le darémos…
– un teléfono celular.
– un coche.
– seguro médico.
– comidas.

¿Hay algo más que usted necesita?

– El supermercado
– El parque
– La parada del autobús
…está __.

3

everyday situations
situaciones de todos los días

everyday situations

back door	*la puerta trasera*
backyard	*el jardín de atras*
basement	*el sótano*
bathroom	*el baño*
door	*la puerta*
downstairs	*abajo*
(to) drive	*manejar*
driveway	*la entrada para coches*
early	*temprano*
family room	*la estancia*
fence	*la cerca*
fireplace	*la chimenea*
front door	*la puerta principal*
front yard	*el jardín de enfrente*
furniture	*los muebles*
garage	*el garaje*
garbage	*la basura*
gate	*el portón*
indoors	*adentro*
kitchen	*la cocina*
late	*tarde*
laundry room	*la lavandería*
lights	*las luces*
lock	*la cerradura*
message	*el mensaje*
outdoors	*afuera*
phone calls	*las llamadas telefónicas*
playroom	*el cuarto de juegos*
pool	*la piscina*
(to) recycle	*reciclar*
telephone	*el teléfono*
television	*la television*
today	*hoy*
tomorrow	*mañana*
upstairs	*arriba*
visitor	*el visitante*
wall	*la pared*
window	*la ventana*
yesterday	*ayer*

work
el trabajo

I need/My spouse needs…	Yo necesito/Mi esposo(a) necesita…
– to go to work early tomorrow.	– ir a trabajar mañana temprano.
– to work late tonight.	– trabajar tarde hoy en la noche.

Can you…
– stay until p 95?
– come at p 95?

¿Puedes…
– quedarte hasta las p 187?
– venir a las p 187?

My…
– husband/wife
– mother
– mother–in–law
– p 92
…will be home by p 95.

Mi…
– esposo(a)
– madre
– suegra
– p 184
…estará en la casa a las p 187.

If I will be late, I will call you on…
– our home phone.
– your cell phone.

Si yo voy a llegar tarde, te llamo…
– a la casa.
– a tu teléfono celular.

I/My spouse will be traveling this week.

Yo estaré/Mi esposo(a) estará viajando esta semana.

I'm sorry I'm late, the traffic was terrible.

Perdón que llegué tarde, el tráfico estaba terrible.

I will call you everyday at p 95 to check in.

Yo te llamaré diario a las p 187 para ver si se te ofrece algo.

My assistant's name is __.

El nombre de mi asistente es __.

If you can't find me, please call my assistant.

Si no me encuentras, por favor llama a mi asistente.

WORKING AT HOME

TRABAJANDO EN LA CASA

Please bring the baby to me at p 95 (am/pm) so I can feed him/her.

Por favor traeme al bebé a las p 187 (am/pm) para que yo le pueda dar de comer.

It is OK for him/her to visit me in my office, but please take him(her) away after a couple of minutes so I can work.

Está bien si él/ella me visita en mi oficina, pero por favor llévatelo(la) después de unos minutos para que pueda trabajar.

If I'm on the phone, please try to keep everyone quiet.

Si estoy hablando por teléfono, trata de mantener a todos en silencio.

I will be leaving at p 95 for a meeting.

Saldré a las p 187 a una reunión.

I'll be gone until around p 95.

Estaré fuera hasta las p 187.

home
la casa

Please do/don't answer the door when I am gone.	*Por favor abre/no abras la puerta cuando no esté en la casa.*
If I am gone, please answer the door for the delivery person, and sign for the package.	*Si no estoy, por favor abrele la puerta al mensajero, y firma el paquete de recibido.*
Do/Do not let him/her play in the...	*Deja/No dejes que él/ella juege en...*
– office.	*– la oficina.*
– living room.	*– la sala.*
– p 99.	*– p 191.*
Keep him(her) away from...	Manténlo(la) lejos de...
– the pool.	– la piscina.
– the steps.	– las escaleras.
– the stove.	– la estufa.
Please put shoes on him/her before he/she goes outside.	*Por favor ponle zapatos cuando él/ella vaya afuera a jugar.*
Please try to keep the children from touching the glass doors or windows.	Por favor no dejes que los niños toquen las puertas de vidrio o las ventanas.
Please take your/his/her shoes off before coming inside.	*Por favor quíta tus/sus zapatos antes de entrar a la casa.*
Our house keys are kept __.	Guardamos las llaves en __.
To use the alarm, press p 95 when you enter the house.	*Para usar la alarma, presiona p 187 cuando entres a la casa.*
We like to leave the...	Nos gusta dejar...
– front door	– la puerta principal
– back door	– la puerta trasera
... open/closed during the day.	...abierta/cerrada durante el día.
Please put/do not put...	*Pon/No pongas...*
– garbage	*– la basura*
– glass	*– el vidrio*
– plastic	*– el plástico*
– paper	*– el papel*
...here.	*...aquí, por favor.*

FOOD — LA COMIDA

Please feed them only at the table.	*Dale comida solamente en la mesa.*
Please do not allow him/her to eat or drink on furniture.	*Por favor no dejes que él/ella coma o beba encima de los muebles.*
Please ask me before you eat something, in case I am planning on using it for dinner.	*Por favor pregúntame antes de que comas algo, por si acaso lo voy a usar en la cena*
Feel free to eat whatever you want.	*Come lo que quieras.*

PHONE

Please take your cell phone with you whenever you leave the house.

Make sure that the battery for the cell phone is charged.

Make sure the cell phone is turned on.

Please do/do not answer our home phone.

You may/may not use our phone for…
 – local phone calls.
 – long distance calls.
 – international calls.

Please write down phone messages on this notepad.

When I call you I will let it ring once, hang up and then call back.

CAR

Make sure you always take…
 – your license
 – insurance papers
 – registration
…when using the car.

You may/may not drive other people in the car we provide.

Please use the…
 – cash
 – gas card

…we provide to keep the car full of gasoline.

GUESTS

It is/is not OK to bring anyone into the house.

Please check with me first if you would like to have someone over to visit.

I would like to know ahead of time who is coming and when.

If you have guests over, please don't let them into p 99.

EL TELÉFONO

Por favor llévate tu teléfono celular contigo siempre que salgas de la casa.

Asegúrate de que la pila del teléfono celular esté cargada.

Asegúrate de que el teléfono celular esté prendido.

Por favor contesta/no contestes el teléfono de la casa.

Puedes/No puedes usar nuestro teléfono para…
 – llamadas locales.
 – llamadas de larga distancia.
 – llamadas internacionales.

Apunta los mensajes telefónicos en esta libreta, por favor.

Cuando te llame, dejaré que suene el teléfono una vez, colgaré, y te llamaré de nuevo.

EL COCHE

Asegúrate de llevarte…
 – tu licencia
 – los papeles del seguro
 – los papeles del registro
…cuando uses el coche.

Puedes/No puedes subir a otras personas en nuestro coche.

Por favor, utiliza…
 – el efectivo
 – la tarjeta de crédito de gasolina
…que te dimos para tener el coche lleno de gasolina.

INVITADOS

Está bien/No está bien traer a gente a la casa.

Pregúntame si quieres invitar a alguien a la casa, por favor.

Me gustaría saber con anticipación quién va a venir y cuándo.

Si tienes invitados, por favor que no entren a p 191.

4

food
comida

food

. . . .

allergy	*la alergia*
bib	*el babero*
(to) boil	*hervir*
bottle	*el biberón*
breakfast	*el desayuno*
breastmilk	*la leche materna*
(to) burp	*repetir*
(to) choke	*ahogarse*
cold	*la gripe*
cup	*la taza*
dinner	*la cena*
dishwasher	*el lavaplatos*
expiration date	*la fecha de vencimiento*
food	*la comida*
fork	*el tenedor*
(to) freeze	*congelar*
fruit	*la fruta*
(to) heat up	*calentar*
highchair	*la silla para comer del bebé*
hot	*caliente*
(to be) hungry	*tener hambre*
juice box	*el jugo de cajita*
knife	*el cuchillo*
(to) leak	*gotear*
lunch	*el almuerzo*
lunchbox	*la lonchera*
milk	*la leche*
mold	*el moho*
napkin	*la servilleta*
nipple	*el chupón*
(to) refrigerate	*refrigerar*
rotten	*podrido(a)*
sippy cup	*el vaso entrenador*
snack	*un refrigerio*
(to) spill	*derramar*
spoon	*la cuchara*
(to) sterilize	*esterilizar*
stomach ache	*el dolor de estómago*
warm	*calientito(a)*

liquids
líquidos

BOTTLES	*BIBERONES*
Please only use this type of bottle.	***Por favor usa este tipo de biberón solamente.***
Do/Don't give him/her a bottle at p 95.	*Dale/No le des un biberón a las p 187.*
Do/Do not give him/her	***Dale/No le des...***
– milk	*– leche*
– soy milk	*– leche de soya*
– tap water	*– agua de la llave*
– bottled water	*– agua embotellada*
– juice	*– jugo*
– **p 104**	*– **p 195***
...in the bottle.	*...en el biberón.*
He/She doesn't like taking a bottle from anyone, so please be patient.	*A él/ella no le gusta el biberón, así que por favor hay que ser paciente.*
Please only use this type of milk.	***Por favor usa este tipo de leche solamente.***
He/She is gassy, so please be sure to lift the bottle so there are no air bubbles.	*Él/Ella padece de gases, así que por favor asegúrate de levantar el biberón para que no haya burbujas.*
Never use the microwave to heat up breast milk.	***Nunca uses el microondas para calentar la leche materna.***
I would like him/her to stop using the bottle.	*Me gustaría que él/ella dejara de usar el biberón.*
Only use the sippy cups from now on.	***De hoy en adelante, usa los vasos entrenadores solamente.***

SIPPY CUPS	*LOS VASOS ENTRENADORES*
Do/Do not give him/her...	***Dale/No le des...***
– milk	*– leche*
– soy milk	*– leche de soya*
– tap water	*– agua de la llave*
– bottled water	*– agua embotellada*
– juice	*– jugo*
...in the sippy cup.	*...en el vaso entrenador.*
Dilute the juice using half water and half juice.	*Diluye el jugo con la mitad de agua y la mitad de jugo.*
Do not put anything carbonated in the sippy cup since it will leak.	***No pongas bebidas carbonosas en el vaso entrenador, porque se gotea.***

solids
sólidos

He/She is...	*Él/Ella es...*
– a good	*– bueno(a)*
– a picky	*– muy especial*
...eater.	*... para comer.*

He/She likes/ dislikes...   *A él/ella le gusta/ no le gusta...*

Do/Do not give him/her ...	*Dale/No le des...*
– soda.	*– refresco.*
– junk food.	*– comida chatarra.*
– p 105.	*– p 196.*

I think he/she is hungry.   *Creo que él/ella tiene hambre.*

SNACKS   LOS REFRIGERIOS

Please don't give him/her snacks in...	*No dejes que coma refrigerios en...*
– the car.	*– el coche.*
– the stroller.	*– la carriola.*
– the morning.	*– la mañana.*
– the afternoon.	*– la tarde.*

Please don't give him/her...	*Por favor no le des...*
– candy	*– dulces*
– cookies	*– galletas*
...for a snack.	*... como refrigerio.*

We like to give him/her...	*Nos gusta darle...*
– fruit	*– fruta*
– p 101	*– p 193*
...for a snack.	*...como refrigerio.*

PREPARING FOOD   PREPARANDO COMIDA

Please cut the portions...	*Por favor corta las porciones...*
– in half.	*– a la mitad.*
– in quarters.	*– en cuartas partes.*
– into little pieces.	*– en pedazos pequeños.*

Please do not add extra...	*Por favor no le pongas más ...*
– salt	*– sal*
– butter	*– mantequilla*
– p 104	*– p 195*
...to the food.	*...a la comida.*

Please make baby food in the food processor and then freeze it in ice cube trays.   *Por favor haz la comida del bebé en la licuadora, y luego congélala en las charolas de hielo.*

Do not use the microwave for the children's food.   *No uses el microondas para calentar la comida de los niños.*

We only use the microwave to heat liquids.   *Solamente usamos el microondas para calentar líquidos.*

SERVING FOOD

Please serve p 102 for...
- breakfast.
- lunch.
- dinner.
- snack.

Wash the children's hands...
- before
- after
...they eat.

Please serve the food warm/cold.

Food is allowed...
- only in the kitchen.
- only at the table.
- anywhere.
- only in the high chair.

He/She does not like his/her food to touch anything else on the plate.

He/She likes...
- white food.
- cold food.
- hot food.

SERVIENDO LA COMIDA

Por favor sirve p 194 para...
- *el desayuno.*
- *el almuerzo.*
- *la cena.*
- *un refrigerio.*

Lávales las manos a los niños...
- *antes*
- *después*
...*de comer.*

Por favor sirve la comida caliente/fría.

La comida se permite...
- *solamente en la cocina.*
- *solamente en la mesa.*
- *en cualquier lugar.*
- *solamente en la silla para comer del bebé.*

A él/ella no le gusta que su comida esté tocando otra comida en su plato.

A él/ella le gusta...
- *la comida blanca.*
- *la comida fría.*
- *la comida caliente.*

cleaning
limpieza

Please sterilize the bottles...

- after each use.
- every few days.

I will sterilize the bottles.

To sterilize the bottles...
- boil them in hot water.
- put them in the dishwasher.
- use the bottle sterilizer.

When you clean the sippy cups make sure you also sterilize the plastic valves.

Please clean the highchair...

- after every meal.
- at end of the day.
- every few days.

Por favor esteriliza los biberones...
- *después de cada uso.*
- *cada tres días.*

Yo esterilizo los biberones.

Para esterilizar los biberones...
- *hiervelos en agua caliente.*
- *ponlos en el lavaplatos.*
- *usa el esterilizador de biberones.*

Cuando laves los vasos entrenadores, asegúrate de esterilizar la válvula de plástico.

Por favor lava la silla para comer del bebé...
- *después de cada comida.*
- *al final del día.*
- *cada tres días.*

shopping
compras

Please do the shopping...
– every day.
– once a week.
– once a month.
– pg96.

Por favor haz las compras...
– todos los días.
– una vez a la semana.
– una vez al mes.
– pg188.

Let me know what you need at the store.

Avísame lo que necesitas de la tienda.

Please buy...
– organic
– whole
– low fat
– non fat
...milk.

Por favor compra leche ...
– orgánica.
– entera.
– semi-descremada.
– descremada.

Please buy...
– butter
– eggs
– juice
– formula
– fruit
– cookies
– bread
– chicken
...today.

Por favor compra...
– mantequilla
– huevos
– jugo
– la formula
– fruta
– galletas
– pan
– pollo
...hoy.

Here is $ __ for the shopping.

Aquí está $ __ para hacer las compras.

Please take him(her) with you when you go shopping.

Por favor llévatelo(la) contigo cuando haces las compras.

Do/Do not give him/her a treat when you are shopping.

Dale/No le des un dulce cuando estás haciendo las compras.

Be careful of him/her in the shopping cart, since he/she sometimes tries to escape.

Ten cuidado con él/ella en el carrito del supermercado, porque a veces trata de escaparse.

The nearest grocery store is called__.

El supermercado más cercano se llama__.

It is located__.

Se encuentra en__.

food safety
precauciones alimenticias

Call 911 if he/she has been exposed to p 104.

Llama al 911 si él/ella ha sido expuesto(a) a p 196.

He/She is allergic to...
– milk.
– peanuts.
– nuts.
– seafood.
– p 104.

Él/Ella es alérgico(a) a...
– la leche.
– los cacahuates.
– las nueces.
– los mariscos.
– p 196.

Do not feed the baby...
- milk
- eggs
- egg whites
- honey
...until after his/her first birthday.

No hay que darle ...
- *leche*
- *huevos*
- *clara de huevo*
- *miel*
...al bebé hasta que cumpla un año.

Please be careful with...
- hot dogs
- carrots
- nuts and seeds
- grapes
- popcorn
- round candies

...because he/she could choke on them.

Ten cuidado con...
- *las salchichas*
- *las zanahorias*
- *las nueces y las semillas*
- *las uvas*
- *las palomitas*
- *los dulces redondos*

...porque él/ella puede ahogarse con este tipo de comida.

Please take the peel off <u>p 102.</u>

Por favor quitale la cáscara a <u>p 193</u>.

If you use the microwave, please be sure to stir the food to make sure there are no hotspots.

Si usas el microondas, no dejes de remover la comida, para que no hayan partes muy calientes.

The meat thermometer is kept __.

El termómetro de la carne se guarda en __.

The following information on food safety is from the United States Department of Agriculture Food Safety and Inspection Service. For more information in English or Spanish visit their website at www.fsis.usda.gov.

La siguiente información sobre precauciones alimenticias es del "United States Department of Agriculture Food Safety and Inspection Service". Para más información en inglés o español, consulte su sitio en el internet: www.fsis.usda.gov.

SHOPPING

Purchase refrigerated or frozen items after selecting your non – perishables.

Check "Sell – By" dates.

Put raw meat and poultry into a plastic bag so meat juices will not cross – contaminate.

THAWING

Refrigerator: The refrigerator allows slow, safe thawing. Make sure thawing meat and poultry juices do not drip onto other food.

Cold water: For faster thawing, place food in a leak – proof plastic bag. Submerge in cold tap water. Change the water every 30 minutes. Cook immediately after thawing.

Microwave: Cook meat and poultry immediately after microwave thawing.

PREPARATION

Always wash hands before and after handling food.

Don't cross – contaminate. Keep raw meat, poultry, fish, and their juices away from other food. After cutting raw meats, wash hands, cutting board, knife, and countertops with hot, soapy water.

Marinate meat and poultry in a covered dish in the refrigerator.

Sanitize cutting boards by using a solution of 1 teaspoon chlorine bleach in 1 quart of water.

COMPRAS

Compre alimentos refrigerados o congelados después de escoger alimentos no perecederos.

Revise la fecha de vencimiento de los alimentos.

Ponga carnes y aves crudas en bolsas de plástico para que sus jugos no contaminen los demás alimentos.

DESCONGELACIÓN

Refrigerador: En el refrigerador se puede descongelar lentamente, sin riesgos. Asegúrese de que los jugos de las carnes y las aves no goteen sobre los otros alimentos.

Agua fría: Para descongelar más rápidamente, coloque el alimento en una bolsa de plástico hermética. Sumérjalo en agua fría de la llave. Cambie el agua cada 30 minutos. Cocínelo inmediatamente después de descongelarlo.

Microondas: Cocine los alimentos inmediatamente después de descongelarlos en el microondas.

PREPARACIÓN

Siempre lávese las manos antes y después de tocar los alimentos.

Prevenga la contaminación. Mantenga carnes, aves y pescados crudos, y sus jugos, aparte de los demás alimentos. Después de cortar carnes crudas, lávese las manos y lave las tablas de cortar, los cuchillos y los mostradores con agua caliente y jabón.

Marine carnes y aves en un envase tapado en el refrigerador.

Desinfecte las tablas de cortar con una solución de 1 cucharadita de cloro en 1 cuarto de agua.

bilingual babycare

COOKING

Cook ground meats to 160 °F; ground poultry to 165 °F.

Beef, veal, and lamb steaks, roasts, and chops may be cooked to 145 °F; all cuts of fresh pork, 160 °F.

Whole poultry should reach 180 °F in the thigh; breasts, 170 °F.

LEFTOVERS

Perishable food should not be left out more than 2 hours at room temperature (1 hour when the temperature is above 90 °F).

Discard any food left out at room temperature for more than 2 hours (1 hour if the temperature was above 90 °F).

Place food into shallow containers and immediately put in the refrigerator or freezer for rapid cooling.

Use cooked leftovers within 4 days.

REFREEZING

Meat and poultry defrosted in the refrigerator may be refrozen before or after cooking. If thawed by other methods, cook before refreezing.

STORAGE

Cook or freeze fresh poultry, fish, ground meats, and variety meats within 2 days; other beef, veal, lamb, or pork, within 3 to 5 days.

When freezing meat and poultry in its original package, maintain quality by wrapping the package again with foil or plastic wrap designed for the freezer.

Discard cans that are dented, leaking, bulging, or rusted.

COCINANDO

Cocine carnes molidas hasta llegar a los 160 °F; aves molidas hasta llegar a los 165 °F.

Filetes de carne de res, ternera y cordero, y chuletas deben de cocinarse hasta llegar a los 145 °F; todos los cortes de puerco fresco, hasta los 160 °F.

Aves enteras deben de llegar a los 180 °F en el muslo y 170 °F en la pechuga.

SOBRAS

Los alimentos perecederos no se deben de dejar afuera del refrigerador por más de 2 horas (1 hora si la temperatura está arriba de 90 °F).

Deseche cualquier alimento que haya estado afuera del refrigerador por más de 2 horas (1 hora si la temperatura está arriba de 90 °F).

Coloque los alimentos en envases poco hondos y póngalos inmediatamente en el refrigerador o el congelador para que se enfríen rápidamente.

Utilice las sobras cocidas en un plazo de 4 días.

RECONGELACIÓN

Las carnes y aves descongeladas en el refrigerador pueden ser recongeladas antes o después de cocinarlas. Si fueron descongeladas con otros métodos, cocínelas antes de recongelarlas.

ALMACENAJE

Cocine o congele aves, pescados, carnes molidas, y vísceras crudos dentro de 2 días; otras carnes de res, ternera, cordero, o cerdo, dentro de 3 a 5 días.

Cuando congela carnes y aves en su paquete original, envuélvalos con algún papel de aluminio o envoltura de plástico diseñado para el congelador.

Deseche latas que estén abolladas, goteando, abultadas, u oxidadas.

USDA COLD STORAGE CHART
TABLA DE ALMACENAJE FRIO DEL USDA

EGGS

fresh, in shell
 (r: 3 – 5 wks; f:do not freeze)

raw yolks & whites
 (r: 2 – 4 days; f:1 year)

hard cooked
 (r: 1 week; f:do not freeze)

egg substitutes (opened)
 (r: 3 days; f:do not freeze)

egg substitutes (unopened)
 (r: 10 days; f:1 year)

DELI & VACUUM PACKED PRODUCTS

store – bought (or homemade)
egg, chicken, ham, tuna, &
macaroni salad
 (r: 3 – 5 days; f:do not freeze)

HOT DOGS

opened package
 (r: 1 week; f:1 – 2 mths)

unopened package
 (r: 2 wks; f: 1 – 2 mths)

LUNCHEON MEAT

opened package
 (r: 3 – 5 days; f:1 – 2 mths)

unopened package
 (r: 2 wks; f: 1 – 2 mths)

BACON & SAUSAGE

bacon
 (r: 7 days; f:1 mth)

sausage, raw from beef, chicken,
turkey, pork
 (r: 1 – 2 days; f:1 – 2 mths)

smoked breakfast links
 (r: 7 days; f: 1 – 2 mths)

hard sausage: pepperoni etc.
 (r: 2 – 3 weeks; f:1 – 2 mths)

HUEVOS

frescos, en cáscara
 (r: 3 – 5 sem.; c: no congelarse)

yemas y blancas crudas
 (r: 2 – 4 días; c:1 año)

cocido
 (r: 1 sem.; c: no congelarse)

sucedáneos de huevos (abierto)
 (r: 3 – 5 dias.; c: no congelarse)

sucedáneos de huevos (sin abrir)
 (r: 10 días; c:1 año)

PRODUCTOS EMPAQUETADOS

ensalada de huevo, pollo, jamón,
atún y macaroni de la tienda (o
hecha en casa)
 (r: 3 – 5 dias; c:no congelarse)

SALCHICHAS

paquete abierto
 (r: 1 semana; c:1 a 2 meses)

paquete cerrado
 (r: 2 semanas; c: 1 a 2 meses)

CARNES FRÍAS

paquete abierto
 (r: 3 a 5 días; c:1 a 2 meses)

paquete cerrado
 (r: 2 semanas; f: 1 a 2 meses)

TOCINO Y SALCHICHAS

tocino
 (r: 7 días; c:1 mes)

salchichas crudas de res, pollo, pavo
y cerdo
 (r: 1 a 2 días; c:1 a 2 meses)

salchichas ahumadas
 (r: 7 días; c: 1 a 2 meses)

salchicha dura: peperoni, etc
 (r: 2 – 3 semanas; c:1 a 2 meses)

HAMBURGER & GROUND MEAT (r: 1 – 2 days; f: 3 – 4 mths)	*HAMBURGUESAS Y CARNE MOLIDA* *(r: 1 a 2 días; c: 3 a 4 meses)*
FRESH BEEF, VEAL, LAMB, PORK **steaks** (r: 3 – 5 days; f:6 – 12 mths) **chops** (r: 3 – 5 days; f:4 – 6 mths) **roasts** (r: 3 – 5 days; f:4 – 12 mths)	*CARNE DE RES, TERNERA, CORDERO Y CERDO FRESCO* *filetes* *(r: 3 a 5 días; c:6 a 12 meses)* *chuletas* *(r: 3 a 5 días; c:4 a 6 meses)* *asados* *(r: 3 a 5 días; c:4 a 12 meses)*
SOUPS & STEWS **vegetable or meat added** (r: 3 – 4 days; f:2 – 3 mths)	*SOPAS Y GUISOS* *de verduras o con carne* *(r: 3 a 4 días; c: 2 a 3 meses)*
COOKED MEAT LEFTOVERS (r: 3 – 4 days; f:2 – 3 mths)	*SOBRAS DE CARNE COCIDA* *(r: 3 a 4 días; c: 2 a 3 meses)*
GRAVY & MEAT BROTH (r: 1 – 2 days; f:2 – 3 mths)	*SALSA Y CALDO DE CARNE* *(r: 1 a 2 días; c: 2 a 3 meses)*
POULTRY **chicken or turkey whole** (r: 1 – 2 days; f:1 year) **chicken or turkey pieces** (r: 1 – 2 days; f: 9 mths) **fried** (r: 3 – 4 days; f: 4 mths) **casseroles** (r: 3 – 4 days; f: 4 – 6 mths) **casseroles with gravy** (r: 1 – 2 days; f: 6 mths) **nuggets** (r: 1 – 2 days; f: 1 – 3 mths)	*AVES* *pollo o pavo, entero* *(r: 1 a 2 días; c: 1 año)* *pollo o pavo, en piezas* *(r: 1 a 2 días; c: 9 meses)* *frito* *(r: 3 a 4 días; c: 4 meses)* *guisados* *(r: 3 a 4 días; c: 4 meses)* *guisados con salsa* *(r: 1 a 2 días; c: 6 meses)* *nugets* *(r: 1 a 2 días; c: 1 a 3 meses)*
PIZZA (r: 3 – 4 days; f:1 – 2 mths)	*PIZZA* *(r: 3 a 4 días; c: 1 a 2 meses)*
MAYONNAISE **refrigerate after opening** (r: 2 mths; f:do not freeze)	*MAYONESA* *refrigerar después de abrir* *(r: 2 meses; c:no congelarse)*
FROZEN DINNERS (f: 3 – 4 mths)	*COMIDAS PREPARADAS CONGELADAS* *(c:3 – 4 meses)*

For more information go to www. fsis.usda.gov

5

outdoor activities
actividades al aire libre

outdoor activities

· ·

art class	*la clase de arte*
backpack	*la mochila*
ballet	*la clase de ballet*
bicycle	*la bicicleta*
birthday	*el cumpleaños*
boy scouts	*los escouts*
car seat	*el asiento del coche*
(to)climb	*escalar*
(to)crawl	*gatear*
dance class	*la clase de baile*
dirty	*sucio(a)*
friends	*los amigos*
(to have) fun	*divertirse*
girl scouts	*las escouts*
Gymboree	*la clase de Gymboree*
gymnastics class	*la clase de gimnasia*
kite	*el papalote*
muddy	*lodoso(a)*
music class	*la clase de música*
park	*el parque*
party	*la fiesta*
(to)play	*jugar*
playground	*los juegos del parque*
present	*el regalo*
sand	*la arena*
sandbox	*el arenero*
scooter/ skateboard	*la patineta*
slide	*la resbaladilla*
soccer	*el fútbol*
stroller	*la carriola*
swimming lesson	*la clase de natación*
swing	*el columpio*
tap dancing class	*la clase de tap*
toys	*los juguetes*
tricycle	*el triciclo*
(to) walk	*caminar*
wagon	*el vagón*
yard	*el jardín*

general activities
actividades generales

He/She is learning how to…	***Él/Ella está aprendiendo a…***
– **roll over.**	– *voltearse.*
– **crawl.**	– *gatear.*
– **walk.**	– *caminar.*
– **talk.**	– *hablar.*

Please take him/her for a walk… | *Por favor llévalo/la a caminar…*
– in the morning. | *– en la mañana.*
– in the afternoon. | *– en la tarde.*
– before nap time. | *– antes de su siesta.*
– after nap time. | *– después de su siesta.*
– now. | *– ahora.*

He/She loves to go to… | ***A él/ella le encanta ir…***
– **the park.** | – *al parque.*
– **the playground.** | – *a los juegos del parque.*
– **the zoo.** | – *al zoológico.*
– **a friend's house.** | – *a la casa de un amigo.*

Please make sure he/she is wearing… | *Por favor asegúrate de que él/ella lleve puesto(a)…*
– a hat. | *– un sombrero.*
– a jacket. | *– una chamarra.*
– a sweater. | *– un suéter.*
– p 108. | *– p 200.*

Please take the… | ***Llévate por favor…***
– **bicycle** | – *la bicicleta*
– **doll** | – *la muñeca*
– **toys** | – *los juguetes*
– **dog** | – *el perro*
…with you. | *… contigo.*

Where did you go? | *¿A dónde fueron?*

Please come home… | ***Por favor regresa a la casa…***
– **before lunch.** | – *antes del almuerzo.*
– **for nap time.** | – *para la hora de la siesta.*
– **by p 95 (am/pm).** | – *a las p 187 (am/pm).*

Before coming back inside, please… | *Antes de entrar a la casa, por favor…*
– take off his/her shoes. | *– quítale sus zapatos.*
– make sure his/her shoes are clean. | *– asegúrate de que sus zapatos estén limpios.*

Let me show you how to… | ***Déjame enseñarte como…***
– **open** | – *abrir*
– **close** | – *cerrar*
– **fasten the seat belts on** | – *abrochar los cinturones de*
– **lock the wheels on** | – *atorar las ruedas de*
– **put the sun cover on** | – *poner la cubierta del sol a*
…the stroller. | *…la carriola.*

He/She likes to…	A él/ella le gusta ir al parque…
– ride the bike	– en bicicleta.
– sit in the wagon	– sentado(a) en el vagón.
– walk	– caminando.
…to the park.	

The baby prefers the front pack to a stroller when fussy. | ***El bebé prefiere la kangurera en lugar de la carriola cuando esté llorando.***

When you are finished with the stroller, please… | *Cuando termines de usar la carriola, por favor…*
– clean it. | *– límpiala.*
– put it away. | *– guárdala.*

parks & playgrounds
parques y paseos

Please let me know…	***Avísame por favor…***
– which park you are going to.	***– a qué parque van a ir.***
– what time you will be at the park.	***– cuándo van a estar en el parque.***
– how long you plan to stay at the park.	***– cuánto tiempo piensan estar en el parque.***

He/She loves…	A él/ella le encanta…
– the slide.	– la resbaladilla.
– the swing.	– el columpio.
– to climb.	– escalar.
– to play in the sand.	– jugar en la arena.

He/She is afraid of…	***Él/Ella le tiene miedo a…***
– dogs.	***– los perros.***
– older children.	***– los niños grandes.***
– other adults.	***– otros adultos.***
– masks or costumes.	***– las máscaras o los disfraces.***
– heights.	***– las alturas.***

Be careful of…	Ten cuidado con…
– bees.	– las abejas.
– big kids.	– los niños grandes.
– dog/ cat poop.	– la popó de perro/gato.
– thorny bushes.	– los arbustos con espinas.

classes & planned activities
clases y actividades

The class begins at…	***La clase empieza a…***
– nine.	***– las nueve.***
– ten.	***– las diez.***
– eleven.	***– las once.***
– twelve.	***– las doce.***
– one.	***– la una.***
– two.	***– las dos.***
– three.	***– las tres.***
– __ thirty.	***– __ y media.***

He/She goes to…	Él/Ella va a…
– a playgroup.	– jugar con un grupo de amigos.
– a gym class.	– clases de gimnasia.

– a dance class.	– clases del baile.
– an art class.	– clases de arte.
– a swim class.	– clases de natación.
– p 106.	– p 197.

The class is on... | **Tiene clase...**
– **Monday.**	– el lunes.
– **Tuesday.**	– el martes.
– **Wednesday.**	– el miércoles.
– **Thursday.**	– el jueves.
– **Friday.**	– el viernes.
– **Saturday.**	– el sábado.
– **Sunday.**	– el domingo.

Please go to the library at p 95 for reading hour. / Por favor ve a la biblioteca a las p 187 para la hora de la lectura.

The class is located__. / **La clase está en__.**

You will have to... / Tienes que ir...
- take the car / – en coche
- take the bus / – en autobús
- walk / – caminando
...to get there. / ...para llegar allí.

The teacher's name is__. / **El nombre del maestro es__.**

Please bring... / Por favor llévate...
- a snack / – un refrigerio
- a bottle of water / – una botella de agua
- p 102 / – p 194
... with you. / ... contigo.

communication & safety
comunicación & seguridad

Make sure you always have... / **Asegúrate de llevar...**
- **a cell phone** / – un teléfono celular
- **our contact information** / – nuestros datos
...with you when you leave the house. / ...contigo siempre que salgas de la casa.

Please let me know... / Por favor avísame...
- where you plan to go today. / – a dónde planeas ir a pasear hoy.
- if you would like to take him/her anywhere. / – si quieres llevarlo(la) a algún lugar.

Please put sunscreen on... / **Por favor ponle protector solar...**

- **before you leave the house.** / – antes de salir de la casa.
- **at the park.** / – cuando llegues al parque.
- **every hour.** / – cada hora.
- **every couple of hours.** / – cada dos horas.

Please put a hat on him/her before you leave the house. / Por favor ponle un sombrero antes de salir de la casa.

Please tell me if you're going... / **Por favor avísame si planeas i...**
- **around the block.** / – a darle la vuelta a la cuadra.
- **to the store.** / – a la tienda.
- **to the park.** / – a al parque.
- **to a friend's house.** / – la casa de un amigo.

Please let me know where you are going by…
– leaving me a note.
– calling me on the phone.

The best place to leave me a note is…
– on the refrigerator.
– by the phone.
– by the door.

Please stay in the house today since it is…
– too hot.
– too cold.
– too windy.
– supposed to rain.
– p 99.

Por favor avísame a dónde vas a ir…
– dejándome una nota.
– hablándome por teléfono.

El mejor lugar para dejarme un mensaje escrito es…
– en el refrigerador.
– cerca del teléfono.
– cerca de la puerta.

Por favor quédate en la casa hoy porque…
– hace demasiado calor.
– hace demasiado frío.
– hay demasiado viento.
– va a llover.
– p 191.

6

indoor activities
actividades adentro de la casa

indoor activities

....

ball	*la pelota*
balloon	*el globo*
boat	*el barco*
book	*el libro*
cartoons	*las caricaturas*
chalk	*los gises*
clay/play doh	*la plastilina*
coloring book	*el libro para colorear*
costume	*el disfráz*
crayons	*las crayolas*
(to) cut	*cortar*
doll	*la muñeca*
(to) draw	*dibujar*
(to) dress up	*disfrazarse*
eraser	*la goma*
football	*el fútbol*
glue	*el pegamento*
jewelry	*las joyería*
magic	*la magia*
(to) make	*hacer*
markers	*los plumones*
mess	*el tiradero*
movie	*la película*
noise	*el ruido*
(to) paint	*pintar*
paper	*el papel*
pencils	*los lápices*
pens	*las plumas*
puzzle	*el rompecabezas*
(to) read	*leer*
scissors	*las tijeras*
(to) share	*compartir*
sticker	*la estampa*
story	*el cuento*
television, tv	*la televisión*
toys	*los juguetes*
(to) turn off	*apagar*
(to) turn on	*prender*

arts & crafts
arte y manualidades

He/She likes to...
– draw.
– paint.
– play with stickers.
– play with beads.

A él/ella le gusta...
– dibujar.
– pintar.
– jugar con estampas.
– jugar con cuentas.

We have…
– paper.
– paint.
– crayons.
– chalk.
– glue.
– tape.
– washable markers.

Tenemos…
– papel.
– pinturas.
– crayolas.
– gises.
– pegamento.
– cinta.
– plumones lavables.

When painting, please…
– put an apron on him/her.
– go outside.
– don't let him/her eat the paint.

Cuando estén pintando…
– ponle un delantal, por favor.
– váyanse afuera, por favor.
– no lo/la dejes que se coma la pintura, por favor.

Try to avoid getting paint on…
– the furniture.
– table.
– the walls.
– the floor.
– the clothes.

Trata de que no caiga pintura…
– en los muebles.
– en la mesa.
– en las paredes.
– en el piso.
– en la ropa.

If paint/marker gets on the furniture, please clean it off with…
– water.
– soap.
– p 101.

Si los muebles se manchan de pintura/plumón, por favor límpialos con…
– agua.
– jabón.
– p 193.

When drawing please only use washable markers.

Solamente usa plumones lavables cuando estén dibujando.

Please keep…
– crayons
– paint
– pens
– beads
...away from the baby.

Por favor mantén…
– las crayolas
– las pinturas
– las plumas
– las cuentas
…lejos del bebé.

Please keep his/her art projects here.

Por favor guarda sus proyectos de arte aquí.

Please play with…
– clay/play doh
– bubbles
– p 106
...outside.

Juega con…
– la plastilina
– las burbujas
– p 198.
…afuera, por favor.

books
libros

He/She likes to read these books.	*A él/ella le gusta leer estos libros.*
Please read to him/her in Spanish?	*¿Podrías leerle en español?*
Please read him/her a book...	*Por favor léele un libro...*
– in the morning.	*– en la mañana.*
– in the afternoon.	*– en la tarde.*
– before nap time.	*– antes de la siesta.*
– p 95.	*– p 187.*
He/She loves pop-up books.	*A él/ella le gustan los libros de los dibujos que se levantan.*
Try not to let him/her...	*Trata de que no...*
– rip the pages.	*– rompa las páginas del libro.*
– draw in the book.	*– dibuje en el libro.*
Please put the books...	*Por favor pon los libros...*
– on the book shelf	*– en el librero*
– in the toy chest	*– en la caja de juguetes*
...at the end of the day.	*...al final del día.*

toys & games
juguetes y juegos

He/She likes/does not like....	*A él/ella le gusta/no le gusta...*
Please play games like p 106 with him/her.	*Por favor juega juegos tipo p 198 con él/ella.*
Please do/do not let him/her play with these toys.	*Por favor deja/no dejes que él/ella juegue con estos juguetes.*
Watch him(her) around other children, he/she might hit them with a toy.	*Hay que estarlo(la) viendo cuando esté con otros niños, porque les puede pegar con un juguete.*
Please keep these toys...	*Por favor guarda estos juguetes...*
– inside.	*– adentro.*
– outside.	*– afuera.*
Please make sure he/she shares the toys with other children.	*Asegúrate de que él/ella comparta los juguetes con los otros niños.*
These toys are old/fragile, so please make sure the children are careful with them.	*Estos juguetes son viejos/frágiles. Por favor asegúrate de que los niños tengan cuidado con ellos.*
Please use this to clean the toys.	*Por favor usa esto para limpiar los juguetes.*
Please clean the toys...	*Por favor limpia los jugetes...*
– at the end of the day.	*– al final del día.*
– if other children have been playing with them.	*– si otros niños han estado jugando con ellos.*

tv & videos
televisión & videos

He/She is allowed to watch p 95 hours of TV a day.	***Él/Ella puede ver p 187 horas de televisión al día.***
Please do not allow him/her to watch TV.	*Por favor no dejes que él/ella vea televisión.*
He/She can watch... **– these videos/dvds.** **– these TV shows.**	***Él/Ella puede ver...*** ***– éstos videos/dvds.*** ***– éstos programas de televisión.***
His/Her favorite video/DVD is...	*Su video/DVD favorito es...*
This is how to use the... **– TV.** **– VCR.** **– DVD.**	***– La televisión*** ***– La videocasetera*** ***– El DVD*** ***... funciona así.***
Please don't watch TV... – until he/she is asleep. – while he/she is awake. – with him/her. – at all.	*Por favor no veas televisión...* *– hasta que él/ella esté dormido(a).* *– mientras él/ella esté despierto(a).* *– con él/ella.* *– nunca.*
Please rewind the videos when you are finished.	***Regresa los videos cuando termines de verlos por favor.***
Please take these videos/DVDs back to the video store.	*Regresa estos videos/DVDs a la tienda de videos por favor.*
The video store is located __.	***La tienda de videos se encuentra en __.***

7

sleep
sueño

sleep

· ·

alarm clock	el despertador
armoire	el armario
asleep	dormido(a)
awake	despierto(a)
bassinet	el bambineto
bed	la cama
bedroom	la recámara
bedspread	la colcha
blanket	la cobija
bookshelf	el librero
changing table	el cambiador
closet	el closet
comforter/quilt	el edredón
crib	la cuna
cribsheet	la sábana de la cuna
(to) cry	llorar
(to) cuddle/hug	abrazar
curtain	la cortina
dark	oscuro
dream	el sueño
(to) fall asleep	quedarse dormido(a)
light	la luz
mattress	el colchón
monitor	el monitor
nap	la siesta
nightmare	la pesadilla
nightstand	la mesita de noche
pacifier	el chupón
pajamas	la pijama
pillowcase	la funda
pillow	la almohada
restless	agitado(a)
rocking chair	la mesedora
sheet	la sábana
(to put to) sleep	acostarse
(to) sleep	dormirse
(to) wake up	despertar

general
general

I think he/she is tired.	***Creo que él/ella está consado(a).***
Please bathe the baby before putting him(her) to sleep.	*Baña al bebé antes de acostarlo(la), por favor.*
Please let him(her) sleep…	***Por favor déjalo(la) dormir…***
– as long as possible.	***– hasta que se despierte.***
– no more than one hour.	***– no más de una hora.***
– no more than two hours.	***– no más de dos horas.***
– no more than three hours.	***– no más de tres horas.***
– for <u>p 95</u> hours.	***– <u>p 187</u> horas.***
He/She is very sensitive to…	*Él/Ella es muy sensible a…*
– light.	*– la luz.*
– noise.	*– el ruido.*
– wet diapers.	*– los pañales mojados.*
Please keep older children away from the baby while he/she is napping.	***Por favor mantén a los niños grandes lejos del/de la bebé cuando esté dormido(a).***
Do not let him/her fall asleep…	*No dejes que él/ella se quede dormido(a)…*
– in the car.	*– en el coche.*
– in the stroller.	*– en la carriola.*
– in the swing.	*– en el columpio.*
– at the park.	*– en el parque.*
He/She is/is not a good sleeper.	***Él/Ella es/no es bueno(a) para dormir.***

naps & bedtime
siestas & la hora de dormir

He/She usually…	***Por lo general, él/ella …***
– takes a nap at <u>p 95</u>.	***– toma una siesta a las <u>p 187</u>.***
– goes to bed at <u>p 95</u>.	***– se acuesta a las <u>p 187</u>.***
– wakes up at <u>p 95</u>.	***– se despierta a las <u>p 187</u>.***
Before putting him/her to sleep, we usually…	*Antes de acostarlo/lla, normalmente…*
– read.	*– leemos.*
– listen to music.	*– escuchamos música.*
– cuddle.	*– nos abrazamos.*
Please play music when you put him/her to sleep.	***Por favor pon música cuando lo/la acuestes.***
This is his/her favorite CD/cassette.	*Éste es su CD/cassette favorito.*
If he/she cries…	***Si él/ella llora..***
– pick him(her) up right away.	***– levántalo(la) en seguida.***
– allow him(her) to cry for <u>p 95</u> minutes.	***– déjalo(la) llorar por <u>p 187</u> minutos.***
Try patting his/her back before…	*Intenta darle palmaditas en su espalda antes de…*
– picking him/her up.	*– levantarlo/lla.*
– giving him/her a pacifier.	*– darle un chupón.*

He/She likes to sleep with...	A él/ella le gusta dormirse con...
– this blanket.	– esta cobija
– this toy.	– este juguete.
– this doll.	– esta muñeca.

He/She likes it when you…	A él/ella le gusta que…
– rock	– lo/la mesas
– sing	– le cantes
...him/her to sleep.	… cuando lo/la estás acostando.

I want him/her to stop taking a morning nap.	Quiero que él/ella deje de tomar una siesta en la mañana.

Please put him(her) to bed at p 95.	Por favor acuéstalo(la) a las p 187.

Please wake him(her) up at p 95.	Por favor despiértalo(la) a las p 187.

cleaning
limpieza

Please change the bed linens...	Por favor cambia las sábanas ...
– once a week.	– una vez a la semana.
– every two weeks.	– cada dos semanas.
– if they are dirty.	– si están sucias.

Please wash soiled bed linens immediately.	Por favor lava las sábanas sucias inmediatamente.

Do not put this in the washer, please wash it by hand.	No pongas esto en la lavadora, por favor lávalo a mano.

safety
seguridad

Please put the baby to sleep on his/her back.	Acuesta al bebé de espaldas, por favor.

Be sure there are no…	Asegúrate de que no hayan…
– extra blankets	– cobijas extras
– pillows	– almohadas
...in his/her crib/bed.	…en su cuna/cama.

Please cover his(her) diaper with pants or pajamas before putting him(her) to sleep.	Ponle(la) un pantalón o una pijama encima de su pañal antes de acostarlo(la) por favor.

Please make sure...	Por favor asegúrate de que...
– you can hear the monitor.	– puedas oir el monitor.
– the crib railing is locked.	– el barandal de la cuna esté cerrado.

bilingual babycare

8

getting dressed
vistiéndose

getting dressed

· ·

bathing suit	*el traje de baño*
blouse	*la blusa*
boots	*las botas*
clothes	*la ropa*
dress	*el vestido*
hat	*el sombrero*
jacket	*la chamarra*
overcoat	*el abrigo*
panties	*los calzones*
pants	*los pantalones*
raincoat	*el impermeable*
shirt	*la camisa*
shoes	*los zapatos*
shorts	*los shorts*
skirt	*la falda*
slippers	*las pantuflas*
socks	*los calcetines*
sportscoat	*el saco*
stockings	*las medias*
suit	*el traje*
sweater	*el suéter*
sweatshirt	*la sudadera*
tennis shoes	*los tenis*
t-shirt	*la camiseta*
underwear	*los calzones*

general
general

Please dress him(her) in...	***Por favor vístelo(la)...***
– play clothes.	***– con ropa para jugar.***
– nice clothes.	***– con ropa de vestir.***
– p 108.	***– en p 200.***

He/She wants to wear...   *Él/Ella quiere ponerse...*

Please let/do not let him/her wear...

Por favor deja/no dejes que se ponga....

He/She likes to dress himself/herself.

A él/ella le gusta vestirse sólo(a).

This is his/her favorite...	***Este es su...***
– pair of pants.	***– pantalón favorito.***
– shirt.	***– camisa favorita.***
– jacket.	***– chamarra favorita.***
– p 108.	***– p 200.***

Please let/do not let the children share clothes.

Por favor deje/no dejes que los niños compartan la ropa.

Please put the clothes that are too small over here.

Por favor pon la ropa que ya no le queda aquí.

outdoors
al aire libre

Please help him put on his/her...	***Por favor ayúdale a ponerse su...***
– bathing suit.	***– traje de baño.***
– wind breaker.	***– rompevientos.***
– sweater.	***– suéter.***
– p 108.	***– p 200.***

Please take this jacket to the park.   *Por favor llévate esta chamarra al parque.*

He/She needs to wear these shoes today.

Él/Ella debe de usar estos zapatos hoy.

Please keep the wet...	*Por favor guarda...*
– rain coats	*– el impermeable mojado*
– boots	*– las botas mojadas*
– umbrellas	*– el paraguas mojado*
...outside.	*...afuera.*

Please put muddy clothes here.   ***Por favor pon la ropa lodosa aquí.***

Here are the...	*Aquí...*
– rain clothes.	*– está la ropa para la lluvia.*
– rubber boots.	*– están las botas de hule.*
– snow boots.	*– están las botas para la nieve.*
– gloves.	*– están los guantes.*

laundry
lavando ropa

Please wash these clothes...	*Por favor lava esta ropa...*
– in the washer.	*– en la lavadora.*
– by hand.	*– a mano.*
– immediately.	*– inmediatamente.*

The p 108 is dirty.

p 200 está sucio(a).

Please do the laundry every pg95.

Por favor lava la ropa sucia cada pg187.

Do/Do not put these clothes in the washer.

Pon/No pongas esta ropa en la lavadora.

The...	*Así funciona...*
– washer	*– la lavadora.*
– dryer	*– la secadora.*
...works like this.	

Please rinse out the p 108 in the shower/sink.

Por favor enjuága p 200 en la regadera/el fregadero.

We keep the...	*Guardamos...*
– detergent	*– el detergente*
– fabric softener	*– el suavizante de ropa*
– stain remover	*– el líquido para las manchas*
– bleach	*– el blanqueador*
...here.	*...aquí.*

Please do/do not use bleach.

Por favor usa/no uses blanqueador.

9

bath time
la hora del baño

bath time

· ·

bath	*el baño*
bathtub	*la tina*
brush	*el cepillo*
bubble bath	*el baño de burbujas*
cold	*frío(a)*
comb	*el peine*
conditioner	*el acondicionador*
dry	*seco(a)*
faucet	*la llave*
(to) groom	*arreglarse*
hairdryer	la *secadora para el pelo*
headband	*la cinta*
infant tub	*la bañera*
hot	*caliente*
lotion	*la crema*
mirror	*el espejo*
ribbon	*el listón de pelo*
shampoo	*el champú*
shower	*la regadera*
shower curtain	*la cortina de baño*
sink	*el lavabo*
slippery	*resbaloso(a)*
soap	*el jabón*
(to) splash	*salpicar*
sponge	*la esponja*
toothpaste	*la pasta de dientes*
towel	*la toalla*
washcloth	*la toallita*
water	*el agua*
wet	*mojado(a)*

general
general

Please give him/her a bath…	***Por favor dale un baño…***
– at the end of the day.	***– al final del día.***
– before nap time.	***– antes de la siesta.***
– every other day.	***– cada dos días.***
– after soiling himself/herself.	***– cuando se ensucie de popó.***

Here… / *Aquí…*
– are the bath toys. / *– están los juguetes de baño.*
– is the shampoo. / *– está el champú.*
– is the conditioner. / *– está el acondicionador.*

Be sure the water is… / ***Asegúrate de que el agua…***
– warm. / ***– esté calientita.***
– cool. / ***– esté fresca.***

Use/Do not use this tub. / *Usa/No uses esta tina.*

He/She likes/does not like… / ***A él/ella le gusta/no le gusta…***
– to take a bath. / ***– bañarse.***
– the shower. / ***– bañarse en la regadera.***
– getting his/her hair wet. / ***– mojarse el pelo.***
– shampoo. / ***– el champú.***
– running around naked. / ***– correr desnudo(a) por todas partes.***

He/She is afraid of… / *Él/Ella tiene miedo…*
– getting his/her hair wet. / *– de mojarse el pelo.*
– shampoo. / *– del champú.*
– the drain. / *– de la coladera.*
– water. / *– del agua.*
– getting soap in his/her eyes. / *– de que el jabón le entre a los ojos.*

We don't let him/her… / ***No lo/la dejamos…***
– splash in the tub. / ***– salpicar en la tina.***
– drink the bath water. / ***– tomar el agua de la tina.***

lotions & potions
jabones y cremas

He/She has sensitive skin. / ***Él/ella tiene la piel sensible.***

Please use this… / *Por favor usa…*
– soap. / *– este jabón.*
– shampoo. / *– este champú.*
– conditioner. / *– este acondicionador.*
– lotion. / *– esta crema.*

Please do not let him/her play with the soap in the water. / ***Por favor no dejes que juege con el jabón en el agua.***

Please do/do not put lotion on him/her after the bath. / *Por favor ponle/no le pongas crema después del baño.*

safety
seguridad

Don't let him/her...
– stand up in the bath.
– stay in the bath without
your supervision.

Please be sure the floor is not
slippery when he/she gets out of
the bath/shower.

Use this thermometer to
measure the temperature of
the water.

Please use these products when
cleaning the tub.

No lo/la dejes...
– pararse durante el baño.
– permanecer en el baño sin tu
supervisión.

Asegúrate de que el piso no esté
resbaloso cuando él/ella salga del
baño por favor.

Utiliza este termómetro para
medir la temperatura del agua.

Usa estos productos de limpieza
para limpiar la tina, por favor.

10

diapers & potties
*pañales y entrenamiento
para usar el excusado*

diapers & potties

. . . .

accident	*el accidente*
bad odor	*olor desagradable*
(to) change	*cambiar*
changing table	*el cambiador*
(to) clean up	*limpiar*
cloth diaper	*el pañal de tela*
cotton balls	*las bolitas de algodón*
delivery person	*el repartidor*
delivery service	*el servicio a domicilio*
detergent	*el detergente*
diaper cover	*el calzón de hule*
diaper pail	*el bote de pañales*
diaper	*el pañal*
dry	*seco(a)*
medicine cabinet	*el botiquín*
ointment	*la pomada*
pins	*los seguros*
poop	*la popó*
training potty	*la basinica*
rash	*la rosadura*
reward	*un premio*
sink	*el lavabo*
skin	*la piel*
(to) smell	*oler*
step stool	*el banquito*
sticker	*la estampa*
talcum powder	*el talco*
toilet paper	*el papel de baño*
toilet	*el excusado*
pull-ups	*los calzones entrenadores*
urine	*la orina*
velcro	*el velcro*
wet	*mojado(a)*
wipes	*las toallitas húmedas*

diapers
pañales

Please dispose of…	*Por favor tira los pañales con…*
– poopie	*– popó*
– pee pee	*– pipí*
…diapers here.	*…aquí.*

Please change his/her diaper… — *Por favor cambia su pañal…*
- every p 95 hours. — *– cada p 187 horas.*
- when it is full. — *– cuando esté lleno.*
- when he/she is crying. — *– cuando él/ella esté llorando.*

Please let me know when we need more… — ***Por favor avísame cuando necesitemos más…***
- **diapers.** — ***– pañales.***
- **wipes.** — ***– toallitas húmedas.***
- **diaper rash ointment.** — ***– pomada para rosaduras.***
- **tissue.** — ***– pañuelos desechables.***

Could you buy more diapers today? — *Podrías comprar más panales hoy?*

Please buy… — ***Por favor compra…***
- **the least expensive diapers.** — ***– los pañales más baratos.***
- **pull ups.** — ***– calzones entrenadores.***
- **swim diapers.** — ***– pañales para nadar.***
- **wipes.** — ***– toallitas húmedas.***
- **these types of diapers.** — ***– este tipo de pañales.***

He/She wears size p 95. — *Él/Ella usa talla p 187.*

Please, change the bag in the diaper pail… — ***Por favor, cambia la bolsa del bote de pañales…***
- **now.** — ***– ahora.***
- **today.** — ***– hoy.***
- **everyday.** — ***– todos los días.***

Please use… — *Por favor usa…*
- warm wipes. — *– toallitas húmedas calientitas.*
- cotton balls instead of wipes. — *– bolitas de algodón en lugar de toallitas húmedas.*

CLOTH DIAPERS
We use cloth diapers.

PAÑALES DE TELA
Nosotros usamos pañales de tela.

We keep… — *Guardamos…*
- clean diapers — *– los pañales limpios*
- dirty diapers — *– los pañales sucios*
- diaper covers — *– los calzones de hule*
…here. — *…aquí.*

Put all soiled diapers in… — ***Pon todos los pañales con popó…***

- **the diaper pail** — ***– en el bote de pañales***
- **the diaper genie** — ***– en el "Diaper Genie"***
…**that is located __.** — ***…que está en __.***

Please dispose of solids (poop) in the toilet. — *Tira la popó en el excusado, por favor.*

Please wash cloth diapers separately from other clothes.	***Lava los pañales de tela aparte de la demás ropa, por favor.***
Please clean diaper covers…	*Por favor limpia los calzones de hule…*
– by hand.	*– a mano.*
– in the washing machine.	*– en la lavadora.*
– once a week.	*– una vez a la semana.*
– every couple days.	*– cada dos días.*
The diaper service picks up diapers on <u>p 95</u> at <u>p 95</u>.	***El servico de pañales recoge los pañales el <u>p 187</u> a las <u>p 187</u>.***
Please be sure the diaper pail is outside on that day.	*Por favor asegúrate de que el bote de pañales esté afuera ese día.*

potty training
entrenamiento para usar el excusado

We would like him/her to start using the potty.	***Nos gustaría que él/ella empezara a usar el excusado.***
Please have him/her sit on the toilet for a little while every day.	*Por favor que se siente un ratito en el excusado todos los días.*
He/She likes…	***A él/ella le gusta…***
– the small potty.	***– la basinica.***
– flushing the toilet.	***– jalarle al excusado.***
– playing with toilet paper.	***– jugar con el papel de baño.***
– the potty seat.	***– la sillita que va encima del excusado.***
If he/she goes potty in the toilet please give him/her a…	*Si él/ella va al baño en el excusado, por favor dale…*
– sticker	*– una estampa*
– treat	*– un dulce*
– a star	*– una estrella*
…as a reward.	*…de premio.*
Please help him/her learn how to use the potty by…	***Por favor ayúdalo(la) a aprender a usar el excusando viendo…***
– watching this video	***– este video***
– reading this book	***– este libro***
…with him/her.	***…con él/ella.***
Please help him(her) wipe his(her) bottom after using the potty.	*Por favor ayúdalo(la) a limpiarse después de ir al baño.*
Only use flushable wipes in the toilet.	*Sólo puedes echar toallitas desechables en el excusado.*
Remind him/her to flush the toilet.	*Recuérdale de jalar el excusado.*
He/She is afraid of…	***Él/Ella tiene miedo…***
– falling in the toilet.	***– de cayerse en el excusado.***
– the sound of flushing.	***– del ruido que hace cuando jalas el excusado.***
Don't flush the toilet if it's only urine.	*No le jales al excusado si es solamente orina.*
Remind her to wipe front to back.	***Recuérdale de limpiarse de adelante hacia atrás.***

Tell him to aim for the toys in the toilet when he goes pee-pee.

Díle que apunte hacia los juguetes en el excusado cuando haga pipí.

Please clean up, if he misses the toilet.

Por favor limpia el excusado si no le atina.

Please soak all soiled clothing in…
– the sink
– the tub
– the toilet
…before washing it.

Por favor remoja la ropa con popó en…
– el fregadero
– la tina
– el excusado
…antes de lavarla.

hygiene
higiene

I think he/she has a dirty diaper.

Creo que él/ella tiene popó.

He/She has…
– a diaper rash.
– a urinary tract infection.

Él/Ella…
– está rosado(a).
– tiene una infección de las vías urinarias.

The diaper rash cream is __.

La pomada para rosaduras está __.

Please apply the diaper rash cream…
– every time you change a diaper.
– after a bath.
– after going to the potty.

Por favor ponle(la) la pomada para rosaduras…
– cada vez que cambias su pañal.
– después del baño.
– después de que vaya al baño.

Please remind him/her to wash his/her hands after using the potty.

Recuérdale que se lave las manos después de ir al baño, por favor.

She has a urinary tract infection because she is not wiping herself well enough.

Ella tiene una infección de las vías urinarias porque no se está limpiando bien.

Please be sure he/she is wearing clean panties.

Por favor asegúrate de que tenga puestos calzones limpios.

11

health & safety
salud y seguridad

health & safety

....

accident	*el accidente*
allergy	*la alergia*
antihistamine	*el antihistaminico*
band-aid	*la curita*
bite	*la mordedura*
(to) bleed	*sangrar*
blister	*la ampolla*
blood	*la sangre*
broken	*roto(a)*
bruise	*el moretón*
burn	*la quemadura*
burned	*quemado(a)*
(to) choke	*ahogarse*
contagious	*contagioso(a)*
(to) cough	*toser*
cough syrup	*el jarabe para la tos*
dehydration	*la deshidratación*
(to) drown	*ahogarse*
(to) fall down	*caerse*
fever	*la fiebre*
fire extinguisher	*el extinguidor*
first aid kit	*la caja de primeros auxilios*
fracture	*la fractura*
frostbite	*el congelamiento*
heatstroke	*la insolación*
infected	*infectado(a)*
insect repellent	*el repelente*
itch	*la comezón*
nosebleed	*la hemorragia nasal*
poisoning	*la intoxicación*
scratch	*el rasguño*
seizure	*el ataque*
(to) sneeze	*estornudar*
sore throat	*el dolor de garganta*
stomach ache	*el dolor de estómago*
sting (insect bite)	*el piquete*
sunburn	*la quemadura de sol*
swollen	*inflamado(a)*
(to) vomit	*vomitar*

general safety
seguridad general

Please be careful of the baby's head when you pick him/her up.

Ten cuidado con la cabeza del/de la bebé cuando lo/la levantes, por favor.

Please do not give him/her medicine without asking me first.

Por favor no le des medicina sin antes preguntarme.

Let me show you how to install the car seat.

Déjame enseñarte cómo se pone el asiento del coche.

Be sure the seat belt is fastened…
– on the high chair.
– on the swing.

Asegúrate de que el cinturón..
– de la silla para comer
– del columpio
…esté abrochado.

Make sure there are plastic covers on every electrical outlet. If you need more they are located in __ .

Asegúrate de que haya una cubierta plastica en cada enchufe eléctrico. Si necesitas más, se encuentran en __ .

Be sure the cords for the curtains are not low enough for the baby to reach.

Asegúrate de que el bebé no puede alcanzar el cordón de las cortinas.

Keep the furniture away from open windows.

Mantén los muebles lejos de las ventanas abiertas.

Be careful, he/she likes to…
– climb the book shelf.
– open the cabinets.
– open the front door.
– lock the bathroom door.
– take off his/her clothes.

Ten cuidado, a él/ella le gusta…
– subirse al librero.
– abrir los gabinetes.
– abrir la puerta principal.
– cerrar la puerta del baño.
– quitarse la ropa.

Please keep the children off the top bunk.

No dejes que los niños se suban a la litera de arriba, por favor.

Be careful, he/she likes to put things in his/her…
– nose.
– mouth.
– eyes.
– ears.

Ten cuidado, a él/ella le gusta meterse cosas en…
– su naríz.
– su boca.
– sus ojos.
– sus oídos.

Be careful, he/she sometimes tries to eat the plants.

Ten cuidado, a veces él/ella trata de comerse las plantas.

These plants are poisonous.

Estas plantas son venenosas.

Please face the pot handle away from the edge of the stove.

Por favor pon el mango del sartén lejos de la orilla de la estufa.

He/She knows how to open the doors.

Él/Ella sabe cómo abrir las puertas.

He/She is not allowed…
– in the front yard
– in the back yard
…alone.

Él/Ella no puede ir al…
– jardín de enfrente
– jardín de atrás
…sólo(a).

Please make sure he/she wears…	Por favor asegúrate de que él/ella lleve puesto(a)…
– a helmet.	– un casco.
– wrist pads.	– muñequeras.
– elbow pads.	– codilleras.
– knee pads.	– rodilleras.

illness
enfermedades

He/She does not feel well today.	***Él/Ella no se siente bien hoy.***
I think he/she…	Creo que él/ella…
– has a fever.	– tiene fiebre.
– has a stomach ache.	– tiene un dolor de estómago.
– has the flu.	– tiene gripe.
– has p 111.	– tiene p 202.
I think he/she is teething.	***Creo que le están saliendo los dientes.***
Please just hold him(her) today as much as possible.	Por favor abrázalo(la) hoy lo más que puedas.
Call me if he/she doesn't look better by p 95.	***Llámame por teléfono si no se mejora para las p 187.***
I am nervous about his/her cough. I think it might be croup.	Su toz me da nervio. Creo que puede ser el crup.
He/She was vomiting…	***Él/Ella estuvo vomitando…***
– this morning.	***– hoy en la mañana.***
– last night.	***– anoche.***
Please give/do not give him/her medicine.	Por favor dale/no le des medicina.
Please give him/her this medication every p 95 hours.	***Por favor dale esta medicina cada p 187 horas.***
Please keep him(her) away from other children.	Por favor manténlo(la) lejos de otros niños.
I think he/she is contagious.	***Creo que él/ella es contagioso(a).***
What color is the mucus?	¿De qué color es el moco?
– green?	– verde?
– yellow?	– amarillo?
– clear?	– claro?
– bloody?	– con sangre?
What color was the poop?	***¿De qué color era la popó?***
– brown?	***– café?***
– light brown?	***– café claro?***
– p 109?	***– p 201.***
I will meet you at the doctor's office.	Yo te alcanzo en la oficina del doctor.
Please take his/her temperature and call me if it is above 100 °F (37.8 Celsius).	***Por favor tómale su temperatura y llámame si está arriba de 100°F (37.8 Celsios).***

accidents
accidentes

Please call 911 if he/she is seriously injured.	***Por favor marca el 911 si él/ella se lastima seriamente.***
Please call me if he/she hurts himself.	*Por favor háblame por teléfono si se lastima.*
He/She fell and hurt his/her...	***Él/Ella se cayó y se lastimó su...***
– head.	***– cabeza.***
– knee.	***– rodilla.***
– elbow.	***– codo.***
– p 112.	***– p 203.***
Please don't let him/her jump off the p 99.	*Por favor no dejes que él/ella salte de p 191.*
He/she slammed his/her finger in the door.	***Él/Ella se machucó el dedo en la puerta.***
If he/she hits his/her head, do not let him/her go to sleep, and watch for any abnormal behavior.	*Si él/ella se pega en la cabeza, no dejes que se duerma, y observa que no se comporte de una forma anormal.*
– The first aid box	***– La caja de primeros auxilios***
– The band-aids	***– Las curitas***
– The antibiotic cream	***– La pomada antibiótica***
– The disinfectant	***– El desinfectante***
– p 111	***– p 203***
...are here.	***...está/están aquí.***

bites & stings
mordeduras y piquetes

He/She was bitten by a...	***A él/ella le/la mordió...***
– dog.	***– un perro.***
– snake.	***– una vívora.***
– p 98.	***– p 190.***
He/She was stung by a...	*A él/ella le/la picó...*
– mosquito.	*– un mosquito.*
– bee.	*– una abeja.*
– wasp.	*– un abispa.*
– p 98.	*– p 190.*
He/She has bites on his/her...	***Él/Ella tiene piquetes en...***
– arms.	***– sus brazos.***
– legs.	***– sus piernas.***
– back.	***– su espalda.***
– face.	***– su cara.***
– p 112.	***– p 203.***
Please use this ointment to soothe the itching.	*Por favor usa esta pomada para quitar la comezón.*
Try to keep him/her from scratching the bites.	***Trata de que él/ella no se rasque sus piquetes.***
Please use this bug repellent when you go outside.	*Por favor usa este repelente cuando vayan afuera.*

ANIMAL BITES
MORDEDURAS DE ANIMALES

Calm the child, and call 911 if you feel they have been severely bitten.

Calme al niño y llame al 911 si cree que ha sido mordido severamente.

If it is a dog bite, keep track of the dog, in case it has rabies.

Si es una mordida de perro, tome los datos del perro, en caso de que tenga rabia.

Hold a clean cloth on the wound and apply pressure until the bleeding stops. If the bite is on the arm or hand hold the wound above the child's heart.

Ponga un trapo limpio en la herida y presione hasta que se pare la sangre. Si la mordida está en el brazo o la mano, mantenga la herida arriba de la altura del corazón del niño.

Place a sterile bandage over the wound and call the child's parents to describe the event and ask if they would like you to take the child to the doctor.

Ponga una venda estéril sobre la herida y llame a los padres del niño para describirles lo que sucedió y preguntarles si quieren que lleve al niño al doctor.

INSECT BITES
PIQUETES DE INSECTOS

Use caution when removing a wasp or bee stinger, because if you push it back into the child's skin, it could inject more venom.

Tenga cuiadado al remover el aguijón de una avispa o abeja, porque si lo llegara a meter más en la piel del niño, se puede injectar más veneno.

Use a dull butter knife or credit card to scrape in the opposite direction of the stinger entry.

Use un cuchillo sin filo o una tarjeta de crédito para raspar en la dirección opuesta de la entrada del aguijón.

Wash the bite with soap and water, or clean it with alcohol. Reduce pain and swelling with a cold compress such as ice wrapped in a wash cloth.

Lave el piquete con agua y jabón, o límpielo con alcohol. Disminuya el dolor y la inflamación con una compresa fría, como un trapo con hielo.

If the child is uncomfortable use a topical antihistamine or apply a paste made from baking soda and water. Apply calamine lotion to help relieve itching and pain. In extreme cases, call the pediatrician and give the child Benedryl for immediate relief of swelling.

Si el niño está incómodo, use un antihistamínico topical o aplique una pasta hecha de bicarbonato y agua. Aplique loción de calamina para ayudar a la comezón y el dolor. En casos extremos, llame al pediátra y dele Benedryl al niño para aliviar de inmediáto la inflamación.

The information below is to be used as a reminder for you and you
provider. The red cross offers first aid and CPR classes in Spanish
cities. Go to www.redcross.org for a location near you.

La siguiente información se debe de usar como un recordatorio
niñera. La Cruz Roja ofrece clases de primeros auxilios y RCP en
todas la ciudades principales. Visite la pagina de Internet www.redcross.
localizar una clase cerca de Usted.

CPR FOR INFANTS (UP TO 1 YR.OLD)
RCP PARA BEBÉS (HASTA 1 AÑO)

Symptoms that indicate that CPR is required:
*No signs of circulation (normal breathing, movement, pulse) and/or breathing.
*The infant is unconscious.

Síntomas que indican la necesidad de RCP:
*Noy hay señales de circulación (respiración normal, movimiento, pulso) y/o respiración.
*El bebé puede estar inconsciente.

Alert someone to call 911, as you position the infant on his or her back on a hard surface, such as a table. Be very careful not to move or twist the head, neck or spine.

Pídale a alguien que llame al 911, mientras que usted acomoda al bebé boca arriba en una superficie dura, como podría ser una mesa. Tenga mucho cuidado de no mover o voltear su cabeza, cuello o columna.

Position your hands for CPR: Imagine a line connecting the infant's nipples; place your middle and ring fingers on this line, on top of the baby's sternum. Use the other hand to tilt the infant's head back slightly and gently lift the chin to open the airway.

Ponga las manos en la posición correcta para RCP: Imagine una linea conectando las tetillas del bebé; ponga dos dedos encima de esta linea, sobre el esternón del bebé. Use la otra mano para inclinar su cabeza hacia atrás, levantándole la barba para abrir la via aérea.

Pushing with your fingers, give the infant 5 chest compressions, to a depth of approximately ½ to 1 inch.

Con los dedos, déle 5 compresiones en el pecho, hasta una profundidad de ½ a 1 pulgada aproximadamente.

Then press your lips around the infant's mouth and nose. Take a breath and breathe slowly into the infant's airway until you see their chest rise.

Después presione sus labios alrededor de la boca y de la nariz de bebé. Tome aire y sople lentamente en la vía aérea del bebé hasta ver que su pecho suba.

Repeat this five – compression, one – breath cycle a total of 20 times. Next check to see if the child has signs of circulation and breathing for a maximum of 10 seconds. If not, continue to administer CPR, until the infant shows signs of circulation and breathing, or until professional medical assistance arrives.

Repita este ciclo de 5 compresiones y un soplo un total de 20 veces. Después revise si el bebé tiene señales de circulación y respiración durantre un máximo de 10 segundos. Si no, continúe con el RCP hasta que el bebé demuestre señales de circulación y respiración, o hasta que llegue ayuda médica profesional.

CPR FOR CHILDREN
RCP PARA NIÑOS

Alert someone to call 911, as you position the child on his or her back on a hard surface.
Be very careful not to move or twist the head, neck or spine.

Place your hands above the sternum:
* Slide your fingers down the breast bone towards the sternum and put the heel of your hand just above (not on top of) the sternum.
* Put the other hand on the child's forehead.

With the heel of your hand, push downward on the chest, using the weight of your upper body for strength.
Compress five times to a depth of approximately ½ to 1 inch.

Tilt the child's head back slightly and gently lift the chin to open the airway.
Softly pinch their nose.
Take a breath and then breathe slowly into the child's mouth, maintaining a seal between your mouth and that of the child's, until you see their chest rise.

Repeat this five – compression, one – breath cycle a total of 12 times.
Next check to see if the child has signs of circulation and breathing for a maximum of 10 seconds.
If not, continue to administer CPR, until the infant shows signs of circulation and breathing, or until professional medical assistance arrives.

*Pídale a alguien que llame al 911, mientras que usted acomoda al niño boca arriba en una superficie dura.
Tenga mucho cuidado de no mover o voltear su cabeza, cuello o columna.*

*Ponga las manos en la posición correcta sobre el esternón:
* Deslice los dedos por el borde de la caja torácica hacía el esternón y pon la base de la mano justo arriba (no encima) de la hendidura del esternón.
Pon la otra mano en la frente del niño.

*Con la base de la mano, comprima el pecho, usando el peso del cuerpo para darle fuerza.
Comprima 5 veces hasta una profundidad de ½ a 1 pulgada aproximadamente.*

*Inclínele su cabeza hacia atrás y levántele la barba para abrir la via aérea.
Tápele la nariz.
Tome aire y sople lentamente en la boca del niño, manteniendo un sello entre su boca y la del niño, hasta ver que su pecho suba.*

*Repita este ciclo de 5 compresiones y un soplo un total de 12 veces.
Después revise si el niño tiene señales de circulación y respiración durante un máximo de 10 segundos.
Si no, continúe con el RCP hasta que el niño demuestre señales de circulación y respiración, o hasta que llegue ayuda médica profesional.*

bilingual babycare

Babies can choke on food or toys left behind by older siblings. It's important to understand the best technique for helping to clear the airway. This information along with many more safety procedures are taught during a red cross first aid course.

Los bebés pueden ahogarse con comida o juguetes que dejen tirados sus hermanos más grandes. Es importante saber cuál es la mejor forma de desbloquear la vía respiratoria. Esta información, además de otras precauciones, se enseña en una clase de primeros auxilios de la Cruz Roja.

CHOKING (FOR BABIES)
EN CASO DE AHOGO (PARA BEBÉS)

Quickly check to see if the baby is breathing: evalute the rise and fall of the chest and listen for the sounds of breathing. Ask someone to call 911. If you are alone, go to the phone with your infant and call 911 as you follow the directions below:

Revise rápidamente si el bebé está respirando: evalúe el movimiento del pecho y escuche por algún sonido de respiración. Pídale a alguién que llame al 911. Si ésta sola, vaya al teléfono con su bebé y llame al 911 mientras siga las siguientes instrucciones:

Place the baby face down lengthwise on your forearm, head pointed toward the ground. Use your thigh for support if necessary as you make sure the baby is positioned firmly against your forearm.

Coloque al bebé boca abajo a lo largo de su antebrazo, con la cabeza apuntada hacia el suelo. Si es necesario, use su pierna como un soporte mientras asegure que el bebé esté posicionado seguramente en su antebrazo.

With the palm of your hand, give the baby five firm back blows between the shoulder blades. If your baby doesn't begin to cry after the back blows, lay him or her face up and administer CPR, as described above. (page 80)

Con la palma de su mano, déle al bebé cinco palmadas firmes en la espalda entre los omóplatos. Si el bebé no empieza a llorar después de las palmadas en la espalda, acuéstelo boca arriba y déle RCP, como se describe anteriormente.

If the airway is still blocked, continue with another set of back blows and CPR until trained medical help arrives.

Si la vía aérea del bebé sigue bloqueada, continúe con otra serie de palmaditas en la espalda y con el RCP hasta que llegue el personal médico.

Earthquakes are unpredictable, therefore being prepared ahead of time is crucial for your child's comfort and safety during and after this frightening experience. Be sure you and your child's caregiver know how to turn off the gas, water and electricity as well as the location of a prepacked earthquake survival kit. Have an out of state contact, such as a friend or relative to relay information to in case the local phone services are not working.

Los terremotos son imprevisibles, por lo tanto es muy importante prepararse con anticipación para asegurar la seguridad y comodidad de su hijo durante y después de esta experiencia tan aterradora. Asegúrese de que usted y su niñera sepan como apagar el gas, el agua y la electricidad así como la ubicación de un botiquín en caso de terremotos. Tenga listo un contacto que no viva en su ciudad, como podría ser un amigo o pariente, para poder comunicarse con él si no están funcionando las líneas de teléfono.

EARTHQUAKE SAFETY
PRECAUCIONES EN CASO DE TERREMOTOS

If you are indoors, stay inside and get yourself and the children underneath a sturdy piece of furniture like a desk or table. Hold on tight and expect to move with it during the shaking. (Or stand against an interior wall with no windows, shelves or attached objects as you cover the children and your head and neck with your arms.)	*Si está adentro, permanezca adentro y métase junto con los niños abajo de un mueble fuerte como un escritorio o una mesa. Agárrese fuertemente y esté preparado para moverse durante el terremoto. (O párese en una esquina o contra una pared interior sin ventanas, repisas u objetos pegados mientas cubra su cabeza, su cuello y a los niños con sus brazos.)*
Stay away from windows, shelves or other areas where objects may fall.	*Manténgase lejos de ventanas, repisas u otras áreas donde se pueden caer objetos.*
If you are in a multi story building without a desk or table nearby, move against an interior wall and protect your head and neck with your arms as well as the children.	*Si está en un edificio y no hay un escritorio o mesa cercana, recárgese en una pared y protega su cabeza, su cuello y a los niños con sus brazos.*
If you are outside, try to get away from trees, buildings, walls, signs and power lines. Lay flat on the ground with the children until the earthquake is over.	*Si está afuera, trate de alejarse de árboles, edificios, paredes, señales y cables de alta tensión. Acuéstese en el suelo con los niños hasta que termine el terremoto.*
If you are in a car, pull over to the side of the road away from overpasses, power lines and tall buildings. Stay in your car until the shaking ends.	*Si está en un coche, orillese a un lado de la carretera lejos de puentes, cables de alta tensión y edificios altos. Quédese en el coche hasta que termine el terremoto.*
If in a crowded store or public area, get away from shelves or other areas where objects may fall. Do not run for the door. Crouch and cover your head and neck with your arms.	*Si está en una tienda o área pública con mucha gente, aléjese de repisas u otras áreas de donde se pueden caer objetos. No corra hacia afuera. Agáchese y cubra su cabeza y su cuello con sus brazos.*

bilingual babycare

Despite warning labels, a number of children die each year from accidental poisoning. Luckily, parents and care givers can call 1 – 800 – 222 – 1222 if they think their child is in immdediate danger. Be sure your nanny is armed with the following information provided by the American Associaton of Poison Control Centers. For more information visit their website at www.poison.org.

A pesar de las advertencias en los productos, cada año un número de niños muere por envenenamiento accidental. Afortunadamente, los padres y la gente que se dedica a cuidar niños pueden llamar a los Centros de Control de Envenenamiento al teléfono 1 – 800 – 222 – 1222 si piensan que su hijo está en peligro. Asegúrese de que su niñera tenga a la mano la siguiente información de la "American Association of Posion Control Centers." Para más información visite la pàgina de Internet www.poison.org.

POISONS
VENENOS

The following medicines and household products are dangerous if used incorrectly:

Las siguientes medicinas y productos caseros son peligrosos si se usan de forma incorrecta:

* Diet pills and stimulants – – pills to help you stay awake.

* Pastillas dietéticas y estimulantes – – pastillas que le ayudan a mantenerse despierto.

* Other medicines, like those that treat depression or high blood pressure.

* Otras medicines, como las que se usan para la depresión y la presión arterial alta.

Use caution with the following:

Hay que tener cuidado con lo siguiente:

* Art supplies: powder clay, instant paper mache, powdered tempera paints , permanent felt tipped markers (use water based), instant glue, model glue or other solvent based adhesives like epoxy.

* Productos de arte: arsilla en polvo, papél maché, pinturas en polvo de témpera, marcadores permanentes (use marcadores de agua), pegamento instantáneo, pegamento para modelos, y otros adhesivos con base de solventes, como el epoxy.

* Dishwasher detergent

* Detergente para el lavaplatos.

* Bleach mixed with ammonia, gasoline, kerosene, paint thinner, antifreeze, and windshield washing fluid.

* Blanqueador mezclado con amoniaco, gasolina, queroseno, tiner, anticongelante, y líquido limpia – parabrisas.

* Beer, wine, liquor and other products with alcohol, like mouthwash, aftershave and colognes.

* Cerveza, vino, licor y otros productos con alcohól como, enjuague bucal, lociones para después de afeitarse y colonias.

* Some houseplants such as: aloe vera, hydrangea, English Ivy and cyclamen, among others.

* Algunas plantas caseras como: áloe vera, hortensia, hiedra inglesa y ciclamen, entre otras.

SYMPTOMS OF POISONING
SINTOMAS DE ENVENENAMIENTO

If you see an open or spilled bottle of pills or other dangerous product, your child may have touched or swallowed poison.

Si ve una botella de pastillas u otro producto peligroso abierto, su niño pudo haber tocado o tragado veneno.

An important sign of poisoning is when children who were well develop unusual symptoms, for example:

Una señal importante de envenenamiento es cuando niños que estaban bien de repente desarrollan síntomas inusuales, por ejemplo:.

* They're sleepy even though it's not nap time.

* Tienen sueño a pesar de que no es su hora de siesta.

* They can't follow you with their eyes.

* No pueden seguirle con la mirada.

* Their eyes go around in circles.

* Sus ojos empiezan a dar vueltas.

* They have burns or stains around the mouth.

* Tienen quemaduras o manchas alrededor de la boca.

* Their breath smells strange.

* Su aliento huele raro.

IF YOU SUSPECT POISONING
SI SOSPECHA UN ENVENENAMIENTO

If you think your child has swallowed, breathed in, or touched poison, call the poison center right away. The number is 1 – 800 – 222 – 1222.

Si piensa que su niño ha tragado, respirado o tocado veneno, llame al Centro de Control de Venenos de inmediato. El número telefónico es el 1 – 800 – 222 – 1222.

If you can, tell them:
– the name of the poison
– the way the poison was taken; (swallowed, breathed in, or splashed on the skin or eyes)

De ser posible, dígales:
– el nombre del veneno
– la forma en que el niño se tomó el veneno, (fuetragado, respirado o salpicado en su cueroo o en sus ojos.)

– if your child has vomited
– your child's age, height & weight
– any health problems your child may have.

– si su niño ha vomitado.
– la edad, altura y peso de su niño
– cualquier problema de salud que tenga su niño.

If you are told to go to the hospital emergency room, take the poison with you.

Si le dicen que vaya a la sala de emergencias del hospital, llévese el veneno consigo.

bilingual babycare

G

glossary
glosario

BABY BASICS
PALABRAS BÁSICAS

special people
personas importantes

BABY – *EL BEBÉ*
BABYSITTER/ NANNY – *LA NIÑERA*
BIG BROTHER – *EL HERMANO GRANDE*
BIG SISTER – *LA HERMANA GRANDE*
CHILD – *EL NIÑO/LA NIÑA*
CHILDREN – *LOS NIÑOS*

LITTLE BROTHER – *EL HERMANO CHICO*
LITTLE SISTER – *LA HERMANA CHICA*
PREMATURE – *PREMATURO*
TRIPLETS – *TRILLIZOS*
TWINS – *GEMELOS*

equipment & toys
equipo y juguetes

BACKPACK – *LA MOCHILA*
BASSINET – *EL BAMBINETO*
BIB – *EL BABERO*
BICYCLE – *LA BICILETA*
BROKEN – *ROTO*
BUBBLES – *LAS BURBUJAS*
BUCKLE – *LA HEBILLA*
CAR SEAT – *EL ASIENTO DEL COCHE*
CHANGING TABLE – *EL CAMBIADOR*
CRIB – *LA CUNA*

FRONT PACK/SLING – *EL*

KANGURERO
HIGHCHAIR – *LA SILLA PARA COMER DEL BEBÉ*
PORTABLE CRIB – *CUNA PORTÁTIL*
ROCKING HORSE – *EL CABALLITO BALANCÍN*
SAFETY STRAP –*EL CINTRUÓN*
STROLLER – *LA CARRIOLA*
SWING – *EL COLUMPIO*
TRICYCLE – *EL TRICÍCLO*
WHEEL – *LA RUEDA*

comfort
consuelo

BLANKET – *LA COBIJA*
BOTTLE – *EL BIBERÓN*
BREASTMILK – *LA LECHE DE MATERNA*
GIVE A BOTTLE – *DAR UN BIBERÓN*
HUG – *EL ABRAZO*
KISS – *EL BESO*
LULLABY – *LA CANCIÓN PARA BEBÉS*

PACIFIER/NIPPLE – *EL CHUPÓN*
QUIET TIME – *TIEMPO PARA DESCANSAR*
ROCKING CHAIR – *LA MECEDORA*
SING A SONG – *CANTAR UNA CANCIÓN*
SIPPY CUP – *EL VASO ENTRENADOR*
SNACK – *EL REFRIGERIO*

diapers
pañales

CHANGE (TO) — *CAMBIAR*
DIAPER – *EL PAÑAL*
DIAPER PAIL – *EL BOTE DE PAÑALES*
DRY – *SECO(A)*
PULL – UPS – *LOS CALZONES*

ENTRENADORES
RASH – *LA ROSADURA*
TOILET – *EL EXUSADO*
TRAINING POTTY — *LA BASINICA*
URINE — *LA ORINA*
WIPES — *LAS TOALLITAS HÚMEDAS*

things babies do
cosas que hacen los ninos

BURP (TO) – *REPETIR*
CRAWL (TO) – *GATEAR*
CRY (TO) – *LLORAR*

CUDDLE (TO) – *ABRAZAR*
FALL (TO) – *CAERSE*
HUNGRY (TO BE) – *TENER HAMBRE*

LAUGH (TO) – *REIRSE*
ROLL OVER (TO) – *VOLTEARSE*
SAY A WORD (TO) – *DECIR UNA PALABRA*
SCREAM (TO) – *GRITAR*
SLEEP (TO) – *DORMIRSE*
SMILE (TO) – *SONREÍRSE*
SUCK HIS/HER THUMB (TO) – *CHUPARSE EL DEDO*
TAKE A NAP (TO) – *TOMAR UNA SIESTA*
TAKE A STEP (TO) – *DAR UN PASO*
TALK (TO) – *HABLAR*
THROW A TANTRUM (TO) – *HACER UN BERRINCHE*
TIRED (TO BE) – *ESTAR CONSADO(A)*
WALK (TO) – *CAMINAR*

EVERYDAY PHRASES
FRASES COMUNES

expressions
expresiones comunes

BLESS YOU (AFTER A SNEEZE) – *SALUD*
CAN I HELP YOU? – *¿PUEDO AYUDARLE?*
CAREFUL – *CUIDADO*
COME HERE – *VENGA*
COME IN – *PÁSE/ADELANTE*
CONGRATULATIONS – *FELICIDADES*
DON'T WORRY – *NO SE PREOCUPE*
EXCUSE ME – *PERDÓN*
FOR EXAMPLE – *POR EJEMPLO*
GOOD – BYE – *ADIOS*
GOOD AFTERNOON – *BUENAS TARDES*
GOOD EVENING – *BUENAS NOCHES*
GOOD LUCK – *BUENA SUERTA*
GOOD MORNING – *BUENOS DÍAS*
GREAT IDEA – *BUENA IDEA*
HAPPY BIRTHDAY – *FELIZ CUMPLEAÑOS*
HAVE A NICE DAY – *QUÉ TENGA BUEN DÍA*
HAVE FUN – *QUE SE DIVIERTA*
HELLO – *HOLA*
HELP – *AYUDA*
HOW ARE YOU? – *¿CÓMO ESTÁ?*
HOW'S IT GOING? – *¿CÓMO LE VA?*
I DON'T KNOW – *NO SÉ*
I'M SORRY – *LO SIENTO*
LET'S GO – *VÁMONOS*
MAY I COME IN – *¿SE PUEDE PASAR?*
MAYBE – *QUIZÁS*
MORE OR LESS – *MÁS O MENOS*
PLEASE – *POR FAVOR*
THANK YOU – *GRACIAS*
THANK YOU VERY MUCH – *MUCHAS GRACIAS*
THAT'S GREAT! – *QUÉ BIEN*
THAT'S TOO BAD – *QUÉ LÁSTIMA*
WELCOME – *BIENVENIDOS*
WHAT HAPPENED? – *¿QUÉ PASO?*
WHAT'S HAPPENING – *¿QUÉ PASA?*
YOU'RE WELCOME – *DE NADA*

questions
preguntas

HOW FAR? – *¿A QUÉ DISTANCIA?*
HOW LONG? – *¿CUÁNTO TIEMPO?*
HOW MANY? – *¿CUÁNTO?*
HOW MUCH? – *¿CUÁNTO?*
HOW? – *¿CÓMO?*
WHAT? – *¿QUÉ?*
WHEN? – *¿CUÁNDO?*
WHO? – *¿QUIÉN?*
WHY? – *¿POR QUÉ?*

where is it?
¿donde está?

THE BOTTLE IS __. *EL BIBERÓN ESTÁ __.*

. . . .

ABOVE – *ARRIBA DE*
BEHIND – *DETRÁS DE*
BETWEEN – *ENTRE*
DOWN – *ABAJO*
EAST – *ESTE*
HERE – *AQUÍ*
IN FRONT OF – *EN FRENTE DE*
INSIDE – *ADENTRO DE*
NEAR – *CERCA DE*
NEXT TO – *AL LADO DE*
NORTH – *NORTE*
ON TOP OF – *ENCIMA DE*
OUTSIDE – *AFUERA DE*
OVER THERE – *ALLÁ*

continued...

SOUTH – *SUR*	TO THE RIGHT – *A LA DERECHA*
STRAIGHT AHEAD – *DERECHO*	UNDER – *ABAJO DE*
THERE – *ALLÍ*	UP – *ARRIBA*
TO THE LEFT – *A LA IZQUIERDA*	WEST – *OESTE*

places to live
lugares para vivir

APARTMENT – *EL APARTAMENTO*	HOUSE – *LA CASA*
CITY – *LA CIUDAD*	STATE – *EL ESTADO*
CONDO – *EL CONDOMINIO*	U.S.A. – *E.U.A.*
COUNTRY – *EL PAÍS*	UNITED STATES OF AMERICA – *LO*
COUNTY – *EL CONDADO*	*ESTADOS UNIDOS*

common words
palabras comunes

A, AN – *UN, UNA*	IF – *SI*
AGAIN – *OTRA VEZ*	NO – *NO*
ALL – *TODOS*	ONLY – *SÓLO/SOLAMENTE*
ALTHOUGH – *AUNQUE*	THAT ONE – *ÉSE/ÉSA*
AND – *Y*	THEN – *ENTONCES*
AT – *A*	THESE – *ESTOS/ESTAS*
BECAUSE – *PORQUE*	THIS ONE – *ÉSTE/ÉSTA*
BEFORE – *ANTES DE*	VERY – *MUY*
EACH – *CADA UNO*	WITH – *CON*
FOR – *PARA*	WITHOUT – *SIN*
FROM – *DE*	YES – *SI*

PEOPLE
PERSONAS

pronouns
pronombres

HE – *ÉL*	WE – *NOSOTROS*
I – *YO*	YOU (FAMILIAR) – *TÚ*
SHE – *ELLA*	YOU (FORMAL) – *USTED*
THEY (FEM.) – *ELLAS*	YOU (PL.) – *USTEDES*
THEY (MASC.) – *ELLOS*	

family
familia

HE/SHE IS MY __. *ÉL/ELLA ES MI __.*
MY __ WILL PICK UP MY CHILD. *MI __ RECOGERÁ A MI NIÑO(A).*
. . . .

AUNT – *TÍA*	GRANDMOTHER – *ABUELA*
BOYFRIEND – *NOVIO*	GRANDSON – *NIETO*
BROTHER – *HERMANO*	HUSBAND – *ESPOSO*
BROTHER-IN-LAW – *CUÑADO*	MOTHER – *MADRE*
COUSIN (FEMALE) – *PRIMA*	MOTHER-IN-LAW – *SUEGRA*
COUSIN (MALE) – *PRIMO*	NEPHEW – *SOBRINO*
DAUGHTER – *HIJA*	NIECE – *SOBRINA*
DAUGHTER-IN-LAW – *NUERA*	PARENTS – *PAPÁS/PADRES*
FATHER – *PADRE*	RELATIVES – *PARIENTES*
FATHER-IN-LAW – *SUEGRO*	SISTER – *HERMANA*
FIANCEE – *NOVIO(A)*	SISTER-IN-LAW – *CUÑADA*
GIRLFRIEND – *NOVIA*	SON – *HIJO*
GRANDDAUGHTER – *NIETA*	SON-IN-LAW – *YERNO*
GRANDFATHER – *ABUELO*	STEPDAUGHTER – *HIJASTRA*

STEPFATHER – *PADRASTRO*
STEPMOTHER – *MADRASTRA*
STEPSON – *HIJASTRO*

UNCLE – *TÍO*
WIFE – *ESPOSA*

types of people
típos de personas

ACQUAINTANCE – *UN(A)*
CONOCIDO(A)
BABY – *UN(A) BEBÉ*
FRIEND – *UN(A) AMIGO(A)*
LITTLE BOY – *UN NIÑO*
LITTLE GIRL – *UNA NIÑA*
MAN – *UN HOMBRE*
OLDER PERSON – *UNA PERSONA
MAYOR*

PERSON – *UNA PERSONA*
SINGLE WOMAN – *UNA SEÑORITA*
TEENAGER – *UN ADOLESCENTE*
WOMAN – *UNA MUJER*
YOUNG BOY – *UN MUCHACHO*
YOUNG GIRL – *UNA MUCHACHA*
YOUNG PERSON – *UN JÓVEN*

physical attributes*
características físicas

THE BABY IS __. *ÉL/LA BEBÉ ES __.*
HE/SHE IS NOT __. *ÉL/ELLA NO ES __.*
I AM __. *YO SOY __.*
ARE YOU __ ? *¿ERES __ ?*

. . . .

BALD – *CALVO(A)*
BIG – *GRANDE*
BLOND – *RUBIO(A)*
DARK – *MORENO(A)*
FAIR – *CLARO(A)*
FAT – *GORDO(A)*
GOOD LOOKING – *GUAPO(A)*
OLD – *VIEJO(A)*
*o = masculine a = feminine

PRETTY – *BONITO(A)*
RED HEAD – *PELIRROJO(A)*
SHORT – *BAJO(A)*
SMALL – *PEQUEÑO(A)*
THIN – *FLACO(A)*
TALL – *ALTO(A)*
UGLY – *FEO(A)*
YOUNG – JÓVEN

descriptions*
palabras descriptivas (ser)

THE BABY IS __. *EL BEBÉ ES __.*
HE/SHE IS NOT __. *ÉL/ELLA NO ES __.*
I AM__. *YO SOY__.*
ARE YOU__ ? *¿ERES __ ?*

. . . .

AGGRESSIVE – *AGRESIVO(A)*
BAD – *MALO(A)*
BRAVE – *VALIENTE*
CREATIVE – *CREATIVO(A)*
DIFFICULT – *DIFÍCIL*
DIVORCED – *DIVORCIADO(A)*
DUMB – TONTO(A)
EASY – *FÁCIL*
FAMOUS – *FAMOSO(A)*
FAST – *RÁPIDO(A)*
FRIENDLY – AMABLE
IMAGINATIVE – *OCCURENTE*
INTELLIGENT – *INTELIGENTE*
MARRIED – *CASADO(A)*
MATURE – *MADURO(A)*
MEAN – *MALDITO(A)*
*o = masculine a = feminine

NEW – *NUEVO(A)*
NICE – *SIMPÁTICO(A)*
PATIENT – *PACIENTE*
PLEASANT – *AGRADABLE*
POLITE – *CORTÉS*
POOR – *POBRE*
PUNCTUAL – *PUNTUAL*
RICH – *RICO(A)*
SHY – *TÍMIDO(A)*
SINGLE – *SOLTERO(A)*
SLOW – *LENTO(A)*
STRANGE – *RARO(A)*
STRONG – *FUERTE*
TWIN(S) – *UN(A) GEMELO(A)*
WELL MANNERED – EDUCADO(A)
WIDOWED – *VIUDO(A)*

descriptions*
palabras descriptivas (estar)

THE BABY IS __. EL BEBÉ ESTÁ __.
HE/SHE IS NOT __. ÉL/ELLA NO ESTÁ __.
I AM __. YO ESTOY __.
ARE YOU __ ? ¿ESTÁS __ ?

. . . .

AVAILABLE – DISPONIBLE
BORED – ABURRIDO(A)
BUSY – OCUPADO(A)
CALM – QUIETO(A)
DEPRESSED – DEPRIMIDA(A)
DRY – SECO(A)
EXCITED – EMOCIONADO(A)
FUNNY – CHISTOSO(A)
GRUMPY – DE MAL HUMOR
HAPPY – CONTENTO(A)/FELÍZ
INTERESTED – INTERESADO(A)
JEALOUS – CELOSO(A)
*o = masculine a = feminine

LAZY – PEREZOSO(A)
NERVOUS – NERVIOSO(A)
PRESSURED – PRESIONADO(A)
QUIET – CALLADO(A)
SAD – TRISTE
SICK – ENFERMO(A)
SPOILED – MIMADO(A)
SURPRISED – SORPRENDIDO(A)
TIRED – CANSADO(A)
WELL – BIEN
WET – MOJADO(A)
WORRIED – PREOCUPADO(A)

careers*
profesiones

I AM __. YO SOY __.
MY HUSBAND/WIFE/PARTNER IS __. MI ESPOSO/ESPOSA/PAREJA ES __.

. . . .

ACTOR – UN ACTOR
ARTIST – UN(A) ARTISTA
ARCHITECT – UN(A) ARQUITECTO(A)
AUTHOR – UN(A) AUTOR(A)
BAKER – UN(A) PANADERO(A)
BANKER – UN(A) BANQUERO(A)
BOSS – UN(A) JEFE(A)
BUSINESSMAN – UN(A) EMPRESARIO(A)
CARPENTER – UN(A) CARPINTERO(A)
CHEF – UN(A) COCINERO(A)
DOCTOR – UN(A) DOCTOR(A)
DENTIST – UN(A) DENTISTA
EMPLOYEE – UN(A) EMPLEADO(A)
ENTREPRENEUR – UN(A) EMPRENDEDOR(A)
FARMER – UN(A) GRANJERO(A)
FIREMAN – UN(A) BOMBERO(A)
FREELANCER – UN(A) PROFESIONAL INDEPENDIENTE
GARDENER – UN(A) JARDINERO(A)
*o = masculine a = feminine

HOMEMAKER – UNA AMA DE CASA
JOURNALIST – UN(A) PERIODISTA
LAWYER – UN(A) ABOGADO(A)
MANAGER – UN(A) GERENTE(A)
MECHANIC – UN(A) MECANICO(A)
MIDWIFE – UNA PARTERA
MUSICIAN – UN MÚSICO
NURSE – UN(A) ENFERMERO(A)
PARAMEDIC – UN(A) PARAMÉDICO(A)
PEDIATRICIAN – UN(A) PEDIATRA
PLUMBER – UN(A) PLOMERO(A)
POLICEMAN – UN(A) POLICÍA
PRIEST – UN SACERDOTE
PRESIDENT – UN PRESIDENTE
PSYCHOLOGIST – UN(A) PSICÓLOGO(A)
TAILOR – UN(A) SASTRE
TEACHER – UN(A) MAESTRO(A)
VETERINARIAN – UN(A) VETERINARIO(A)
WRITER – UN(A) ESCRITOR(A)

religion
la religión

BIBLE – LA BIBLIA
CHURCH – LA IGLESIA
CATHEDRAL – LA CATEDRAL
CHAPEL – LA CAPILLA
CROSS – LA CRUZ
DEVIL – EL DIABLO
GOD – DIOS
HEAVEN – EL CIELO

HELL – EL INFIERNO
MASS – LA MISA
PRIEST – EL SACERDOTE
SAINTS – LOS SANTOS
SOUL – EL ALMA
SYNAGOGUE – LA SINAGOGA
VIRGIN (THE) – LA VIRGEN

bilingual babycare

I AM __. *YO SOY __.*

. . . .

AGNOSTIC – *AGNÓSTICO(A)*
ATHEIST – *ATEO(A)*
CHRISTIAN – *CRISTIANO(A)*
CATHOLIC – *CATÓLICO(A)*

JEWISH – *JUDÍO(A)*
MORMON – *MORMÓN(A)*
MUSLEM – *MUSULMÁN(A)*
PROTESTANT – *PROTESTANTE*

TIME, DIGITS & DAYS
TIEMPOS, DÍGITOS Y DÍAS

numbers
números

1 – *UNO*
2 – *DOS*
3 – *TRES*
4 – *CUATRO*
5 – *CINCO*
6 – *SEIS*
7 – *SIETE*
8 – *OCHO*
9 – *NUEVE*
10 – *DIEZ*
11 – *ONCE*
12 – *DOCE*
13 – *TRECE*
14 – *CATORCE*
15 – *QUINCE*
16 – *DIECISÉIS*
17 – *DIECISIETE*
18 – *DIECIOCHO*
19 – *DIECINUEVE*
20 – *VIENTE*
21 – *VIENTIUNO*
22 – *VIENTIDÓS*
23 – *VIENTITRÉS*
24 – *VIENTICUATRO*

25 – *VIENTICINCO*
26 – *VIENTISÉIS*
27 – *VIENTISIETE*
28 – *VIENTIOCHO*
29 – *VIENTINUEVE*
30 – *TREINTA*
40 – *CUARENTA*
50 – *CINCUENTA*
60 – *SESENTA*
70 – *SETENTA*
80 – *OCHENTA*
90 – *NOVENTA*
100 – *CIEN*
200 – *DOSCIENTOS*
300 – *TRESCIENTOS*
400 – *CUATROCIENTOS*
500 – *QUINIENTOS*
600 – *SIESCIENTOS*
700 – *SETECIENTOS*
800 – *OCHOCIENTOS*
900 – *NOVECIENTOS*
1,000 – *MIL*
MILLION – *MILLÓN*

hours of the day
horas del día

IT IS TWO O'CLOCK – *SON LAS DOS*
IT IS TWO THIRTY – *SON LAS DOS Y MEDIA*
IT IS FIVE TO TWO – *SON CINCO PARA LAS DOS*

IT IS A QUARTER TO TWO – *ES CUARTO PARA LAS DOS*
IT IS FIVE PAST TWO – *SON LAS DOS Y CINCO*
IT IS QUARTER AFTER TWO – *SON LOS DOS Y CUARTO*

days of the week
días de la semana

MONDAY – *LUNES*
TUESDAY – *MARTES*
WEDNESDAY – *MIÉRCOLES*
THURSDAY – *JUEVES*
FRIDAY – *VIERNES*

SATURDAY – *SABADO*
SUNDAY – *DOMINGO*

months of the year
meses del ano

JANUARY – *ENERO*	JULY – *JULIO*
FEBRUARY – *FEBRERO*	AUGUST – *AGOSTO*
MARCH – *MARZO*	SEPTEMBER – *SEPTIEMBRE*
APRIL – *ABRIL*	OCTOBER – *OCTUBRE*
MAY – *MAYO*	NOVEMBER – *NOVIEMBRE*
JUNE – *JUNIO*	DECEMBER – *DICIEMBRE*

time related words
palabras relacionadas con el tiempo

AFTER – *DESPUES DE*	NEVER – *NUNCA*
AFTERNOON – *LA TARDE*	NEXT MONTH – *EL PRÓXIMO MES*
AFTERWARDS – *DESPUÉS DE*	NEXT ONE – *EL(LA) PRÓXIMO(A)*
AGAIN – *OTRA VEZ*	NEXT TIME – *LA PRÓXIMA VEZ*
ALREADY – *YA*	NIGHT – *LA NOCHE*
ALWAYS – *SIEMPRE*	NOON – *EL MEDIODÍA*
BEFORE – *ANTES DE*	NOW – *AHORA*
DAILY – *DIARIO*	ONCE – *UNA VEZ*
DAY AFTER TOMORROW – *PASADO MAÑANA*	RIGHT NOW – *AHORITA*
DURING – *MIENTRAS*	SOMEDAY – *ALGÚN DÍA*
DUSK – *EL ANOCHECER*	SOON – *PRONTO*
EACH DAY – *CADA DÍA*	SUNRISE – *EL AMANECER*
EARLY – *TEMPRANO*	SUNSET – *LA PUESTA DEL SOL*
EVENING – *LA NOCHE*	THEN – *ENTONCES*
EVERY TIME – *CADA VEZ*	TIME – *TIEMPO*
FIRST – *PRIMERO*	TODAY – *HOY*
LAST – *EL(LA) ÚLTIMO(A)*	TOMORROW – *MAÑANA*
LAST MONTH – *EL MES PASADO*	TOMORROW MORNING – *MAÑANA POR LA MAÑANA*
LAST NIGHT – *ANOCHE*	TONIGHT – *HOY EN LA NOCHE*
LAST WEEK – *LA SEMANA PASADA*	TWICE – *DOS VECES*
LATE – *TARDE*	UNTIL – *HASTA*
LATER – *LUEGO*	WEEKEND – *EL FIN DE SEMANA*
MIDNIGHT – *MEDIA NOCHE*	YEAR – *EL AÑO*
MONTH – *MES*	YESTERDAY – *AYER*
MORNING – *LA MAÑANA*	

measurements
medidas

CENTIMETER – *UN CENTÍMETRO*	METER – *UN METRO*
FOOT – *UN PIE*	MILE – *UNA MILLA*
GRAM – *UN GRAMO*	MILLIMETER – *UN MILÍMETRO*
INCH – *UNA PULGADA*	OUNCE – *UNA ONZA*
KILO – *UN KILO*	POUND – *UNA LIBRA*
LITER – *UN LITRO*	YARD – *UNA YARDA*

quantative words*
palabras cuantitativas

A DOZEN – *UNA DOCENA*	HALF – *LA MITAD*
A LITTLE – *UN POCO*	MANY – *MUCHOS(AS)*
A LOT – *MUCHO*	MANY TIMES – *MUCHAS VECES*
ALL – *TODO*	MORE – *MÁS*
ALMOST – *CASI*	NO ONE – *NADIE*
ANOTHER – *OTRO(A)*	NONE – *NINGUNO(A)*
ANY – *CUALQUIER(A)*	NOTHING – *NADA*
BOTH – *AMBOS*	QUARTER – *UN CUARTO*
DOUBLE – *EL DOBLE*	REST OF – *LO DEMÁS*
EACH – *CADA UNO*	SAME – *EL(LA) MISMO(A)*
ENOUGH – *SUFICIENTE*	SEVERAL – *VARIOS(AS)*

bilingual babycare

SOME – *ALGUNOS(AS)*
TOGETHER – *JUNTOS(AS)*
*o = masculine a = feminine

TOO MUCH – *DEMASIADO(A)*

seasons & holidays
temporadas del año y días festivos

ASH WEDNESDAY – *EL MIÉRCOLES DE CENIZA*
CHRISTMAS – *LA NAVIDAD*
COLUMBUS DAY – *EL DÍA DE LA RAZA*
DAY OF THE DEAD – *EL DÍA DE LOS MUERTOS*
EASTER – *LA PASCUA*
FALL – *EL OTOÑO*
GOOD FRIDAY – *EL VIERNES SANTO*
HALLOWEEN – *EL HALLOWEEN*
HANUKAH – *LA HANUKAH*
HAPPY NEW YEAR – *FELIZ AÑO NUEVO*
JANUARY 6 – *EL DÍA DE LOS SANTOS REYES*
JULY 4TH – *EL 4 DE JULIO*
KWANZAA – *EL KWANZAA*
LABOR DAY – *EL DÍA DEL TRABAJO*
MARTIN LUTHER KING DAY – *EL DÍA DE MARTIN LUTHER KING*
MAY 5TH – *EL CINCO DE MAYO*

MEMORIAL DAY – *EL DÍA DE LOS CAÍDOS*
MERRY CHRISTMAS – *FELIZ NAVIDAD*
NEW YEARS DAY – *EL AÑO NUEVO*
PASSOVER – *EL PASSOVER*
RAMADAN – *EL RAMADÁN*
ROSH HASHANA – *EL ROSH HASHANA*
SPRING – *LA PRIMAVERA*
SPRING BREAK – *LAS VACACIONES DE PRIMAVERA*
ST. PATRICK'S DAY – *EL DÍA DE SAN PATRICIO*
SUMMER – *EL VERANO*
THANKSGIVING – *EL DÍA DE ACCIÓN DE GRACIAS*
VACATION – *LA VACACIÓN*
VALENTINES DAY – *EL DÍA DE LOS NOVIOS/SAN VALENTÍN*
WINTER – *EL INVIERNO*
YOM KIPPUR – *EL YOM KIPPUR*

NATURE
NATURALEZA

garden
jardín

BENCH – *LA BANCA*
BUSH – *EL ARBUSTO*
BRANCH – *LA RAMA*
BUD – *EL CAPULLO*
CACTUS – *EL CACTUS*
DANDELION – *EL DIENTE DE LEÓN*
DIRT – *LA TIERRA*
DUST – *EL POLVO*
FERN – *EL HELECHO*
FLOWER – *LA FLOR*
GRASS/LAWN – *EL PASTO*
GRAVEL – *LA GRAVA*
GROUND – *EL SUELO*
HAMMOCK – *LA HAMACA*

IVY – *LA HIEDRA*
LEAF – *LA HOJA*
MUD – *EL LODO*
PATIO – EL PATIO
PLANT – *LA PLANTA*
ROCK – *LA PIEDRA*
ROOT – *LA RAÍZ*
SAND – *LA ARENA*
SHADE – *LA SOMBRA*
SEED – *LA SEMILLA*
STICK – *EL PALO*
TREE – *EL ÁRBOL*
WEED – *LA MALA HEIRBA*

flowers
flores

DAISY – *LA MARGARITA*
GERANIUM – *EL GERANIO*
LAVENDER – LA LAVANDA
LILAC – *LA LILA*
PETUNIA – *LA PETUNIA*

POPPY – *LA AMAPOLA*
ROSE – *LA ROSA*
SUNFLOWER – *EL GIRASOL*
TULIP – *EL TULIPÁN*
VIOLET – *LA VIOLETA*

bugs & crawlers
insectos

ANT – *LA HORMIGA*
BEE – *LA ABEJA*
BEETLE – *EL ESCARABAJO*
BUG – EL BICHO
BUTTERFLY – *LA MARIPOSA*
CATEPILLAR – *LA ORUGA*
CRICKET – *EL GRILLO*
DRAGONFLY – *LA LIBÉLULA*
FLEA – *LA PULGA*
FLY – *LA MOSCA*
GRASSHOPPER – *EL SALTAMONTES*

HORNET – *EL AVISPÓN*
LADYBUG – *LA MARIQUITA*
MOSQUITO – *EL MOSQUITO*
MOTH – *LA POLILLA*
ROLY-POLY – *EL ESCARABAJO*
SCORPION – *EL ESCORPIÓN*
SNAIL – *EL CARACOL*
SPIDER – *LA ARAÑA*
WASP – *LA AVISPA*
WORM – *EL GUSANO*

pets
mascotas

CANARY – *EL CANARIO*
CAT – *EL GATO*
CHICKEN – *EL POLLO*
COW – *LA VACA*
CRAB – *EL CANGREJO*
DOG – *EL PERRO*
DONKEY – *EL BURRO*
DUCK – *EL PATO*
FISH – *EL PEZ*
FROG – *EL SAPO*
GOAT – *EL CHIVO*
GOOSE – *EL GANSO*

HAMSTER – *EL HÁMSTER*
HORSE – *EL CABALLO*
KITTEN – *EL GATITO*
LAMB – *EL CORDERO*
MOUSE – *EL RATÓN*
PARAKEET – *EL PERÍCO*
PARROT – *EL PERÍCO*
PIG – *EL COCHINO*
PUPPY – *EL CACHORRO*
RABBIT – *EL CONEJO*
SHEEP – *EL BORREGO*

wild animals
animales salvajes

ALLIGATOR – *EL CAIMÁN*
BEAR – *EL OSO*
BEAVER – *EL CASTOR*
BIRD – *EL PÁJARO*
CAMEL – *EL CAMELLO*
COYOTE – *EL COYOTE*
CROCODILE – *EL COCODRILO*
CROW – *EL CUERVO*
DEER – *EL VENADO*
DINOSAUR – *EL DINOSAURIO*
EAGLE – *EL AGUILA*
ELEPHANT – *EL ELEFANTE*
FOX – *EL ZORRO*
HAWK – *EL HALCÓN*
HIPPO – *EL HIPOPOTAMO*
GIRAFFE – *LA JIRAFA*

KANGAROO – *EL CANGURO*
LION – *EL LEÓN*
LIZARD – *EL LAGARTO*
MONKEY – *EL CHANGO*
OWL – *EL BÚHO*
RACCOON – *EL MAPACHE*
RAT – *LA RATA*
RHINO – *EL RINOCERONTE*
SNAKE – *EL SERPIENTE*
SQUIRREL – *LA ARDILLA*
TIGER – *EL TIGRE*
WOLF – *EL LOBO*
WOODPECKER – *EL PICAPOSTE*
UNICORN – *EL UNICORNIO*
ZEBRA – *LA CEBRA*

ocean animals
animales del oceáno

DOLPHIN – *EL DELFÍN*
FISH – *EL PEZ*
LOBSTER – *LA LANGOSTA*
MERMAID – *LA SIRENA*
SAND DOLLAR – *EL ERIZO DE MAR*
SEAHORSE – *EL CABALLO MARINO*

SHARK – *EL TIBURÓN*
STARFISH – *LA ESTRELLA MARINA*
TURTLE – *LA TORTUGA*
WALRUS – *LA MORSA*
WHALE – *LA BALLENA*

bilingual babycare

weather
el tiempo

COLD – *EL FRÍO*
CLOUDS – *LAS NUBES*
DRIZZLE – *LA LLOVIZNA*
FOG – *LA NIEBLA*
FROST – *LA HELADA*
HAIL – *EL GRANIZO*
HEAT – *EL CALOR*
HUMIDITY – *LA HUMEDAD*
HURRICANE – *EL HURACÁN*
ICE – *EL HIELO*

LIGHTNING – *EL RELÁMPAGO*
NICE WEATHER – *BUEN TIEMPO*
PUDDLE – *EL CHARCO*
RAIN – *LA LLUVIA*
STORM – *LA TORMENTA*
SNOW – *LA NIEVE*
SUN – *EL SOL*
THUNDER – *EL TRUENO*
TORNADO – *EL CICLÓN*
WIND – *EL VIENTO*

IT'S SUPPOSED TO BE ___. *VA A ESTAR ___.*

COLD – *FRÍO*
CLEAR – *DESPEJADO*
CLOUDY – *NUBLADO*
DRIZZLING – *LLOVIZNANDO*
HAILING – *GRANIZANDO*
HOT – *CALUROSO*
HUMID – *HÚMEDO*

LIGHTNING – *RELAMPAGEANDO*
NICE – *BONITO*
RAINING – *LLOVIENDO*
SNOWING – *NEVANDO*
SUNNY – *SOLEADO*
WINDY – *CON VIENTO*

geographic terms
términos geográficos

AIR – *EL AIRE*
DIRT/EARTH – *LA TIERRA*
EARTHQUAKE – *EL TERREMOTO*
FIRE – *EL FUEGO*
FLOOD – *LA INUNDACIÓN*
GROUND – *EL SUELO*

MOON – *LA LUNA*
MUD – *EL LODO*
SKY – *EL CIELO*
STARS – *LAS ESTRELLAS*
TIDE – *LA MAREA*
WATER – *EL AGUA*

HOUSE WORDS
PALABRAS REFERENTES A LA CASA

places in a house
lugares en una casa

IT IS IN THE ___. *ESTÁ EN ___.*
KEEP THE KIDS OUT OF ___. *MANTÉN LOS NIÑOS FUERA DE ___.*
THIS IS ___. *ESTO ES ___.*

ATTIC – *EL ÁTICO*
BACKYARD – *EL JARDÍN*
BALCONY – *EL BALCÓN*
BATHROOM – *EL BAÑO*
BACK DOOR – *LA PUERTA TRASERA*
BAR – *EL BAR*
BASEMENT – *EL SÓTANO*
BEDROOM – *LA RECÁMARA*
CHILDREN'S ROOM – *EL CUARTO DE LOS NIÑOS*
CHIMNEY/FIREPLACE – *LA CHIMENEA*
DINING ROOM – *EL COMEDOR*
DOWNSTAIRS – *ABAJO/PLANTA BAJA*

DRIVEWAY – *LA ENTRADA PARA COCHES*
FAMILY ROOM – *LA ESTANCIA*
FENCE – *LA CERCA*
FRONT DOOR – – *LA PUERTA PRINCIPAL*
FRONT YARD – *EL JARDÍN DE ENFRENTE*
FURNITURE – *LOS MUEBLES*
GARAGE – *EL GARAJE*
GATE – *EL PORTÓN*
GUEST ROOM – *EL CUARTO DE VISTAS*
HALLWAY – *EL PASILLO*
INDOORS – *ADENTRO*

continued...

KITCHEN – *LA COCINA*
LAUNDRY ROOM – *LA LAVANDERÍA*
LIBRARY – *LA BIBLIOTECA*
LIVING ROOM – *LA SALA*
NURSERY – *EL CUARTO DEL BEBÉ*
OFFICE – *LA OFICINA*
OUTDOORS – *AFUERA*

PLAYROOM – *EL CUARTO DE JUEGOS*
POOL – *LA PISCINA*
PORCH – *LA TERRAZA*
ROOF – *EL TECHO*
WINDOW – *LA VENTANA*
UPSTAIRS – *ARRIBA/PLANTA ALTA*

kitchen
la cocina

ALUMINUM FOIL – *EL PAPEL DE ALUMINIO*
BIB – *EL BABERO*
BOWL – *EL PLATO HONDO*
CABINET – *EL GABINETE*
COFFEE MAKER – *LA CAFETERA*
CUP – *LA TAZA*
DISHES – *LA VAJILLA*
DISHWASHER – *EL LAVAPLATOS*
FAUCET – *LA LLAVE*
FORK – *EL TENEDOR*
FREEZER – *EL CONGELADOR*
GARBAGE – *LA BASURA*
GARBAGE CAN – *EL BASURERO*
GAS RANGE – *LA PARILLA DE GAS*
GLASS – *EL VASO*
HIGHCHAIR – *LA SILLA PARA COMER DEL BEBÉ*

HOT – *CALIENTE*
KNIFE – *EL CUCHILLO*
MICROWAVE – *EL MICROONDAS*
NAPKIN – *LA SERVILLETA*
OVEN – *EL HORNO*
PLASTIC WRAP – *EL PAPEL DE PLÁSTICO*
POT – *LA OLLA*
REFRIDGERATOR – *EL REFRIGERADOR*
SIPPY CUP – *EL VASO ENTRENADOR*
SILVERWARE – *LOS CUBIERTOS*
SPLASH MAT – *EL PLÁSTICO*
SPOON – *LA CUCHARA*
TABLE – *LA MESA*
TOASTER – *EL TOSTADOR*
WAX PAPER – *EL PAPEL DE CERA*

bathroom
el baño

BATHROOM – *EL BAÑO*
BATHTUB – *LA TINA*
FAUCET – *LA LLAVE*
INFANT TUB – *LA BAÑERA*
MEDICINE CABINET – *EL BOTIQUÍN*
SHOWER – *LA REGADERA*
SHOWER CURTAIN – *LA CORTINA*

DE BAÑO
SINK – *EL LAVABO*
STEP STOOL – *EL BANQUITO*
TOILET – *EL EXCUSADO*
TOILET PAPER – *EL PAPEL DE BAÑO*
TOWEL – *LA TOALLA*
WASHCLOTH – *LA TOALLITA*

bedroom
la recámara

ALARM CLOCK – *EL DESPERTADOR*
ARMOIRE – *EL ARMARIO*
BASSINET – *EL BAMBINETO*
BED – *LA CAMA*
BEDSPREAD – *LA COLCHA*
BLANKET – *LA COBIJA*
BOOKSHELF – *EL LIBRERO*
CHANGING TABLE – *EL CAMBIADOR*
CLOSET – *EL CLOSET*
CRIBSHEETS – *LAS SÁBANAS DE LA CUNA*
CRIB – *LA CUNA*
DRESSER – *EL BUREAU*

MATTRESS – *EL COLCHÓN*
MIRROR – *EL ESPEJO*
MONITOR – *EL MONITOR*
NIGHTSTAND – *LA MESITA DE NOCHE*
NIGHT LIGHT – *LA LUCESITA*
ROCKING CHAIR – *LA MECEDORA*
PILLOWS – *LA ALMOHADA*
PILLOWCASE – *LA FUNDA*
PORT-A-CRIB – *PORTACUNA*
SHEET – *LA SÁBANA*
QUILT/COMFORTER – *EL EDREDÓN*

living/play room
la sala/ el cuarto de juegos

CEILING – *EL TECHO*
CHAIR – *LA SILLA*
CURTAIN – *LA CORTINA*

DOOR – *LA PUERTA*
FLOOR – *EL PISO*
KEY – *LA LLAVE*

LAMP – *LA LÁMPARA*
LOCK – *LA CERRADURA*
RADIO – *EL RADIO*
SHUTTERS – *LAS PERSIANAS*
SOFA – *EL SOFÁ*
TABLE – *LA MESA*

TELEPHONE – *EL TELÉFONO*
TV – *LA TELEVISIÓN*
VCR – *LA VIDEOCASETERA*
WALL – *LA PARED*
WINDOW – *LA VENTANA*

cleaning products
productos de limpieza

PLEASE USE __ TO CLEAN __. *POR FAVOR USA __ PARA LIMPIAR __.*
DON'T USE __ TO CLEAN __. *NO USES __ PARA LIMPIAR __.*
THE __ IS IN THE CLOSET. *__ESTÁ EN EL CLOSET.*

. . . .

AMMONIA – *EL AMONÍACO*
BROOM – *LA ESCOBA*
BRUSH – *EL CEPILLO*
BUCKET – *LA CUBETA*
DISENFECTANT – *EL DESINFECTANTE*
DUSTPAN – *EL RECOGEDOR DE BASURA*
FEATHER DUSTER – *EL PLUMERO*
FLOOR POLISH – *LA CERA PARA EL PISO*
FURNITURE POLISH – *LA CERA PARA LOS MUEBLES*
GLOVE – *EL GUANTE*
LADDER – *LA ESCALERA*

LIQUID – *EL LÍQUIDO*
MOP – *EL TRAPEADOR*
PAPER TOWELS – *LAS TOALLAS DE PAPEL*
RAG – *EL TRAPO*
SOAP – *EL JABÓN*
SPONGE – *LA ESPONJA*
TOWEL – *LA TOALLA*
TRASH – *LA BASURA*
TRASH BAG – *LA BOLSA DE BASURA*
VACUUM – *LA ASPIRADORA*
VINEGAR – *EL VINAGRE*
WINDOW CLEANER – *EL LIMPIAVIDRIOS*

. . . .

PLEASE __ THE FLOOR. *POR FAVOR __ EL PISO.*

. . . .

CLEAN – *LIMPIA*
DUST – *DESEMPLOVA*
MOP – *TRAPEA*
POLISH – *PULE*

SWEEP – *BARRE*
VACUUM – *ASPIRA*
WASH – *LAVA*

FOOD
COMIDA

meat, poultry, fish & shellfish
carne, aves, pescados y mariscos

BACON – *EL TOCINO*
BEEF – *LA CARNE DE RES*
CHICKEN – *EL POLLO*
CLAM – *LA ALMEJA*
CRAB – *EL CANGREJO*
DUCK – *EL PATO*
FISH – *EL PESCADO*
GOOSE – *EL GANSO*
HAM – *EL JAMÓN*
HAMBURGER – *LA HAMBURGUESA*
HOT DOG – *LA SALCHICHA*
LAMB – *EL CORDERO*

LOBSTER – *LA LANGOSTA*
MEATBALL – *LA ALBÓNDIGA*
PORK – *EL CERDO*
ROAST BEEF – *EL ROSBIF*
SALMON – *EL SALMÓN*
SAUSAGE – *LA SALCHICHA*
STEAK – *EL BISTEC*
TUNA – *EL ATÚN*
TURKEY – *EL PAVO*

fruit
frutas

PLEASE WASH/SLICE __. *POR FAVOR LAVA/CORTA __.*
PLEASE SERVE __ TO EAT TODAY. *POR FAVOR SIRVE __ DE COMER HOY.*

. . . .

APPLE – *LA MANZANA*
APRICOT – *EL CHABACANO*
AVOCADO – *EL AGUACATE*
BANANA – *EL PLÁTANO*
BLACKBERRIES – *LAS ZARZAMORAS*
BLUEBERRIES – *LOS ARÁNDANOS*
RASPBERRIES – *LAS FRAMBUESAS*
STRAWBERRIES – *LAS FRESAS*
CANTALOUPE – *EL MELÓN*
CHERRIES – *LAS CEREZAS*
COCONUT – *EL COCO*
DATES – *LOS DÁTILES*
FIGS – *LOS HIGOS*
GRAPES – *LAS UVAS*
GRAPEFRUIT – *LA TORONJA*
GUAVA – *LA GUAYAVA*
KIWI – *EL KIWI*
LEMON – *EL LIMA*

LIME – *EL LIMÓN*
MANDARIN – *LA MANDARINA*
MANGO – *EL MANGO*
MELON – *EL MELÓN*
NECTARINE – *EL NECATARÍN*
ORANGE – *LA NARANJA*
PAPAYA – *LA PAPAYA*
PEAR – *LA PERA*
PEACH – *EL DURAZNO*
PINEAPPLE – *LA PIÑA*
PLUM – *LA CIRUELA*
POMEGRANATE – *LA GRANADA*
PRUNE – *LA CIRUELA PASA*
RAISINS – *LAS PASAS*
WATERMELON – *LA SANDIA*

vegetables
verduras

PLEASE WASH/SLICE __.   *POR FAVOR LAVA/CORTA __.*
PLEASE SERVE __ TO EAT TODAY. *POR FAVOR SIRVE __ DE COMER HOY.*

. . . .

ARTICHOKE – *LA ALCACHOFA*
ASPARAGUS – *LOS ESPÁRRAGOS*
BEANS – *LOS FRIJOLES*
GREEN BEANS – *LOS EJOTES*
BEETS – *EL BETABEL*
BELL PEPPER – *EL CHILE MORRÓN*
BOK CHOY – *EL BOK CHOY*
BROCCOLI – *EL BRÓCOLI*
BRUSSEL SPROUTS – *LAS COLES DE BRUSELAS*
CABBAGE – *LA COL*
CARROT – *LA ZANAHORIA*
CAULIFLOWER – *LA COLIFLOR*
CELERY – *EL ÁPIO*
CHARD – *LA ACELGA*
CHILI PEPPER – *EL CHÍLE*
CORN – *EL ELOTE*
CUCUMBERS – *EL PEPINO*
EGGPLANT – *LA BERENJENA*
FENNEL – *EL HINOJO*
GARLIC – *EL ÁJO*
GREEN ONIONS – *LAS CEBOLLITAS*

GREEN PEPPER – *EL PIMIENTO VERDE*
GREEN TOMATOES – *EL TOMATILLO*
JICIMA – *LA JICAMA*
LEEK – *EL PUERRO*
LETTUCE – *LA LECHUGA*
MUSHROOMS – *LOS HONGOS*
ONION – *LA CEBOLLA*
PEAS – *LOS CHICHARROS*
POTATOES – *LAS PAPAS*
  – BAKED – *LAS PAPAS AL HORNO*
  – BOILED – *LAS PAPAS COCIDAS*
  – FRIED – *LAS PAPAS FRITAS*
  – MASHED – *EL PURÉ DE PAPA*
RADISHES – *EL RÁBANO*
RED PEPPER – *EL PIMIENTO ROJO*
SPINACH – *LA ESPINACA*
SQUASH – *LA CALABAZA*
SWEET POTATO – *EL CAMOTE*
TOMATO – *EL JITOMATE*
WATERCRESS – *EL BERRO*
YAM – *EL CAMOTE*
ZUCCHINI – *LA CALABAZA VERDE*

dairy
productos lácteos

BUTTER – *LA MANTEQUILLA*
CHEESE – *EL QUESO*
  – BLUE CHEESE – *EL QUESO ROQUEFORT*
  – BRIE CHEESE – *EL QUESO TIPO*

BRIE
  – CHEDDAR – *EL QUESO AMARILLO*
  – FETA – *EL QUESO TIPO FETA*
  – GOAT – *EL QUESO DE CABRA*
  – JACK – *EL QUESO BLANCO*

– PARMESAN – *EL QUESO PARMESANO*
COTTAGE CHEESE – *EL QUESO COTÁJ*
CREAM – *LA CREMA*
CREAM CHEESE – *EL QUESO CREMA*
EGG – *EL HUEVO*
– FRIED – *EL HUEVO FRITO*
– HARD BOILED – *EL HUEVO DURO*
– SCRAMBLED – *EL HUEVO REVUELTO*

– WHITE – *EL BLANCO DEL HUEVO*
– YOLK – *LA YEMA*
ICE CREAM – *EL HELADO/LA NIEVE*
MARGARINE – *LA MARGINA*
MILK – *LA LECHE*
– LOWFAT – *SEMI – DESCREMADA*
– NONFAT – *DESCREMADA*
– WHOLE – *ENTERA*
SOY MILK – *LA LECHE DE SOYA*
SOUR CREAM – *LA CREMA ÁCIDA*
YOGURT – *EL YOGHOURT*

breads and grains
panes, cereales y granos

BREAD – *EL PAN*
– CORN – *EL PAN DE MAÍZ*
– RYE – *EL PAN DE CENTENO*
– WHITE BREAD – *EL PAN BLANCO*
– WHOLE WHEAT – *EL PAN INTEGRAL*
CEREAL – *EL CEREAL*
– OATMEAL – *LA AVENA*
CRACKER – *LA GALLETA SALADA*
RICE – *EL ARROZ*

– BROWN RICE – *EL ARROZ INTEGRAL*
– FRIED RICE – *EL ARROZ FRITO*
– WILD RICE – *EL ARROZ SALVAJE*
TOAST – *EL PAN TOSTADO*
– FRENCH TOAST – *EL PAN FRANCES*
PANCAKES – *LOS HOTCAKES*
PASTA – *LOS FIDEOS/LA PASTA*
WAFFLES – *LOS WAFLES*

condiments
condimentos

BARBEQUE SAUCE – *LA SALSA DE BARBACÓA*
BALSAMIC VINEGAR – *EL VINAGRE BALSÁMICO*
HOT PEPPER – *EL CHILE*
KETCHUP – *LA CATSUP*
MAYONNAISE – *LA MAYONESA*

MUSTARD – *LA MOSTAZA*
OLIVE OIL – *EL ACIETE DE OLÍVA*
PICKLE – *EL PEPINO*
SAUCE – *LA SALSA*
SOY SAUCE – *LA SALSA DE SOYA*
SYRUP – *EL JARÁBE*
VINEGAR – *EL VINAGRE*

preparations
preparaciones

ORGANIC – *ORGÁNICO*
FAT-FREE – *SIN GRASA*
SALT-FREE – *SIN SAL*
SUGAR-FREE – *SIN AZÚCAR*

WITHOUT SEASONING – *SIN CONDIMENTO*
VEGETARIAN – *VEGETARIANO*

. . . .

PLEASE __ THE VEGETABLES. *POR FAVOR __ LAS VERDURAS.*

. . . .

BAKE – *HORNÉA*
BBQ – *COCINA EN EL ASADOR*
BLEND – *LICÚA*
BOIL – *HIERVE*
COOK – *COCINA*
CUT – *CORTA*
DEFROST – *DESCONGELA*
DRY – *SECA*
FRY – *FRÍE*

FREEZE – *CONGELA*
GRATED – *RALLA*
GROUND – *MUELE*
KOSHER – *PREPARA TIPO KOSHER*
PEEL – *PELA*
ROAST – *ROSTIZA/ASA*
SLICE – *REBANA*
STEAM – *COCINA AL VAPOR*

taste
sabores

BITTER – *AMARGO*
COOKED – *COCIDO*
DELICIOUS – *DELICIOSO*

DRY – *SECO*
FRESH – *FRESCO*
MOIST – *HÚMEDO*

continued...

RAW – *CRUDO*
RIPE – *MADURO*
SALTY – *SALADO*
SOUR – *AGRIO*

SPICY – *PICANTE*
SWEET – *DULCE*
TASTY – *SABROSO*

baking ingredients
ingredientes para hornear

BAKING POWDER – *EL POLVO DE HORNEAR*
BAKING SODA – *EL BICARBONATO*
COCOA – *EL COCÓA*
CORNSTARCH – *LA MAIZENA*
CHOCOLATE – *EL CHOCOLATE*
HONEY – *LA MIEL*

FLOUR – *LA HARINA*
NUTS – *LAS NUECES*
OIL – *EL ACEITE*
SALT – *LA SAL*
SUGAR – *EL AZÚCAR*
VANILLA – *LA VAINILLA*

beverages
bebidas

COFFEE – *EL CAFÉ*
JUICE – *EL JUGO*
 – APPLE JUICE – *EL JUGO DE MANZANA*
 – GRAPE JUICE – *EL JUGO DE UVA*
 – ORANGE JUICE – *EL JUGO DE NARANJA*
MILK – *LA LECHE*
 – CHOCOLATE – *EL CHOCOLATE FRÍO*
 – COLD – *LE LECHE FRÍA*
 – HOT – *LE LECHE CALIENTE*

 – HOT CHOCOLATE – *EL CHOCOLATE CALIENTE*
SODA – *EL REFRESCO*
TEA – *EL TÉ*
 – BLACK – *EL TÉ NEGRO*
 – CHAMOMILE – *EL TÉ DE MANZANILLA*
 – MINT – *EL TÉ DE MENTA*
WATER – *EL AGUA*
 – MINERAL WATER – *EL AGUA MINERAL*

herbs & spices
hierbas & especies

BASIL – *LA ALBAHACA*
CAPERS – *LAS ALCAPARRAS*
CINNAMON – *LA CANELA*
CLOVE – *EL CLAVO*
CHIVE – *EL CEBOLLÍN*
DILL – *EL ENELDO*
MINT – *LA MENTA*
NUTMEG – *LA NUEZ MOSCADO*

OREGANO – *EL ORÉGANO*
PARSELY – *EL PEREJIL*
PEPPER – *LA PIMIENTA*
ROSEMARY – *EL ROMERO*
SAGE – *LA SALVIA*
SALT – *LA SAL*
THYME – *EL TOMILLO*

bottles
biberones

BOTTLE – *EL BIBERÓN*
NIPPLE – *EL CHUPÓN*
BOILING WATER – *EL AGUA HERVIDA*
COLD – *FRÍO(A)*
WARM – *CALIENTITO(A)*
HOT – *CALIENTE*

BREASTMILK – *LA LECHE DE PECHO*
FORMULA – *LA FORMULA*
MILK – *LA LECHE*
BOTTLE BRUSH – *EL SEPILLO PARA BOTELLAS*
REFLUX – *EL REFLUJO*
GAS(BURPS ETC.) – *EL GAS*

· ·

PLEASE __ THE BOTTLE. *POR FAVOR __ EL BIBERÓN.*

· ·

REFRIDGERATE – *REFRIGÉRA*
HEAT UP – *CALIÉNTA*

WASH – *LAVA*
STERILIZE – *ESTERILÍZA*

nuts & seeds
nueces y semillas

ALMOND – *LA ALMENDRA*
CASHEW – *LA NUEZ DE LA INDIA*
COCONUT – *EL COCO*
MACADAMIA – *LA MACADAMIA*
PEANUT – *EL CACAHUATE*
PEANUT BUTTER – *LA CREMA DE CACAHUATE*
PECAN – *LA NUEZ*

PINE NUTS – *LOS PIÑONES*
PISTACHIO – *LOS PISTACHOS*
SESAME SEED – *EL AJONJOLÍ*
SUNFLOWER SEED – *LA SEMILLA DE GIRASOL*
TOFU – *EL TOFU*
WALNUT – *LA NUEZ DE CASTILLA*

legumes
frijoles

BLACK BEANS – *LOS FRIJOLES NEGROS*
CHICK PEAS – *LOS GARBANZOS*
KIDNEY BEANS – *LOS FRIJOLES ROJAS*
LENTILS – *LAS LENTEJAS*
LIMA BEANS – *LOS FRIJOLES DE MEDIA LUNA*

PINTO BEANS – *LOS FRIJOLES BAYOS*
REFRIED – *LOS FRIJOLES REFRITOS*
WHITE BEANS – *LAS HAICHULAS BLANCAS*

sweets & treats
postres y dulces

CAKE – *EL PASTEL*
 – CARROT CAKE – *EL PASTEL DE ZANAHORIA*
 – CHOCOLATE CAKE – *EL PASTEL DE CHOCOLATE*
 – WHITE CAKE – *EL PASTEL BLANCO*
CANDY – *LOS DULCES*

CHOCOLATE – *EL CHOCOLATE*
COOKIE – *LA GALLETA*
GUM – *EL CHICLE*
ICE CREAM – *EL HELADO*
 – IN A CUP – *EN VASO*
 – ON A CONE – *EN BARQUILLO*
PIE – *LA TARTA*
PUDDING – *EL BUDÍN*

food safety
precauciones alimenticias

ALLERGY – *LA ALERGIA*
BOIL (TO) – *HERVIR*
CHOKE (TO) – *AHOGARSE*
EXPIRATION DATE – *LA FECHA DEL VENCIMIENTO*
FOOD – *LA COMIDA*
FREEZE (TO) – *CONGELAR*
GERMS – *LOS MICROBIOS*

HOT SPOTS – *LOS LUGARES CALIENTES*
MOLD – *EL MOHO*
PERISHABLES – *LOS ALIMENTOS PERECEDEROS*
ROTTEN – *PODRIDO(A)*
STERILIZE (TO) – *ESTERILIZAR*

ACTIVITIES
ACTIVIDADES

out of the house
afuera de la casa

PLEASE TAKE MY CHILD TO __. *POR FAVOR LLEVA MI NIÑO(A) A __.*
BE CAREFUL OF __. *CUIDADO CON __.*
DON'T FORGET __. *NO SE TE OLVIDE __.*

. . . .

ART CLASS – *LA CLASE DE ARTE*
BACKPACK – *LA MOCHILA*

BATHROOM – *EL BAÑO*
CAT POOP – *LA POPÓ DE GATO*

continued...

CHILDRENS MUSEUM – *EL MUSEO DEL NIÑO*
CLIMB A TREE (TO) – *ESCALAR UN ÁRBOL*
DANCE CLASS – *LA CLASE DE BAILE*
DOG POOP – *LA POPÓ DE PERRO*
GRASS – *EL PASTO*
LUNCHBOX – *LA LUNCHERA*
MUSIC CLASS – *LA CLASE DE MÚSICA*
PARADE – *EL DESFILE*
PARK – *EL PARQUE*
RIDE A BIKE (TO) – *ANDAR EN BICICLETA*
RIDE A HORSE (TO) – *MONTAR A CABALLO*
RIDE A SCOOTER (TO) – *ANDAR E PATINETA*
RIDE A SKATEBOARD (TO) – *ANDA EN PATINETA*
SANDBOX – *EL ARENERO*
SLIDE – *LA RESBALADIA*
SNACK – *EL REFRIGERIO*
STORY TIME AT THE LIBRARY – *L HORA DE LA LECTURA EN LA BIBLIOTECA*
STROLLER – *LA CARRIOLA*
SWING – *EL COLUMPIO*
ZOO – *EL ZOOLÓGICO*

hobbies
pasatiempos

HE/SHE LIKES __. *A ÉL/ELLA LE GUSTA __.*
HE/SHE IS LEARNING __. *ÉL/ELLA ESTÁ APRENDIENDO __.*

. . . .

ART – *EL ARTE*
BALLET – *EL BALLET*
BOATING – *PASEAR EN BARCO*
DANCING – *EL BAILE*
DRAWING – *EL DIBUJO*
FISHING – *LA PESCA*
HIKING – *LA CAMINATA*
JOGGING – *CORRER*
MUSIC – *LA MÚSICA*
MOVIES – *LAS PELÍCULAS*
PAINTING – *LA PINTURA*
PHOTOGRAPHY – *LA FOTOGRAFÍA*
READING – *LA LECTURA*

toys & games
juguetes & juegos

HE/SHE LIKES TO PLAY WITH __. *LE GUSTA JUGAR CON __.*
HE/SHE NEEDS TO SHARE __. *ÉL/ELLA NECESITA COMPARTIR __.*
__ IS BROKEN. *__ ESTÁ ROTO(A).*

. . . .

AIRPLANE – *EL AVIÓN*
ANIMALS – *LOS ANIMALES*
BALL – *LA PELOTA*
BALLOON – *EL GLOBO*
BASKETBALL – *EL BALONCESTO*
BASEBALL – *EL BÉISBOL*
BICYCLE – *LA BICICLETA*
BLOCKS – *LOS CUBOS DE MADERA*
BOAT – *EL BARCO*
BOOK – *EL LIBRO*
CARTOONS – *LAS CARICATURAS*
CHALK – *LOS HISES*
CHECKERS – *EL JUEGO DE DAMAS*
CHESS – *EL AJEDREZ*
COLORED PENCILS – *LOS LAPICES DE COLORES*
COLORING BOOK – *EL LIBRO PARA COLOREAR*
COSTUME – *EL DISFRAZ*
CRAYONS – *LAS CRAYOLAS*
DOLL – *LA MUÑECA*
FOOTBALL – *EL FÚTBOL*
JUMP ROPE – *LA CUERDA PARA BRINCAR*
KITE – *EL PAPALOTE*
MARBLES – *LAS CANICAS*
MONOPOLY – *EL MONOPOLIO*
NOISE – *EL RUIDO*
PLAYING HOUSE – *JUGAR A LA CASITA*
PUPPET – *EL TITERE*
PUZZLE – *EL ROMPECABEZAS*
RADIO – *LA RADIO*
SKATES – *LOS PATÍNES*
SKATEBOARD – *LA PATINETA*
SONG – *LA CANCIÓN*
STEREO – *EL ESTÉREO*
STORY – *EL CUENTO*
STUFFED ANIMAL – *EL PELUCHE*
TEA SET – *EL JUEGO DE TÉ*
TEDDY BEAR – *EL OSITO DE PELUCHE*
TELEVISION – *LA TELEVISIÓN*
TRAIN – *EL TREN*
TRUCK – *EL CAMIÓN*
TRICYCLE – *EL TRICICLO*
TRUCKS – *EL CAMION*
 – FIRE TRUCK – *EL CAMION DE LC BOMBEROS*
 – DUMP TRUCK – *EL CAMION DE VOLTEO*
 – TRACTOR – *EL TRACTOR*
WAGON – *EL VAGÓN*
VIDEOS – *LOS VIDEOS*

bilingual babycare

HE/SHE LIKES TO __. *A ÉL/ELLA LE GUSTA __.*

. . . .

CLAP HANDS – *APLAUDIR*
DRESS UP – *DISFRAZARSE*
– CROWN – *LA CORONA*
– FAIRY – *EL HADA/HADO*
– KING – *EL REY*
– MONSTER – *EL MONSTRUO*
– QUEEN – *LA REINA*

HIDE-AND-GO-SEEK – *LAS ESCONDIDAS*
MAGIC – *LA MAGIA*
MAKING COOKIES – *HACER GALLETAS*
PLAY CHASE – *JUGAR A LAS TRAES*
PRETEND – *FINJIR*
RACE – *LAS CARRERAS*

outdoor destinations
destinos al aire libre

WE ARE GOING TO __. *VAMOS A __.*
I LIVE NEAR THE __. *VIVO CERCA DE __.*
PLEASE TAKE THE CHILDREN TO __. *POR FAVOR LLEVA LOS NIÑOS A __.*

. . . .

BEACH – *LA PLAYA*
CAVE – *LA CUEVA*
COAST – *LA COSTA*
DESERT – *EL DESIERTO*
FIELD – *EL CAMPO*
FOREST – *EL BOSQUE*
HILL – *EL CERRO*
JUNGLE – *LA SELVA*
LAKE – *EL LAGO*

MOUNTAIN – *LA MONTAÑA*
OCEAN – *EL MAR*
POND – *LA LAGUNA*
POOL – *LA PISCINA*
RANCH – *EL RANCHO*
RIVER – *EL RÍO*
STREAM – *EL ARROYO*
SWAMP – *EL PANTANO*
VALLEY – *EL VALLE*

musical instruments
instrumentos musicales

HE/SHE LIKES __. *A ÉL/ELLA LE GUSTA __.*
HE/SHE IS LEARNING __. *ÉL/ELLA ESTÁ APRENDIENDO __.*

. . . .

CLARINET – *EL CLARINETE*
DRUM – *EL TAMBOR*
GUITAR – *LA GUITARRA*
ORGAN – *EL ÓRGANO*
PIANO – *EL PIANO*

SAXOPHONE – *EL SAXÓFONO*
TROMBONE – *EL TROMBÓN*
TRUMPET – *LA TROMPETA*
VIOLIN – *EL VIOLÍN*

urban destinations
destinos urbanos

WE ARE GOING TO __. *VAMOS A __.*
I LIVE NEAR THE __. *VIVO CERCA DE __.*
PLEASE TAKE THE CHILDREN TO __. *POR FAVOR LLEVA LOS NIÑOS A __.*

. . . .

AIRPORT – *EL AEROPUERTO*
BANK – *EL BANCO*
BRIDGE – *EL PUENTE*
CHURCH – *LA IGLESIA*
DOWNTOWN – *EL CENTRO*
GAS STATION – *LA GASOLINERA*
GYMNASIUM – *EL GIMNASIO*
HOSPITAL – *EL HOSPITAL*
LIBRARY – *LA BIBLIOTECA*
MARKET – *EL SUPERMERCADO*
MOVIES – *EL CINE*
MUSEUM – *EL MUSEO*

OFFICE – *LA OFICINA*
PARK – *EL PARQUE*
PATH – *EL CAMINO*
PLAYGROUND – *EL CAMPO DE RECREO*
POST OFFICE – *EL CORREO*
RESTAURANT – *EL RESTAURANTE*
STREET – *LA CALLE*
SCHOOL – *LA ESCUELA*
SIDEWALK – *LA BANQUETA*
STORE – *LA TIENDA*
TOWN – *EL PUEBLO*

beach & swimming
la playa & la natación

BIKINI – *EL BIKINI*
BOAT – *EL BARCO*
CURRENT – *LA CORRIENTE*
DARK GLASSES – *LOS LENTES OSCUROS*
DUNE – *LA DUNA*
FLIP FLOPS – *LAS CHANCLAS*
FLIPPERS – *LAS ALETAS*
GOGGLES – *LOS GOGLES*
HIGH TIDE – *LA MAREA ALTA*
LIFE JACKET – *EL CHALECO SALVAVIDAS*
LOW TIDE – *LA MAREA BAJA*
MASK – *LAS GAFAS DE BUCEO*

SAND – *LA ARENA*
SAND PAIL – *LA CUBETA*
SEA – *EL MAR*
SWIMMING RING – *LA LLANTITA*
SWIMSUIT – *EL TRAJE DE BAÑO*
SHOVEL – *LA PALA*
SNORKEL – *EL SNÓRQUEL*
SUNBURN – *LA QUEMADURA*
SUNSCEEN – *EL PROTECTOR SOLA*
SUNSTROKE – *LA INSOLACIÓN*
TOWEL – *LA TOALLA*
WATER WINGS – *LOS FLOTADORES*
WAVES – *LAS OLAS*

snow play
jugando en la nieve

GLOVES/MITTENS – *LOS GUANTES*
HAT – *EL SOMBRERO/LA CACHUCHA*
ICE – *EL HIELO*
ICICLES – *LOS CARÁMBANOS*
JACKET – *LA CHAMARRA*
LONG UNDERWEAR – *ROPA INTERIOR*
SCARF – *LA BUFANDA*

SKIS – *LOS ESKIS*
SNOW – *LA NIEVE*
SNOWBALL – *LA BOLA DE NIEVE*
SNOWBOARD – *LA SNOWBOARD*
SNOWMAN – *EL MUÑECO DE NIEVE*
SNOWMOBILE – *EL MOTONIEVE*
SLED – *EL TRINEO*

sports
deportes

HE/SHE LIKES TO PLAY __. *A ÉL/ELLA LE GUSTA JUGAR __.*
PLEASE PLAY __ WITH HIM/HER. *POR FAVOR JUEGA __ CON ÉL/ELLA.*
. . . .

BASEBALL – *EL BÉISBOL*
BASKETBALL – *EL BASQUETBOL*
BOWLING – *EL BOLICHE*
BOXING – *EL BOXEO*
FOOTBALL – *EL FÚTBOL AMERICANO*

GOLF – *EL GOLF*
RUNNING – *LA CARRERA*
SAILING – *LA VELEADA*
SOCCER – *EL FÚTBOL*
TENNIS – *EL TENIS*
VOLLEYBALL – *EL VÓLIBOL*

CLOTHES
LA ROPA

dressing
vistiéndose

THIS IS HIS/HER FAVORITE __. *ESTO ES SU __ FAVORITO(A).*
PLEASE WASH THE __. *POR FAVOR LAVA __.*
THE __ IS DIRTY. *__ ESTÁ SUCIO(A).*
. . . .

BATHING SUIT – *EL TRAJE DE BAÑO*
BLOUSE – *LA BLUSA*
BOOTS – *LAS BOTAS*
DRESS – *EL VESTIDO*
JACKET – *LA CHAMARRA*
OVERCOAT – *EL ABRIGO*
PAJAMA – *LA PIJAMA*

PANTS – *LOS PANTALONES*
RAINCOAT – *EL IMPERMEABLE*
SHIRT – *LA CAMISA*
SHOES – *LOS ZAPATOS*
SHORTS – *LOS SHORTS*
SKIRT – *LA FALDA*
SLIPPERS – *LAS PANTUFLAS*

SOCKS – *LOS CALCETINES*
SPORTSCOAT – *EL SACO*
STOCKINGS – *LAS MEDIAS*
SUIT – *EL TRAJE*
SWEATER – *EL SUÉTER*

SWEATSHIRT – *LA SUDADERA*
TENNIS SHOES – *LOS TENIS*
T-SHIRT – *LA CAMISETA*
UNDERWEAR – *LOS CALZONES*

fabrics
telas

CANVAS – *LA LONA*
COTTON – *EL ALGODÓN*
CORDUROY – *LA PANA*
DENIM – *LA MEZCLILLA*
FUR – *LA PIEL*
KNIT – *EL TEJIDO*

LACE – *EL ENCAJE*
LEATHER – *EL CUERO*
LINEN – *EL LINO*
SILK – *LA SEDA*
VELVET – *EL TERCIOPELO*
WOOL – *LA LANA*

diapers
pañales

CHANGING TABLE – *EL CAMBIADOR*
CLOTH DIAPER – *EL PAÑAL DE TELA*
DELIVERY PERSON – *EL REPARTIDOR*
DELIVERY SERVICE – *EL SERVICIO A DOMICILIO*
DIAPER – *EL PAÑAL*
DIAPER BAG – *LA PAÑALERA*
DIAPER COVERS – *EL CALZÓN DE HULE*

DIAPER PAIL – *EL BOTE DE PAÑALES*
DIAPER RASH CREAM – *LA POMADA PARA ROSADURAS*
PINS – *LOS SEGUROS*
TALCUM POWDER – *EL TALCO*
TRAINING PANTS – *LOS CALZONES ENTRENADORES*
VELCRO – *EL VELCRO*
WIPES – *LAS TOALLITAS HUMEDAS*

accesories
accesorios

BELT – *EL CINTURÓN*
BRACELET – *LA PULSERA*
BUTTON – *EL BOTÓN*
CAP – *LA GORRA*
DIAMONDS – *LOS DIAMANTES*
EARRINGS – *LOS ARETES*
GLOVES – *LOS GUANTES*
GOLD – *EL ORO*
HAT – *EL SOMBRERO*

NECKLACE – *EL COLLAR*
PEARLS – *LAS PERLAS*
POCKET – *EL BOLSILLO*
PURSE – *LA BOLSA*
RING – *EL ANILLO*
SCARF – *LA BUFANDA*
TIE – *LA CORBATA*
WALLET – *LA CARTERA*
ZIPPER – *EL CIERRE*

colors
colores

BLACK – *NEGRO*
BLUE – *AZUL*
CHECKERED – *DE CUADROS*
DARK – *OSCURO*
GRAY – *GRIS*
GREEN – *VERDE*
LIGHT – *CLARO*

ORANGE – *ANARANJADO*
PINK – *ROSA*
POLKA – DOTTED – *DE PUNTITOS*
PURPLE – *MORADO*
RED – *ROJO*
WHITE – *BLANCO*
YELLOW – *AMARILLO*

sizes
tamaños

SMALL – *CHICO*
MEDIUM – *MEDIANO*
LARGE – *GRANDE*

EXTRA LARGE – *EXTRA GRANDE*
TOO SMALL – *DEMASIADO CHICO*
TOO BIG – *DEMASIADO GRANDE*

grooming
arreglo personal

BARRET – EL BROCHE
BRUSH – EL CEPILLO
BUBBLE BATH – EL BAÑO DE BURBUJAS
COMB – EL PEINE
CONDITIONER – EL ACONDICIONADOR
HAIRDRYER – LA SECADORA PARA EL PELO
HEADBAND – LA CINTA
LIPSTICK – EL PINTALABIOS
LOTION – LA CREMA

MAKEUP – EL MAQUILLAJE
MIRROR – EL ESPEJO
NAIL POLISH – EL ESMALTE DE UÑAS
PERFUME – EL PERFUME
RIBBON – EL LISTÓN
SHAMPOO – EL CHAMPÚ
SOAP – EL JABÓN
SPONGE – LA ESPONJA
TOOTHPASTE – LA PASTA DE DIENTES
TWEEZERS – LAS PINZAS

laundry
lavado de ropa

PLEASE DON'T USE __. POR FAVOR NO USES __.
PLEASE USE __ WITH THESE CLOTHES. POR FAVOR USA __ CON ESTA ROPA
. . . .

BLEACH/CLOROX – EL BLANQUEADOR/EL CLORO
CLEANING PRODUCTS – PRODUCTOS DE LIMPIEZA
COLD WATER – AGUA FRÍO
COLORS – LA ROPA DE COLOR
DELICATE CYCLE – EL CICLO PARA ROPA DELICADA
DETERGENT – EL DETERGENTE
DIRTY LAUNDRY – LA ROPA SUCIA
DRYER – LA SECADORA
FOLD – DOBLAR
HAND WASH – LAVAR A MANO
HANG – COLGAR
HANGERS – LOS GANCHOS
HOT WATER – AGUA CALIENTE
IRON – LA PLANCHA

LAUNDROMAT – LA LAVANDERÍA
LINE DRY – SECAR AL AIRE
OFF – APAGADO
ON – PRENDIDO
RINSE – ENJUAGAR
SOAK – REMOJAR
SPIN – GIRAR
START – EMPEZAR
STOP – PARAR
STAIN – LA MANCHA
STAIN REMOVER – EL QUITAMANCHAS
STARCH – EL ALMIDÓN
WASHER – LA LAVADORA
WHITES – LA ROPA BLANCA

HEALTH & SAFETY
SALUD Y SEGURIDAD

injuries
heridas

ACCIDENT – EL ACCIDENTE
ANIMAL BITE – LA MORDEDURA
BITE – EL PIQUETE/LA MORDEDURA
BLEEDING – SANGRANDO
BLISTER – LA AMPOLLA
BROKEN – ROTO(A)
BRUISE – EL MORETÓN
BURN – LA QUEMADURA
BURNED – QUEMADO(A)
CAT BITE – LA MORDEDURA DE GATO
CHOKING – AHOGANDO
CONVULSION – LA CONVULSIÓN
DEHYDRATION – LA

DESHIDRATACIÓN
DOG BITE – LA MORDEDURA DE PERRO
DROWNING – AHOGANDO
FRACTURE – LA FRACTURA
FROSTBITE – EL CONGELAMIENTO
HEATSTROKE – LA INSOLACIÓN
INSECT BITE – EL PIQUETE
NOSEBLEED – LA HEMORRAGIA NASAL
SNAKE BITE – LA MORDEDURA DE VIVORA
SWELLING – LA INFLAMACIÓN
WOUND – LA HERIDA

symptoms and medical conditions
síntomas y condiciones médicas

HE/SHE HAS __. *ÉL/ELLA TIENE __.*
CALL ME IF HE/SHE HAS __. *LLÁMAME SI ÉL/ELLA TIENE __.*

. . . .

ALLERGY – *LA ALERGIA*
BACKACHE – *EL DOLOR DE ESPALDA*
BOIL – *EL FURÚNCULO*
BRONCHITIS – *EL BRONQUITIS*
CANCER – *EL CANCER*
CHICKEN POX – *LA VARICELA*
CHILLS – *LOS ESCALOFRIOS*
COLD – *EL GRIPE*
CONSTIPATION – *EL ESTRENIMIENTO*
COUGH – *LA TOS*
CROUP – *EL KRUP*
DIABETES – *EL DIABETES*
DIAPER RASH – *LA ROSADURA*
DIARREA – *LA DIARREA*
FEVER – *EL FIEBRE/LA CALENTURA*
FLU – *LA INFLUENZA*
GAS – *EL GAS*
HAY FEVER – *LA ALERGIA*
HEADACHE – *EL DOLOR DE CABEZA*
HEART ATTACK – *EL ATAQUE DEL CORAZÓN*
HEART PROBLEMS – *LOS PROBLEMAS CARDIACOS*

HEARTBURN – *EL ACIDEZ*
INFECTION – *LA INFECCIÓN*
JAUNDICE – *LA ICTERICIA*
MEASLES – *EL SARAPIÓN*
MIGRAINE – *LA MIGRAÑA*
MUMPS – *LAS PAPERAS*
NAUSEA – *LA NAUSEA*
POISONING – *EL ENVENENAMIENTO*
RASH – *EL SALPULLIDO*
REFLUX – *EL REFLUJO*
SALMONELLA – *LA SALMONELA*
SEIZURE – *EL ATAQUE*
SMALLPOX – *LA VIRUELA*
SORE THROAT – *EL DOLOR DE GARGANTA*
STOMACH ACHE – *EL DOLOR DE ESTÓMAGO*
SUNBURN – *LA QUEMADURA DEL SOL*
SWELLING – *LA INFLAMACIÓN*
TONSILLITIS – *EL AMIGDALITIS*
ULCER – *LA ULCERA*
VOMIT – *EL VÓMITO*

giving medication
dosis de medicinas

AT NIGHT – *EN LA NOCHE*
BEFORE BREAKFAST – *ANTES DEL DESAYUNO*
BETWEEN MEALS – *ENTRE COMIDAS*
EVERY FOUR HOURS – *CADA CUATRO HORAS*

HALF – TEASPOON – *MEDIA CUCHARADITA*
TWICE A DAY – *DOS VECES POR DÍA*
TEASPOON – *UNA CUCHARADITA*
WITH FOOD – *CON COMIDA*

medicine cabinet
medicinas

ANTIHISTAMINE – *LA ANTIHISTAMINA*
ASPRIN – *LA ASPIRINA*
BAND-AID – *LA CURITA*
CAST – *EL YESO*
COUGH DROPS – *LAS PASTILLAS PARA LA GARGANTA*
COUGH SYRUP – *EL JARABE PARA LA TOS*
CRUTCHES – *LAS MULETAS*
DISINFECTANT – *EL DISENFECTANTE*
EYE DROPS – *LAS GOTAS PARA LOS OJOS*
INSECT REPELLENT – *EL REPELENTE*
INSULIN – *LA INSULINA*
LAXATIVE – *EL LAXANTE*
OINTMENT – *LA POMADA*
OINTMENT FOR BURNS – *LA POMADA PARA LAS QUEMADURAS*
THERMOMETER – *EL TERMÓMETRO*
VASELINE – *LA VASELINA*
WHEELCHAIR – *LA SILLA DE RUEDAS*

parts of the body
partes del cuerpo

ANKLE – *EL TOBILLO*
ARM – *EL BRAZO*
BACK – *LA ESPALDA*
BLOOD – *LA SANGRE*
BONE – *EL HUESO*
BUTTOCK – *LA POMPA*
CALF – *LA PANTORRILLA*
CHEST – *EL PECHO*
EAR – *LA OREJA*
ELBOW – *EL CODO*
EYE – *EL OJO*
EYEBROW – *LA CEJA*
EYELID – *EL PÁRPADO*
FACE – *LA CARA*
FINGER – *EL DEDO*
FOOT – *EL PIE*
HEAD – *LA CABEZA*
HEART – *EL CORAZÓN*
HEEL – *EL TALÓN*

HIP – *LA CADERA*
JAW – *LA MANDÍBULA*
KNEE – *LA RODILLA*
LEG – *LA PIERNA*
LIP – *EL LABIO*
MOUTH – *LA BOCA*
NECK – *EL CUELLO*
NOSE – *LA NARÍZ*
PENIS – *EL PENE*
RIB – *LA COSTILLA*
SHOULDER – *EL HOMBRO*
SKIN – *LA PIEL*
STOMACH – *EL ESTÓMAGO*
TONGUE – *LA LENGUA*
TOOTH – *EL DIENTE*
THIGHS – *LOS MUSLOS*
TOE – *EL DEDO DEL PIE*
VAGINA – *LA VAGINA*
WRIST – *LA MUÑECA*

emergency items
artículos de emergencias

THE __ IS HERE. __ *ESTÁ AQUÍ.*
THIS IS HOW TO TURN OFF __. *ASÍ SE APAGA __.*
. . . .

ALARM – *LA ALARMA*
FIRE EXTINGUISHER – *EL EXTINGUIDOR*
FIRST AID KIT – *LA CAJA DE PRIMEROS AUXILLOS*

FUSE BOX – *LA CAJA DE FUSIBLES*
GAS METER – *EL MEDIDOR DE GAS*
WATER VALVE – *LA VÁLVULA DE AGUA*

people to contact
contactos en caso de emergencia

AMBULANCE – *LA AMBULANCIA*
CLINIC – *LA CLÍNCIA*
FIRE DEPARTMENT – *EL DEPARTAMENTO DE BOMBEROS*
HOSPITAL – *EL HOSPITAL*

NEIGHBOR – *EL VECINO*
PARAMEDIC – *EL PARAMÉDICO*
POLICE – *LA POLICÍA*
TOW TRUCK – *LA GRÚA*

CONJUGATED VERBS
ALGUNOS VERBOS

to be
ser*

I AM – *YO SOY*
YOU ARE (INFORMAL) – *TÚ ERES*
YOU ARE (FORMAL) – *USTED ES*
HE/SHE IS – *ÉL/ELLA ES*

WE ARE – *NOSOTROS SOMOS*
YOU ARE (PLURAL) – *USTEDES SON*
THEY ARE – *ELLOS/ELLAS SON*

*"to be" verb generally used for permanent conditions.

bilingual babycare

to be
*estar**

I AM – *YO ESTOY*	WE ARE – *NOSOTROS ESTAMOS*
YOU ARE (INFORMAL) – *TÚ ESTÁS*	YOU ARE (PLURAL) – *USTEDES*
YOU ARE (FORMAL) – *USTED ESTÁ*	*ESTÁN*
HE/SHE IS – *ÉL /ELLA ESTÁ*	THEY ARE – *ELLOS/ELLAS ESTÁN*

*"to be" verb generally used for temporary conditions.

to speak
hablar

I SPEAK – *YO HABLO*	WE SPEAK – *NOSOTROS HABLAMOS*
YOU SPEAK (INFORMAL) – *TÚ HABLAS*	YOU SPEAK (PLURAL) – *USTEDES HABLAN*
YOU SPEAK (FORMAL) – *USTED HABLA*	THEY SPEAK – *ELLOS/ELLAS HABLAN*
HE/SHE SPEAKS – *ÉL/ELLA HABLA*	

to eat
comer

I EAT – *YO COMO*	WE EAT – *NOSOTROS COMEMOS*
YOU EAT (INFORMAL) – *TÚ COMES*	YOU EAT (PLURAL) – *USTEDES COMEN*
YOU EAT (FORMAL) – *USTED COME*	THEY EAT – *ELLOS/ELLAS COMEN*
HE/SHE EATS – *ÉL/ELLA COME*	

to write
escribir

I WRITE – *YO ESCRIBO*	WE WRITE – *NOSOTROS ESCRIBIMOS*
YOU WRITE (INFORMAL) – *TÚ ESCRIBES*	YOU WRITE (PLURAL) – *USTEDES ESCRIBEN*
YOU WRITE (FORMAL) – *USTED ESCRIBE*	THEY WRITE – *ELLOS/ELLAS ESCRIBEN*
HE/SHE WRITES – *ÉL/ELLA ESCRIBE*	

to need
necesitar

I NEED – *YO NECESITO*	WE NEED – *NOSOTROS NECESITAMOS*
YOU NEED (INFORMAL) – *TÚ NECESITAS*	YOU NEED (PLURAL) – *USTEDES NECESITAN*
YOU NEED (FORMAL) – *USTED NECESITA*	THEY NEED – *ELLOS/ELLAS NECESITAN*
HE/SHE NEEDS – *ÉL/ELLA NECESITA*	

other common verbs
verbos comunes

ASK – *PREGUNTAR*
BELIEVE – *CREER*
BUY – *COMPRAR*
CAN – *PODER*
COME – *VENIR*
CLEAN – *LIMPIAR*
DO – *HACER*
DRIVE – *MANEJAR*
EAT – *COMER*
FEEL – *SENTIR*
FIND – *ENCONTRAR*
GET – *OBTENER*
GIVE – *DAR*
GO – *IR*
HAVE – *TENER*
HEAR – *OÍR*
KNOW – *SABER*
LET – *DEJAR*
LIKE – *GUSTAR*
LISTEN – *ESCUCHAR*
LOOK FOR – *BUSCAR*

MUST – *DEBER*
READ – *LEER*
RECOMMEND – *RECOMENDAR*
RUN – *CORRER*
SAY – *DECIR*
SEE – *VER*
SELL – *VENDER*
SLEEP – *DORMIR*
SMELL – *OLER*
SPEAK – *HABLAR*
SWEEP – *BARRER*
TAKE – *TOMAR*
TASTE – *SABOREAR*
TELL – *CONTAR*
THINK – *PENSAR*
QUIT – *RENUNCIAR*
WASH – *LAVAR*
WATCH – *MIRAR*
WORK – *TRABAJAR*
WRITE – *ESCRIBIR*

A-Z

vocabulary
vocabulario

alphabetical: English – Spanish
alfabético: inglés – español

A LITTLE	POCO, UN	ANCHOVY	ANCHOA
A LOT (MORE)	MUCHO	AND	Y
A TINY BIT	POQUITO, UN	ANESTHESIA	ANESTESIA
A, AN	UN, UNA	ANGEL	ÁNGEL, EL
ABOUT	ACERCA DE	ANGLE	ÁNGULO, EL
ABOVE	ARRIBA DE	ANGRY	ENOJADA
ABSCESS	ABSCESO, EL	ANIMAL BITE	MORDEDURA, LA
ACCESSORIES	ACCESORIOS, LOS	ANIMAL	EL ANIMAL
ACCIDENT	ACCIDENTE, EL	ANIMALS	ANIMALES , LOS
ACCOMPANY (TO)	ACOMPAÑAR	ANKLE	TOBILLO, EL
ACCTRESS	ACTRIZ, LA	ANNIVERSARY	ANIVERSARIO
ACID	ÁCIDO, EL	ANNOUNCEMENT	ANUNCIO
ACQUAINTANCE	CONOCIDO , EL	ANNOYED	MOLESTO
ACRYLIC	ACRÍLICO	ANOTHER	OTR0 (A)
ACTOR	ACTOR, EL	ANSWER	RESPUESTA, LA
ADD (TO)	AÑADIR	ANT	HORMIGA, LA
ADDRESS	DIRECCIÓN, LA	ANTIHISTAMINE	ANTIHISTAMINA, LA
AEROBICS	EJERICICIOS AEROBICÓS	ANTIQUE	ANTIGÜEDAD, LA
AFTER	DESPUES DE	ANY	CUALQUIER (A)
AFTERNOON	TARDE, LA	ANYONE	CUALQUIERA PERSONA
AFTERWARDS	DESPUÉS DE	ANYTHING	CUALQUIERA COSA
AGAIN	OTRA VEZ	ANYWHERE	CUALQUERA PARTE
AGAINST	CONTRA	APARTMENT	APARTAMENTO, EL
AGE	EDAD, LA	APPLE JUICE	JUGO DE MANZANA, EL
AGENCY	AGENCIA, LA	APPLE	MANZANA, LA
AGGRESSIVE	AGRESIVO (A)	APPLIANCE	APARATO, EL
AGNOSTIC	AGNÓSTICO (A)	APPLICATION	APLICACIÓN, LA
AHEAD	ADELANTE DE	APPOINTMENT	CITA, LA
AIR CONDITIOINING		APRICOT	CHABACANO, EL
AIRE ACONDICIONADO, EL		APRIL	ABRIL
AIR	AIRE, EL	APRON	DELANTAL
AIRPLANE	AVIÓN, EL	AQUARIUM	ACUARIO, EL
AIRPORT	AEROPUERTO, EL	ARCHITECT	ARQUITECTO, EL
ALARM CLOCK	DESPERTADOR, EL	AREA CODE	CÓDIGO DE ÁREA, EL
ALARM	ALARMA, LA	ARM	BRAZO, EL
ALGAE	ALGA, EL	ARMOIRE	ARMARIO, EL
ALL	TODOS	ARMY	EJÉRCITO, EL
ALLERGY	ALERGIA, LA	AROUND	ALREDEDOR DE
ALLEY	CALLEJÓN	ARRANGE (TO)	ARREGLAR
ALLIGATOR	CAIMÁN, EL	ARREST (TO)	ARRESTAR
ALMOND	ALMENDRA, LA	ARRIVE (TO)	LLEGAR
ALMOST	CASI	ART CLASS	CLASE DE ARTE, LA
ALONE	SOLO	ART	ARTE, EL
ALONG	A LO LARGO DE	ARTICHOKE	ALCACHOFA, LA
ALREADY	YA	ARTIST	ARTISTA, EL
ALTAR	ALTAR	AS	COMO
ALTER (TO)	CAMBIAR	ASH	CENIZA, LA
ALTHOUGH	AUNQUE	ASHTRAY	CENICERO, EL
ALUMINUM FOIL	PAPEL DE ALUMINIO, EL	ASK FOR	PEDIR
ALWAYS	SIEMPRE	ASK (TO)	PREGUNTAR
AMAZING	ASOMBROSO	ASLEEP	DORMIDO (A)
AMBITIOUS	AMBICIOSO	ASPARAGUS	ESPÁRRAGOS, LOS
AMBULANCE	AMBULANCIA, LA	ASPHALT	ASFALTO, EL
AMERICAN	AMERICANO, EL	ASPRIN	ASPIRINA, LA
AMMONIA	AMONÍACO, EL	ASSISTANT	ASISTENTE, EL
AMOUNT	CANTIDAD, LA	ASTHMA	ASMA, EL
AMUSING	DIVERTIDO	AT	A

bilingual babycare

ATHEIST	ATEO (A)
ATHLETE	ATLETA, EL
ATTEND (TO)	ASISTIR
ATTIC	ÁTICO, EL
AUGUST	AGOSTO
AUNT	TÍA, LA
AUTHOR	AUTOR, EL
AUTO INSURANCE	SEGURO DE AUTO, EL
AUTO	AUTO, EL
AUTOMATIC	AUTOMÁTICO(A)
AUTUMN	OTOÑO, EL
AVAILABLE	DISPONIBLE
AVENUE	AVENIDA, LA
AVOCADO	AGUACATE, EL
AVOID (TO)	EVITAR
AWAKE	DESPIERTO (A)
AWESOME	IMPRESIONANTE
AWHILE	RATO, UN
AX	HACHA, EL
BABY CREAM	CREMA PARA BEBÉS, LA
BABY FOOD	ALIMENTO PARA BEBÉ
BABY	BEBÉ, EL
BABYSITTER	NIÑERA, LA
BABYSIT (TO)	CUIDAR NIÑOS
BACK DOOR	PUERTA TRASERA, LA
BACK	ESPALDA, LA
BACKACHE	DOLOR DE ESPALDA, EL
BACKPACK	MOCHILA, LA
BACKYARD	JARDÍN, EL
BACON	TOCINO, EL
BAD	MALO (A)
BADGE	INSIGNIA, LA
BADMINTON	BADMINTON, EL
BAG	BOLSA, LA
BAKE (TO)	HORNÉAR
BAKED	COCIDO EN EL HORNO
BAKER	PANADERO, EL
BAKING POWDER	POLVO DE HORNEAR, EL
BAKING SODA	BICARBONATO, EL
BALCONY	BALCÓN, EL
BALD	CALVO (A)
BALL	PELOTA, LA
BALLET	BALLET, EL
BALLOON	GLOBO, EL
BALSAMIC VINEGAR	VINAGRE BALSÁMICO, EL
BANANA	PLÁTANO, EL
BAND-AID	CURITA, LA
BANDAGE	VENDAJE, EL
BANK	BANCO, EL
BANKER	BANQUERO, EL
BAR	BAR, EL
BARBER SHOP	PELUQUERÍA, LA
BARGAIN	GANGA, LA
BARRETS	BROCHE, EL
BASEBALL	BÉISBOL, EL
BASEMENT	SÓTANO, EL
BASIC	BÁSICO(A)
BASIL	ALBAHACA, LA
BASKETBALL	BASQUETBOL, EL
BASSINET	BAMBINETO, EL
BATHING SUIT	TRAJE DE BAÑO, EL
BATHROOM	BAÑO, EL
BATHTUB	TINA, LA
BATTERY	PILA, LA
BAY LEAF	HOJA DE LAUREL, LA
BAY	BAHÍA, LA
BBQ	ASADOR, EL
BBQ SAUCE	SALSA DE BARBACÓA, LA
BE (TO)	ESTAR
BE (TO)	SER
BEACH	PLAYA, LA
BEANS	FRIJOLES, LOS / HABICHUELAS, LOS
BEAR	OSO, EL
BEAUTIFUL	PRECIOSO(A)
BEAUTY SALON	SALÓN DE BELLEZA, EL
BEAVER	CASTOR, EL
BECAUSE	PORQUE
BED	CAMA, LA
BEDROOM	RECÁMARA, LA
BEDSPREAD	COLCHA, LA
BEE	ABEJA, LA
BEEF	CARNE DE RES, EL
BEER	CERVESA, LA
BEETLE	ESCARABAJO, EL
BEETS	BETABEL, EL
BEFORE	ANTES DE
BEGIN (TO)	EMPEZAR
BEGINNER	PRINCIPIANTE, EL
BEHAVE (TO)	COMPORTARSE
BEHIND	DETRÁS DE
BELIEVE (TO)	CREER
BELL PEPPER	CHILE MORRÓN, EL
BELT	CINTURÓN, EL
BENCH	BANCA, LA
BEND (TO)	DOBLAR
BESIDES	ADEMÁS
BETWEEN	ENTRE
BEVERAGES	BEBIDAS
BIB	BABERO, EL
BIBLE	BIBLIA, LA
BICYCLE	BICICLETA, LA
BIG	GRANDE
BIKINI	BIKINI, EL
BILL	CUENTA, LA
BILLION	MIL MILLONES
BINOCULARS	BINOCULARES, LOS
BIOLOGIST	BIÓLOGO, EL
BIRD	PÁJARO, EL
BIRTH	NACIMIENTO, EL
BIRTHDAY	CUMPLEAÑOS, EL
BIRTHPLACE	LUGAR NATAL, EL
BITE	MORDEDURA, LA
BITE (TO)	MORDER
BITTER	AMARGO(A)
BLACK BEANS	FRIJOLES NEGROS, LOS

BLACK	NEGRO(A)
BLACKBERRIES	ZARZAMORAS, LAS
BLACKBOARD	PIZZARÓN, EL
BLADDER	VEJIGA, EL
BLAME	CULPA, LA
BLANKET	COBIJA, LA
BLEACH	BLANQUEADOR, EL
BLEND, TO	LICÚAR
BLENDER	LIQUADORA, LA
BLESS YOU (AFTER A SNEEZE)	SALUD
BLINDS	PERSIANSAS, LAS
BLISTER	AMPOLLA, LA
BLOCK (CITY)	CUADRA, LA
BLOCKS	CUBOS DE MADERA, LOS
BLOND	RUBIO (A)
BLOOD	SANGRE, LA
BLOUSE	BLUSA, LA
BLUE CHEESE	QUESO ROQUEFORT, EL
BLUE	AZUL
BLUEBERRIES	ARÁNDANOS, LOS
BOAT	BARCO, EL
BOATING	PASEAR EN BARCO
BOIL (SKIN)	FURÚNCULO, EL
BOIL (TO)	HERVIR
BOILING WATER	AGUA HERVIDA, EL
BOK CHOY	BOK CHOY, EL
BOLT	PERNO, EL
BONE	HUESO, EL
BOOK	LIBRO, EL
BOOKKEEPER	CONTABLE, EL
BOOKSHELF	LIBRERO, EL
BOOTS	BOTAS, LAS
BORDER	FRONTERA, LA
BORED	ABURRIDO (A)
BOSS	JEFE, EL
BOTH	AMBOS(AS)
BOTTLE BRUSH	SEPILLO PARA BOTELLAS
BOTTLE	BIBERÓN, LA
BOWL	PLATO HONDO, EL
BOWLING	BOLICHE, EL
BOX (CONTAINER)	CAJA, LA
BOXING	BOXEO, EL
BOY SCOUTS	ESCOUTS, LOS
BOYFRIEND	NOVIO, EL
BRACELET	PULSERA, LA
BRACES (TEETH)	ABRAZADERA DENTAL, LA
BRAIN	CEREBRO, EL
BRANCH	RAMA, LA
BRASSIERE	SOSTÉN, EL
BRAVE	VALIENTE
BREAD	PAN, EL
BREAK (TO)	QUEBRAR / ROMPER
BREAKFAST	DESAYUNO, EL
BREAST	SENO, EL
BREASTMILK	LECHE MATERNA, LA
BREATHE (TO)	RESPIRAR
BRICK	LADRILLO, EL
BRIDE	NOVIA, LA
BRIDGE	PUENTE, EL
BRIE CHEESE	QUESO TIPO BRIE, EL
BRIEFCASE	MALETÍN, EL
BRIGHT	BRILLANTE
BRING (TO)	TRAER
BROCCOLI	BRÓCOLI, EL
BROKEN	ROTO (A)
BRONCHITIS	BRONQUITIS, EL
BROOK	ARROYO, EL
BROOM	ESCOBA, LA
BROTH	CALDO, EL
BROTHER – IN – LAW	CUÑADO, EL
BROTHER	HERMANO, EL
BROWN RICE	ARROZ INTEGRAL, EL
BROWN	PARDO/ CAFÉ
BRUISE	EL MORETÓN
BRUSH	CEPILLO, EL
BRUSSEL SPROUTS	COLES DE BRUSELAS, LAS
BUBBLE BATH	BAÑO DE BURBUJAS, EL
BUCKET	CUBETA, LA
BUCKLE	HEBILLA, LA
BUD	CAPULLO, EL
BUG BITE	PIQUETE, EL
BUG	BICHO, EL
BUILDING	EDIFICIO, EL
BUNGALOW	CASITA, LA
BURN	QUEMADURA, LA
BURNED	QUEMADO (A)
BURP (TO)	REPETIR
BUS STOP	PARADA DEL AUTOBÚS, LA
BUS	AUTOBÚS, EL
BUSH	ARBUSTO, EL
BUSINESS MEETING	CITA DE NEGOCIOS, LA
BUSINESSMAN	EMPRESARIO, EL
BUSY	OCUPADO (A)
BUT	PERO
BUTCHER	CARNICERO, EL
BUTTER	MANTEQUILLA, LA
BUTTERFLY	MARIPOSA, LA
BUTTOCK	POMPA, LA
BUTTON	BOTÓN, EL
BUY (TO)	COMPRAR
CABBAGE	COL, LA
CABIN	CABAÑA, LA
CABINET	GABINETE, EL
CACTUS	CACTUS, EL
CAKE	PASTEL, EL
CALF	PANTORRILLA, LA
CALM	QUIETO (A)
CAMEL	CAMELLO, EL
CAMERA	CÁMARA, LA
CAMPER	AUTOCARAVANA, EL
CAMPSITE	CAMPAMENTO, EL
CAN OPENER	ABRELATAS, EL
CAN	LATA, LA
CAN (BE ABLE)	PODER
CANAL	CANAL, EL
CANARY	CANARIO, EL

CANCER	CANCER, EL
CANDLESTICK	CANDELERO, EL
CANDY	DULCE, EL
CANOE	CANOA, LA
CANTALOUPE	MELÓN, EL
CANVAS	LONA, LA
CAP	GORRA, LA
CAPERS	ALCAPARRAS, LAS
CAPPUCCINO	CAPUCHINO, EL
CAR SEAT	ASIENTO DEL COCHE, EL
CAR	COCHE, EL
CAREFUL	CUIDADO
CARPENTER	CARPINTERO, EL
CARROT CAKE	PASTEL DE ZANAHORIA, EL
CARROT	ZANAHORIA, LA
CARTOONS	CARICATURAS, LAS
CASHEW	NUEZ DE INDIA, LA
CAST	YESO, EL
CAT BITE	MORDEDURA DE GATO, LA
CAT POOP	POPÓ DE GATO, LA
CAT	GATO, EL
CATEPILLAR	ORUGA, LA
CATHEDRAL	CATEDRAL, LA
CATHOLIC	CATÓLICO (A)
CAULIFLOWER	COLIFLOR, LA
CAVE	CUEVA, LA
CEILING	TECHO, EL
CELEBRATE (TO)	CELEBRAR
CELERY	ÁPIO, EL
CENTIMETER	CENTÍMETRO, EL
CEREAL	CEREAL, EL
CHAIR	SILLA, LA
CHALK	HISES, LOS
CHAMOMILE	TÉ DE MANZANILLA, EL
CHANGE (TO)	CAMBIAR
CHANGING TABLE	CAMBIADOR, EL
CHAPEL	CAPILLA, LA
CHARD	ACELGA, LA
CHECKBOOK	CHEQUERA, LA
CHECKERED	DE CUADROS
CHECKERS	JUEGO DE DAMAS, EL
CHEDDAR	QUESO AMARILLO, EL
CHEESE	QUESO, EL
CHEF	CHEF, EL
CHERRIES	CEREZAS, LAS
CHESS	AJEDREZ, EL
CHEST	PECHO, EL
CHICK PEAS	GARBANZOS, LOS
CHICKEN POX	VARICELA, LA
CHICKEN	POLLO, EL
CHILD	NIÑO, EL
CHILDREN	NIÑOS, LOS
CHILDRENS MUSEUM	MUSEO DEL NIÑO, EL
CHILDREN'S ROOM	CUARTO DE LOS NIÑOS, EL
CHILI PEPPER	CHÍLE, EL
CHILLS	ESCALOFRIOS, LOS
CHIMNEY/FIREPLACE	CHIMENEA, LA
CHIVE	CEBOLLÍN, EL
CHOCOLATE CAKE	PASTEL DE CHOCOLATE, EL
CHOCOLATE	CHOCOLATE, EL
CHOKE (TO)	AHOGARSE
CHRISTIAN	CRISTIANO (A)
CHRISTMAS	NAVIDAD, LA
CHURCH	IGLESIA, LA
CINNAMON	CANELA, LA
CIRCUS	CIRCO, EL
CITY	CIUDAD, LA
CLAM	ALMEJA, LA
CLAP HANDS (TO)	APLAUDIR
CLARINET	CARINETE, EL
CLAY/PLAY DOH	PLASTILINA, LA
CLEAN	LIMPIO (A)
CLEAN (TO)	LIMPIAR
CLEAR	DESPEJADO(A)
CLIMB A TREE	ESCALAR UN ÁRBOL
CLIMB (TO)	ESCALAR
CLINIC	CLÍNCIA, LA
CLOSET	CLOSET, EL
CLOTH DIAPER	PAÑAL DE TELA, EL
CLOTHES	ROPA, LA
CLOUDS	NUBES, LAS
CLOUDY	NUBLADO(A)
CLOVE	CLAVO, EL
COAST	COSTA, LA
COCOA	COCÓA, EL
COCONUT	COCO, EL
COFFEE MAKER	CAFETERA, LA
COFFEE	CAFÉ, EL
COLD (SICK)	GRIPE, EL
COLD WATER	AGUA FRÍO
COLD	FRÍO (A)
COLORS	COLORES
COMB	PEINE, EL
COME (TO)	VENIR
COMFORTABLE	CÓMODO
COMFORTER/QUILT	EDREDÓN, EL
COMPENSATION	COMPENSACIÓN, LA
CONDITIONER	ACONDICIONADOR, EL
CONDO	CONDOMINIO, EL
CONGRATULATIONS	FELICIDADES
CONSTIPATION	ESTRENIMIENTO, EL
CONTAGIOUS	CONTAGIOSO (A)
CONTRACT	CONTRATO, EL
CONVULSION	CONVULSIÓN, LA
COOK(TO)	COCINAR
COOKED	COCIDO
COOKIE	GALLETA, LA
CORDUROY	PANA, LA
CORN	ELOTE, EL
CORNER	ESQUINA, LA
CORNSTARCH	MAIZENA, LA
COSTUME	DISFRAZ, EL
COTTAGE CHEESE	QUESO COTÁJ, EL
COTTON BALLS	BOLITAS DE ALGODÓN, LAS

COTTON .... ALGODÓN, EL
COUGH ....TOS, LA
COUNTRY .... PAÍS, EL
COUNTY ....CONDADO, EL
COUSIN (FEMALE).......................... PRIMA. LA
COUSIN (MALE) ....PRIMO, EL
COW.. VACA, LA
COYOTE ....COYOTE, EL
CRAB ....CANGREJO, EL
CRACKER....................GALLETA SALADA, LA
CRAWL (TO).....................................GATEAR
CRAYONS............................CRAYOLAS, LAS
CREAM CHEESE...............QUESO CREMA, EL
CREAM ....CREMA, LA
CREATIVE .... CREATIVO (A)
CRIB .... CUNA, LA
CRIBSHEETS ....SÁBANAS DE CUNA, LAS
CRICKET.. GRILLO, EL
CROCODILE .... COCODRILO, EL
CROSS .... CRUZ, LA
CROUP.. KRUP, EL
CROW..CUERVO, EL
CROWN .... CORONA, LA
CRUTCHES..........................MULETAS, LAS
CRY (TO) ....LLORAR
CUCUMBERS .... PEPINO, EL
CUDDLE/HUG (TO).......................ABRAZAR
CUP... TAZA, LA
CURRENT .... CORRIENTE, LA
CURTAIN...................................CORTINA, LA
CUT (TO) ....CORTAR
CUTE...MONO(A)
DAILY..DIARIO
DAISY............................MARGARITA, LA
DANCE CLASS .... CLASE DE BAILE, LA
DANCING ....BAILE, EL
DANDELION................... DIENTE DE LEÓN, EL
DANGEROUS .... PELIGROSO(A)
DARK GLASSES..........LENTES OSCUROS, LOS
DARK .... OSCURO(A)
DATES.......................................DÁTILES, LOS
DAUGHTER-IN-LAW ....NUERA, LA
DAUGHTER.....................................HIJA, LA
DECEMBER .... DICIEMBRE
DEER .... VENADO, EL
DEFROST (TO) .... DESCONGELAR
DEHYDRATION .... DESHIDRATACIÓN, LA
DELICATE CYCLE ....CICLO PARA ROPA
   DELICADA, EL
DELICIOUS .... DELICIOSO(A)
DELIVERY PERSON .... REPARTIDOR, EL
DELIVERY SERVICE ....
   SERVICIO A DOMICILIO, EL
DENIM .... MEZCLILLA, LA
DENTIST .... DENTISTA, EL
DEPRESSED .... DEPRIMIDA (A)
DESERT .... DESIERTO, EL
DETERGENT ....DETERGENTE, EL

DEVIL ....DIABLO, EL
DIABETES ....DIABETES, EL
DIAMOND .... DIAMANTES, EL
DIAPER BAG ....PAÑALERA, LA
DIAPER COVERS .... CALZÓN DE HULE, EL
DIAPER PAIL.................BOTE DE PAÑALES, EL
DIAPER RASH...................... ROSADURA, LA
DIAPER...PAÑAL, EL
DIARREA ....DIARREA, LA
DIFFICULT ....DIFÍCIL
DILL..ENELDO, EL
DINING ROOM .... COMEDOR, EL
DINNER ....CENA, LA
DINOSAUR..........................DINOSAURIO, EL
DIRT .... TIERRA, LA
DIRTY LAUNDRY...................ROPA SUCIA, LA
DIRTY..SUCIO (A)
DISENFECTANT ..............DESINFECTANTE, EL
DISHES.....................................VAJILLA, LA
DISHWASHER .... LAVAPLATOS, EL
DISINFECTANT ...............DISENFECTANTE, EL
DIVORCED .... DIVORCIADO (A)
DO (TO)..HACER
DOCTOR.................................... DOCTOR, EL
DOG BITE........... MORDEDURA DE PERRO, LA
DOG POOP ....POPÓ DE PERRO, LA
DOG .... PERRO, EL
DOLL......................................MUÑECA, LA
DOLPHIN ....DELFÍN, EL
DONKEY .... BURRO, EL
DOOR ....PUERTA, LA
DOORMAN..................................PORTERO, EL
DOUBLE .... DOBLE, EL
DOWN... ABAJO
DOWNSTAIRS ....ABAJO/PLANTA BAJA
DOWNTOWN........................... CENTRO, EL
DRAGONFLY............................LIBÉLULA, LA
DRAW...DIBUJAR
DRAWING................................. DIBUJO, EL
DREAM .... SUEÑO, EL
DRESS UP (TO) ....DISFRAZARSE
DRESS .... VESTIDO, EL
DRESSER .... BUREAU , EL
DRIVE (TO) .... MANEJAR
DRIVER'S LICENCE ....
   LICENCIA DE MANEJAR, LA
DRIVEWAY ...... ENTRADA PARA COCHES, LA
DRIZZLE.................................... LLOVIZNA, LA
DRUM.. TAMBOR, EL
DRY CLEANERS.................... TÍNTORERIA, LA
DRY ....SECO (A)
DRYER ....SECADORA, LA
DUCK ....PATO, EL
DUMB.. TONTO (A)
DUMP TRUCK..........CAMION DE VOLTEO, EL
DUNE ....DUNA, LA
DURING ....MIENTRAS
DUSK ....ANOCHECER, EL

DUST (TO)	DESEMPLOVAR
DUSTPAN	RECOGEDOR DE BASURA, EL
EACH DAY	CADA DÍA
EACH	CADA UNO (A)
EAGLE	AGUILA, EL
EAR	OREJA, LA
EARLY	TEMPRANO
EARRINGS	ARETES, LOS
EARTH	TIERRA, LA
EARTHQUAKE	TERREMOTO, EL
EAST	ESTE
EASTER	PASCUA, LA
EASY	FÁCIL
EAT (TO)	COMER
EGG	HUEVO, EL
EGGPLANT	BERENJENA, LA
ELBOW	CODO, EL
ELEPHANT	ELEFANTE, EL
EMPLOYEE	EMPLEADO. EL
EMPTY (TO)	VACIAR
ENOUGH	SUFICIENTE
ENTREPRENEUR	EMPRENDEDOR, EL
ENVELOPE	SOBRE, EL
ERASER	GOMA, LA
ERRAND	ENCARGO, EL
EVENING	NOCHE, LA
EVERYBODY	TODO EL MUNDO
EVERYTHING	TODOS
EXCITED	EMOCIONADO (A)
EXPIRATION DATE	
FECHA DEL VENCIMIENTO, LA	
EXTRA LARGE	EXTRA GRANDE
EYE DROPS	GOTAS PARA OJOS, LAS
EYE	OJO, EL
EYEBROW	CEJA, LA
EYELID	PÁRPADO, EL
FABRIC	TELA, LA
FACE	CARA, LA
FAIR	CLARO (A)
FAIRY	HADA, EL
FALL ASLEEP (TO)	QUEDARSE DORMIDO (A)
FALL	OTOÑO, EL
FAMILY ROOM	ESTANCIA, LA
FAMILY	FAMILIA, LA
FAMOUS	FAMOSO (A)
FARMER	GRANJERO, EL
FAST	RÁPIDO (A)
FAT-FREE	SIN GRASA
FAT	GORDO (A)
FATHER-IN-LAW	SUEGRO, EL
FATHER	PADRE, EL
FAUCET	LLAVE, LA
FEATHER DUSTER	PLUMERO, EL
FEBRUARY	FEBRERO
FEEL (TO)	SENTIR
FENCE	CERCA, LA
FENNEL	HINOJO, EL
FERN	HELECHO, EL
FETA	QUESO TIPO FETA, EL
FEVER	FIEBRE/ CALENTURA, LA
FIANCÉE	NOVIO (A), EL (LA)
FIELD	CAMPO, EL
FIGHT (TO)	PELEAR
FIGS	HIGOS, LOS
FIND (TO)	ENCONTRAR
FINGER	DEDO, EL
FINISH	TERMINAR
FIRE (TO)	DESPEDIR
FIRE DEPARTMENT	
DEPARTAMENTO DE BOMBEROS, EL	
FIRE EXTINGUISHER	EXTINGUIDOR, EL
FIRE TRUCK	
CAMION DE LOS BOMBEROS, EL	
FIRE	FUEGO, EL
FIREMAN	BOMBERO, EL
FIREPLACE	CHIMINEA, LA
FIRST AID KIT	
CAJA DE PRIMEROS AUXILLOS, LA	
FIRST	PRIMERO (A)
FISH	PESCADO, EL
FISHING	PESCA, LA
FLEA	PULGA, LA
FLIP FLOPS	CHANCLAS, LAS
FLIPPERS	ALETAS, LAS
FLOOD	INUNDACIÓN, LA
FLOOR POLISH	CERA PARA PISO, LA
FLOOR	PISO, EL
FLOUR	HARINA, LA
FLOWER	FLORE, LA
FLU	INFLUENZA, LA
FLUSHABLE WIPES	
TOALLITAS DESECHABLES EN EL	
EXUSADO, LAS	
FLY	MOSCA, LA
FOG	NIEBLA, LA
FOLD (TO)	DOBLAR
FOOD	COMIDA, LA
FOOT	PIE, EL
FOOTBALL	FÚTBOL AMERICANO, EL
FOR EXAMPLE	POR EJEMPLO
FOR	PARA
FOREST	BOSQUE, EL
FORGET (TO)	OLVIDAR
FORK	TENEDOR, EL
FORMULA	FORMULA, LA
FOX	ZORRO, EL
FRACTURE	FRACTURA, LA
FREELANCER	PROFESIONAL
INDEPENDIENTE, EL	
FREEZE (TO)	CONGELAR
FREEZER	CONGELADOR, EL
FRENCH TOAST	PAN FRANCES, EL
FRESH	FRESCO(A)
FRIDAY	VIERNES, EL
FRIEND	AMIGO, EL
FRIENDLY	AMABLE

FRIENDS	AMIGOS, LOS
FROG	SAPO, EL
FROM	DE
FRONT DOOR	PUERTA PRINCIPAL, LA
FRONT YARD	JARDÍN DE ENFRENTE, EL
FROST	HELADA, LA
FROSTBITE	CONGELAMIENTO, EL
FRUIT	FRUTA, LA
FRY (TO)	FRÍER
FULL TIME	TIEMPO COMPLETO
FULL	LLENO(A)
FUN (TO HAVE)	DIVERTIRSE
FUNNY	CHISTOSO (A)
FUR	PIEL, LA
FURNITURE POLISH	
CERA PARA LOS MUEBLES, LA	
FURNITURE	MUEBLES, LOS
FUSE BOX	CAJA DE FUSIBLES, LA
GARAGE	GARAJE, EL
GARBAGE CAN	BASURERO, EL
GARBAGE	BASURA, LA
GARDEN	JARDÍN, EL
GARDENER	JARDINERO, EL
GARGBAGE DISPOSAL	DESECHADOR, EL
GARLIC	ÁJO, EL
GAS (BURPS)	GAS, EL
GAS METER	MEDIDOR DE GAS, EL
GAS RANGE	PARILLA DE GAS, LA
GAS STATION	GASOLINERA, LA
GATE	PORTÓN, EL
GERANIUM	GERANIO, EL
GERMS	MICROBIOS, LOS
GET (TO)	OBTENER
GIRAFFE	JIRAFA, LA
GIRL SCOUTS	ESCOUTS , LAS
GIRLFRIEND	NOVIA, LA
GIVE (TO)	DAR
GLASS	VASO, EL
GLOVE	GUANTE, EL
GLOVES/MITTENS	GUANTES, LOS
GLUE	PEGAMENTO, EL
GO (TO)	IR
GOAT	CHIVO, EL
GOD	DIOS
GODCHILD	AHIJADO, EL
GOGGLES	GOGLES, LOS
GOLD	ORO, EL
GOLF	GOLF, EL
GOOD-BYE	ADIÓS
GOOD AFTERNOON	BUENAS TARDES
GOOD EVENING	BUENAS NOCHES
GOOD LOOKING	GUAPO (A)
GOOD LUCK	BUENA SUERTA
GOOD MORNING	BUENOS DÍAS
GOOSE	GANSO, EL
GRAM	GRAMO, EL
GRANDDAUGHTER	NIETA, LA
GRANDFATHER	ABUELO, EL

GRANDMOTHER	ABUELA, LA
GRANDSON	NIETO, EL
GRAPE JUICE	JUGO DE UVA, EL
GRAPEFRUIT	TORONJA, LA
GRAPES	UVAS, LAS
GRASS/LAWN	PASTO, EL
GRASSHOPPER	SALTAMONTES, EL
GRATE (TO)	RALLA
GRAVEL	GRAVA, LA
GRAY	GRIS
GREEN BEANS	EJOTES, LOS
GREEN ONIONS	CEBOLLITAS, LAS
GREEN PEPPER	PIMIENTO VERDE, EL
GREEN TOMATOES	TOMATILLO, EL
GREEN	VERDE
GROCERIES	COMESTIBLES, LOS
GROOM (TO)	ARREGLARSE
GROUND	SUELO, EL
GRUMPY	DE MAL HUMOR
GUAVA	GUAYAVA, LA
GUEST ROOM	CUARTO DE VISTAS, EL
GUITAR	GUITARRA, LA
GUM	CHICLE, EL
GYMNASIUM	GIMNASIO, EL
HAIL	GRANIZO, EL
HAIR DRYER	SECADOR PARA EL PELO
HALF	MITAD, LA
HALLOWEEN	HALLOWEEN, EL
HALLWAY	PASILLO, EL
HAM	JAMÓN, EL
HAMBURGER	HAMBURGUESA, LA
HAMMOCK	HAMACA, LA
HAMSTER	HÁMSTER, EL
HAND WASH (TO)	LAVAR A MANO
HANG (TO)	COLGAR
HANGERS	GANCHOS, LOS
HAPPY BIRTHDAY	FELIZ CUMPLEAÑOS
HAPPY	CONTENTO(A)/FELÍZ
HAT	SOMBRERO, EL
HAVE (TO)	TENER
HAWK	HALCÓN, EL
HAY FEVER	ALERGIA, LA
HE	ÉL
HEAD	CABEZA, LA
HEADACHE	DOLOR DE CABEZA, EL
HEADBAND	CINTA, LA
HEAR (TO)	OÍR
HEART ATTACK	ATAQUE DEL CORAZÓN, EL
HEART PROBLEMS	
PROBLEMAS CARDIACOS, LOS	
HEART	CORAZÓN, EL
HEARTBURN	ACIDEZ, LA
HEAT UP (TO)	CALENTAR
HEAT	CALOR, EL
HEATSTROKE	INSOLACIÓN, LA
HEAVEN	CIELO, EL
HEEL	TALÓN, EL
HELL	INFIERNO, EL

bilingual babycare

HELLO	HOLA
HELMET	CASCO, EL
HELP (TO)	AYUDAR
HERE	AQUÍ
HIDE-AND-GO-SEEK	ESCONDIDILLAS, LAS
HIDE (TO)	ESCONDER
HIGH TIDE	MAREA ALTA, LA
HIGHCHAIR	SILLA PARA COMERDEL BEBÉ, LA
HIKING	CAMINATA, LA
HILL	CERRO, EL
HIP	CADERA, LA
HIPPO	HIPOPOTAMO, EL
HIRE (TO)	CONTRATAR
HIT (TO)	GOLPEAR
HOLIDAYS	DIAS FESTIVOS, LOS
HOMEMAKER	AMA DE CASA, LA
HONEY	MIEL, LA
HORNET	AVISPÓN, EL
HORSE	CABALLO, EL
HOSPITAL	HOSPITAL, EL
HOT CHOCOLATE	CHOCOLATE CALIENTE, EL
HOT DOG	SALCHICHA, LA
HOT PEPPER	CHILE, EL
HOT WATER	AGUA CALIENTE, EL
HOT	CALIENTE
HOURLY	POR HORA
HOURS	HORAS, LAS
HOUSE CLEANING	LIMPIEZA DE CASA, LA
HOUSE	CASA, LA
HOW	¿CÓMO?
HUG (TO)	ABRAZAR
HUMID	HÚMEDO(A)
HUMIDITY	HUMEDAD, LA
HURRICANE	HURACÁN, EL
HURRY (TO)	APURARSE
HURT (TO)	HERIR
HUSBAND	ESPOSO
I	YO
ICE CREAM	HELADO/EL, NIEVE, LA
ICE	HIELO, EL
ICICLES	CARÁMBANOS, LOS
IF	SI
IMAGINATIVE	OCCURENTE
INCH	PULGADA, LA
INDOORS	ADENTRO
INFANT TUB	BAÑERA, LA
INFECTED	INFECTADO (A)
INFECTION	INFECCIÓN, LA
INJURY	HERIDA
INSECT BITE	PIQUETE, EL
INSECT REPELLENT	REPELENTE, EL
INSIDE	ADENTRO DE
INSULIN	INSULINA, LA
INTELLIGENT	INTELIGENTE
INTERESTED	INTERESADO (A)
INTERVIEW	ENTREVISTA, LA
IRON	PLANCHA, LA
ITCH	COMEZÓN, LA
IVY	HIEDRA, LA
JACKET	CHMARRA, LA
JANUARY	ENERO
JAUNDICE	ICTERICIA, LA
JAW	MANDÍBULA, LA
JEALOUS	CELOSO (A)
JEWELRY	JOYERÍA, LAS
JEWISH	JUDÍO (A)
JICIMA	JICAMA, LA
JOG(TO)	CORRER
JOURNALIST	PERIODISTA, EL
JUICE BOX	JUGO DE CAJITA, EL
JUICE	JUGO, EL
JULY	JULIO
JUMP ROPE	CUERDA PARA BRINCAR, LA
JUNE	JUNIO
JUNGLE	SELVA, LA
KANGAROO	CANGURO, EL
KEEP (TO)	GUARDAR
KETCHUP	CATSUP, LA
KEY	LLAVE, LA
KICK (TO)	PATEAR
KILO	KILO, EL
KING	REY, EL
KISS	BESO, EL
KITCHEN	COCINA, LA
KITE	COMETA, LA
KITTEN	GATITO, EL
KIWI	KIWI, EL
KNEE	RODILLA, LA
KNIFE	CUCHILLO, EL
KNIT	TEJIDO, EL
KNOW (TO)	SABER
KOSHER	TIPO KOSHER
LACE	ENCAJE, EL
LADDER	ESCALERA, LA
LADYBUG	MARIQUITA, LA
LAKE	LAGO, EL
LAMB	CORDERO, EL
LAMP	LÁMPARA, LA
LARGE	GRANDE
LAST MONTH	MES PASADO, EL
LAST NIGHT	ANOCHE
LAST WEEK	SEMANA PASADA, LA
LAST	ÚLTIMO (A), EL(LA)
LATE	TARDE
LATER	LUEGO
LAUGH (TO)	REÍRSE
LAUNDRY ROOM	LAVANDERÍA, LA
LAUNDRY	ROPA SUCIA, LA
LAVENDER	LAVANDA, LA
LAWYER	ABOGADO, EL
LAXATIVE	LAXANTE, EL
LAZY	PEREZOSO(A)
LEAF	HOJA, LA
LEAK (TO)	GOTEAR
LEARN (TO)	APRENDER

LEASH .... CORREA, LA
LEATHER .... CUERO, EL
LEEK ....PUERRO, EL
LEG .... PIERNA, LA
LEGAL RESIDENT........... RESIDENTE LEGAL, EL
LEGUMES............................... FRIJOLES, LOS
LEMON .... LIMA, EL
LENTILS ....LENTEJAS, LAS
LET (TO).......................................DEJAR
LETTUCE ....LECHUGA, LA
LIBRARY .... BIBLIOTECA, LA
LICENSE ....LICENCIA, LA
LIE (TO)..MENTIR
LIFE JACKET ....CHALECO SALVAVIDAS, EL
LIFT (TO)....................................LEVANTAR
LIGHT (COLOR) .... CLARO(A)
LIGHTNING .... RELÁMPAGO, EL
LIGHTS ....LUCES, LAS
LIKE (TO) ....GUSTAR
LILAC ....LILA, LA
LIMA BEANS ..FRIJOLES DE MEDIA LUNA, LOS
LIME ....LIMÓN, EL
LINE DRY .... SECAR AL AIRE
LINEN ....LINO, EL
LION..LEÓN, EL
LIP .... LABIO, EL
LIPSTICK ....PINTALABIOS, EL
LIQUID.....................................LÍQUIDO, EL
LISTEN (TO) ....ESCUCHAR
LITER ....LITRO, EL
LITTLE BOY.....................................NIÑO, EL
LITTLE GIRL.....................................NIÑA,LA
LIVING ROOM...............................SALA, LA
LIZARD ....LAGARTO, EL
LOBSTER ....LANGOSTA, LA
LOCK .... CERRADURA, LA
LONG UNDERWEAR .... ROPA INTERIOR, LA
LONG ....LARGO(A)
LOOK FOR (TO) .... BUSCAR LOS
LOST .... PERDIDO(A)
LOTION ....CREMA, LA
LOW TIDE.......................... MAREA BAJA, LA
LUNCH...............................ALMUERZO, EL
LUNCHBOX..........................LUNCHERA, LA
MACADAMIA................... MACADAMIA, LA
MAGIC................................ MAGIA, LA
MAID .... CRIADA, LA
MAIL CARRIER .... CARTERO, EL
MAIL.......................................CORREO, EL
MAILBOX.................................BUZÓN, EL
MAKE (TO)....................................HACER
MAKE THE BED................. TENDER LA CAMA
MAKE (TO)....................................HACER
MAKEUP.......................MAQUILLAJE, EL
MAKING COOKIES ....HACER GALLETAS
MAN .... HOMBRE, EL
MANAGER...................................GERENTE, EL
MANDARIN.......................MANDARINA, LA

MANGO .... MANGO, EL
MANY................................. MUCHOS(AS)
MARBLES .... CANICAS, LAS
MARCH ....MARZO
MARGARINE................. MARGARINA , LA
MARKERS .... PLUMONES, LOS
MARKET .... SUPERMERCADO, EL
MARRIED .... CASADO (A)
MARRY (TO) .... CASARSE
MASK .... GAFAS DE BUCEO, LAS
MASS....................................MISA, LA
MATTRESS ....COLCHÓN, EL
MATURE .... MADURO (A)
MAY .... MAYO
MAYBE ....QUIZÁS
MAYONNAISE ....MAYONESA, LA
MEAL(S) .... COMIDA(S), LA(S)
MEAN .... MALDITO (A)
MEASLES .... SARAPIÓN, EL
MEASUREMENTS....................MEDIDAS, LAS
MEATBALL.....................ALBÓNDIGA, LA
MECHANIC ....MECANICO, EL
MEDICINE CABINET ....BOTIQUÍN, EL
MEDIUM..............................MEDIANO(A)
MELON ....MELÓN, EL
MERMAID.................................SIRENA, LA
MESS ....TIRADERO, EL
MESSAGE ....MENSAJE, EL
METER ....METRO, EL
MICROWAVE .... MICROONDAS, EL
MIDDLE.................................EN MEDIO
MIDNIGHT .... MEDIA NOCHE, LA
MIDWIFE .... PARTERA, LA
MIGRAINE..........................MIGRAÑA, LA
MILDEW ....MOHO, EL
MILE..MILLA, LA
MILK.......................................LECHE, LA
MILLIMETER .... MILÍMETRO, EL
MINERAL WATER...........AGUA MINERAL, EL
MINT....................................MENTA, LA
MIRROR ....ESPEJO, EL
MOIST................................ HÚMEDO(A)
MOLD ....MOHO, EL
MONDAY ....LUNES, EL
MONEY .... DINERO, EL
MONITOR ....MONITOR, EL
MONKEY .... CHANGO, EL
MONOPOLY ....MONOPOLIO, EL
MONSTER.............................MONSTRUO, EL
MONTH ....MES, EL
MOON .... LUNA, LA
MOP ....TRAPEADOR, EL
MOP (TO)....................................TRAPEAR
MORE OR LESS .... MÁS O MENOS
MORE ....MÁS
MORMON .... MORMÓN (A)
MORNING............................... MAÑANA, LA
MOSQUITO........................... MOSQUITO, EL

124   bilingual babycare

MOTH	POLILLA, LA
MOTHER – IN – LAW	SUEGRA, LA
MOTHER	MADRE, LA
MOUNTAIN	MONTAÑA, LA
MOUSE	RATÓN, EL
MOUTH	BOCA, LA
MOVE (TO)	MOVER
MOVIE	PELÍCULA, LA
MOVIES	CINE, EL
MUD	LODO, EL
MUDDY	LODOSO (A)
MUMPS	PAPERAS, LAS
MUSEUM	MUSEO, EL
MUSHROOMS	HONGOS, LOS
MUSIC CLASS	CLASE DE MÚSICA, LA
MUSIC	MÚSICA, LA
MUSICIAN	MÚSICO, EL
MUSLEM	MUSULMÁN (A)
MUST	DEBER
MUSTARD	MOSTAZA, LA
NAIL POLISH	ESMALTE DE UÑAS, EL
NAIL	CLAVO, EL
NAME	NOMBRE, EL
NANNY	NIÑERA, LA
NAP	SIESTA, LA
NAPKIN	SERVILLETA, LA
NATIONALITY	NACIONALIDAD, LA
NATURE	NATURALEZA, LA
NAUSEA	NAUSEA, LA
NEAR	CERCA DE
NECK	CUELLO, EL
NECKLACE	COLLAR, EL
NECTARINE	NECATARÍN, EL
NEED (TO)	NECESITAR
NEEDLE	AGUJA, LA
NEIGHBOR	VECINO, EL
NEIGHBORHOOD	COLONIA/VECINDAD, LA
NEPHEW	SOBRINO, EL
NERVOUS	NERVIOSO (A)
NEST	NIDO, EL
NEVER	NUNCA
NEW	NUEVO (A)
NEXT MONTH	PRÓXIMO MES, EL
NEXT ONE	PRÓXIMO (A), EL(LA)
NEXT TIME	PRÓXIMA VEZ, LA
NEXT TO	AL LADO DE
NICE	SIMPÁTICO (A)
NIECE	SOBRINA, LA
NIGHT LIGHT	LUCESITA, LA
NIGHT	NOCHE, LA
NIGHTMARE	PESADILLA, LA
NIGHTSTAND	MESITA DE NOCHE, LA
NIPPLE	CHUPÓN, EL
NO ONE	NADIE
NO	NO
NOISE	RUIDO, EL
NONE	NINGUNO (A)
NOODLE	FIDEO, EL

NOON	MEDIODÍA, EL
NORTH	NORTE
NOSE	NARÍZ, LA
NOSEBLEED	HEMORRAGIA NASAL, LA
NOTHING	NADA
NOVEMBER	NOVIEMBRE
NOW	AHORA
NUMBER	NÚMERO, EL
NURSE	ENFERMERA, LA
NURSERY(CHILDREN)	CUARTO DEL BEBÉ, EL
NUTMEG	NUEZ MOSCADO, LA
NUTS	NUECES, LAS
OATMEAL	AVENA, LA
OBEY (TO)	OBEDECER
OCEAN	MAR, EL
OCTOBER	OCTUBRE
ODOR	OLOER, EL
OFF	APAGADO(A)
OFFICE	OFICINA, LA
OIL	ACEITE, EL
OINTMENT	POMADA, LA
OLD	VIEJO (A)
OLDER PERSON	PERSONA MAYOR, LA
OLDER	MAYOR
OLIVE OIL	ACIETE DE OLÍVA, EL
ON A CONE	EN BARQUILLO
ON TOP OF	ENCIMA DE
ON	PRENDIDO(A)
ONCE	VEZ, UNA
ONION	CEBOLLA, LA
ONLY	SÓLO/SOLAMENTE
OR	O
ORANGE (COLOR)	ANARANJADO(A)
ORANGE (FRUIT)	NARANJA, LA
ORANGE JUICE	JUGO DE NARANJA, EL
OREGANO	ORÉGANO, EL
ORGAN	ÓRGANO, EL
ORGANIC	ORGÁNICO(A)
OUNCE	ONZA, LA
OUTDOORS	AFUERA
OUTSIDE	AFUERA DE
OVEN	HORNO, EL
OVERCOAT	ABRIGO, EL
OWL	BÚHO, EL
PACIFIER	CHUPÓN, EL.
PAINT (TO)	PINTAR
PAINTING	PINTURA, LA
PAJAMA	PIJAMA, LA
PANCAKES	HOTCAKES, LOS
PANTIES	CALZONES, LOS
PANTS	PANTALONES, LOS
PAPAYA	PAPAYA, LA
PAPER TOWELS	TOALLAS DE PAPEL, LAS
PAPER	PAPEL, EL
PARADE	DESFILE, EL
PARAMEDIC	PARAMÉDICO, EL
PARENTS	PAPÁS/PADRES, LOS
PARK	PARQUE, EL

PARMESAN	QUESO PARMESANO, EL
PARROT	PERÍCO, EL
PARSELY	PEREJIL, EL
PARTY	FIESTA, LA
PASSPORT	PASAPORTE, EL
PASTA	PASTA, LA
PATH	CAMINO, EL
PATIENT	PACIENTE
PATIO	PATIO, EL
PAY (TO)	PAGAR
PEACH	DURAZNO, EL
PEANUT BUTTER	CREMA DE CACAHUATE, LA
PEANUT	CACAHUATE, EL
PEAR	PERA, LA
PEARLS	PERLAS, LAS
PEAS	CHICHARROS, LOS
PECAN	NUEZ, LA
PEDIATRICIAN	PEDIATRA, EL
PEEL	PELA , LA
PENCILS	LÁPICES, LOS
PENIS	PENE, EL
PENS	PLUMAS, LAS
PEOPLE	PERSONAS, LA
PEPPER	PIMIENTA, LA
PERFUME	PERFUME, EL
PERISHABLES	ALIMENTOS PERECEDEROS, LOS
PERSON	PERSONA, UNA
PET	MASCOTA, LA
PETUNIA	PETUNIA, LA
PHOTOGRAPHY	FOTOGRAFÍA, LA
PIANO	PIANO, EL
PICKLE	PEPINO, EL
PICNIC	PICNIC, EL
PIE	TARTA, LA
PIG	COCHINO, EL
PILLOW	ALMOHADA, LA
PILLOWCASE	FUNDA, LA
PINE NUTS	PIÑONES, LOS
PINEAPPLE	PIÑA, LA
PINK	ROSA
PINS	SEGUROS, LOS
PINTO BEANS	FRIJOLES BAYOS, LOS
PISTACHIO	PISTACHOS, LOS
PLAN (TO)	PLANEAR
PLANT	PLANTA, LA
PLASTIC WRAP	PAPEL DE PLÁSTICO, EL
PLAY CHASE	JUGAR A LAS TRAES
PLAY (TO)	JUGAR
PLAYGROUND	JUEGOS DEL PARQUE, LOS
PLAYING HOUSE	JUGAR A LA CASITA
PLAYROOM	CUARTO DE JUEGOS, EL
PLEASANT	AGRADABLE
PLEASE	POR FAVOR
PLUM	CIRUELA, LA
PLUMBER	PLOMERO, EL
POCKET	BOLSILLO, EL
POISONING	ENVENENAMIENTO, EL
POLICE	POLICÍA, LA
POLICEMAN	POLICÍA, EL
POLISH (TO)	PULIR
POLITE	CORTÉS
POLKA-DOTTED	DE PUNTITOS
POMEGRANATE	GRANADA, LA
POND	LAGUNA, LA
POOL	PISCINA, LA
POOP	POPÓ, LA
POOR	POBRE
POPPY	AMAPOLA, LA
PORCH	TERRAZA, LA
PORK	CERDO, EL
POST OFFICE	CORREO, EL
POT (COOKING)	OLLA, LA
POTATOES	PAPAS, LAS
POUND	LIBRA, LA
PREGNANT	EMBARAZADA
PREMATURE	PREMATURO(A)
PRESCRIPTION	RECETA, LA
PRESENT	REGALO, EL
PRESIDENT	PRESIDENTE, EL
PRESSURED	PRESIONADO (A)
PRETEND (TO)	FINJIR
PRETTY	BONITO (A)
PRIEST	SACERDOTE, EL
PROFESSION	PROFESIÓN, LA
PRONOUNS	PRONOMBRES, LOS
PROTESTANT	PROTESTANTE, EL
PRUNE	CIRUELA PASA, LA
PSYCHOLOGIST	PSICÓLOGO, EL
PUDDING	BUDÍN, EL
PUDDLE	CHARCO, EL
PULL UPS	CALZONES ENTRENADORES, LOS
PUNCTUAL	PUNTUAL
PUNISH (TO)	CASTIGAR
PUNISHMENT	CASTIGO, EL
PUPPET	TITERE, EL
PUPPY	CACHORRO, EL
PURPLE	MORADO(A)
PURSE	BOLSA, LA
PUZZLE	ROMPECABEZAS, EL
QUARTER	CUARTO, EL
QUEEN	REINA, LA
QUESTION	PREGUNTA LA
QUIET	CALLADO (A)
QUINTUPLETS	QUINTILLIZOS
QUIT (TO)	RENUNCIAR
RABBIT	CONEJO, EL
RACCOON	MAPACHE, EL
RACE	CARRERA, LA
RADIO	RADIO, EL
RADISHES	RÁBANO , EL
RAG	TRAPO, EL
RAILING	BARANDAL, EL
RAIN	LLUVIA, LA

126

RAINCOAT	IMPERMEABLE, EL
RAISINS	PASAS, LAS
RANCH	RANCHO, EL
RASH	SALPULLIDO, EL
RASPBERRIES	FRAMBUESAS, LAS
RAT	RATA, LA
RAW	CRUDO(A)
READ (TO)	LEER
READING	LECTURA, LA
RECOMMEND (TO)	RECOMENDAR
RECYCLE (TO)	RECICLAR
RED HEAD	PELIRROJO (A)
RED PEPPER	PIMIENTO ROJO, EL
RED	ROJO(A)
REFLUX	REFLUJO, EL
REFRIDGERATE (TO)	REFRIGÉRAR
REFRIDGERATOR	REFRIGERADOR, EL
REFRIED BEANS	FRIJOLES REFRITOS
RELATIVES	PARIENTES, LOS
RELIGION	RELIGION, LA
RELOCATE (TO)	MUDARSE
REPLACE (TO)	REEMPLAZAR
REST OF	LO DEMÁS
RESTAURANT	RESTAURANTE, EL
RESTLESS	AGITADO (A)
REWARD	PREMIO, EL
RHINO	RINOCERONTE, EL
RIB	COSTILLA, LA
RIBBON	LISTÓN, EL
RICE	ARROZ, EL
RICH	RICO (A)
RIGHT NOW	AHORITA
RING	ANILLO, EL
RINSE	ENJUAGAR
RIPE	MADURO(A)
RIVER	RÍO, EL
ROAST BEEF	ROSBIF, EL
ROAST (TO)	ROSTIZAR/ASAR
ROCK	PIEDRA, LA
ROCKING CHAIR	MECEDORA, LA
ROLL (TO)	ENROLLAR
ROLY-POLY	ESCARABAJO, EL
ROOF	TECHO, EL
ROOT	RAÍZ, LA
ROSE	ROSA, LA
ROSEMARY	ROMERO, EL
ROTTEN	PODRIDO (A)
RUN (TO)	CORRER
SAD	TRISTE
SAFETY STRAP	CORREA, LA
SAFETY	SEGURIDAD, LA
SAGE	SALVIA, LA
SAIL (TO)	VELEAR
SAINT	SANTO, EL
SALARY	SALARIO, EL
SALMON	SALMÓN, EL
SALMONELLA	SALMONELA, LA
SALT-FREE	SIN SAL
SALT	SAL, LA
SALTY	SALADO(A)
SAME	MISMO (A), EL(LA)
SAND DOLLAR	ERIZO DE MAR, EL
SAND PAIL	CUBETA, LA
SAND	ARENA, LA
SANDBOX	ARENERO, EL
SATURDAY	SABADO, EL
SAUCE	SALSA, LA
SAUSAGE	SALCHICHA, LA
SAXOPHONE	SAXÓFONO, EL
SAY (TO)	DECIR
SCARF	BUFANDA, LA
SCHOOL	ESCUELA, LA
SCISSORS	TIJERAS, LAS
SCOOTER/ SKATEBOARD	PATINETA, LA
SCORPION	ESCORPIÓN, EL
SCRATCH	RASGUÑO, EL
SEA	MAR, EL
SEAHORSE	CABALLO MARINO, EL
SEASONS	TEMPORADAS DEL AÑO, LAS
SEE (TO)	VER
SEED	SEMILLA, LA
SEIZURE	ATAQUE, EL
SELL (TO)	VENDER
SEPTEMBER	SEPTIEMBRE
SESAME SEED	AJONJOLÍ, EL
SEVERAL	VARIOS(AS)
SHADE	SOMBRA, LA
SHAMPOO	CHAMPÚ, EL
SHARE (TO)	COMPARTIR
SHARK	TIBURÓN, EL
SHE	ELLA
SHEEP	BORREGO, EL
SHEET	SÁBANA, LA
SHIRT	CAMISA, LA
SHOES	ZAPATOS, LOS
SHORT	BAJO (A)
SHORTS	SHORTS, LOS
SHOULDER	HOMBRO, EL
SHOVEL	PALA, LA
SHOWER CURTAIN	CORTINA DE BAÑO, LA
SHOWER	REGADERA, LA
SHUTTERS	PERSIANAS, LAS
SHY	TÍMIDO (A)
SICK	ENFERMO (A)
SIDEWALK	BANQUETA, LA
SILK	SEDA, LA
SILVERWARE	CUBIERTOS, LOS
SING (TO)	CANTAR
SINGLE WOMAN	SEÑORITA, LA
SINGLE	SOLTERO (A)
SINK	LAVABO, EL
SIPPY CUP	VASO ENTRENADOR, EL
SISTER-IN-LAW	CUÑADA,LA
SISTER	HERMANA, LA
SIZES	TAMAÑOS, LAS
SKATEBOARD	PATINETA, LA

SKATES	PATÍNES, LOS
SKIN	PIEL, LA
SKIRT	FALDA, LA
SKIS	ESKIS, LOS
SKUNK	ZORRILLO, EL
SKY	CIELO, EL
SLED	TRINEO, EL
SLEEP (TO PUT TO)	ACOSTAR
SLEEP (TO)	DORMIRSE
SLICE (TO)	REBANAR
SLIDE	RESBALADIA, LA
SLIPPERS	PANTUFLAS, LAS
SLIPPERY	RESBALOSO (A)
SLOW	LENTO (A)
SMALL	CHICO(A)
SMALLPOX	VIRUELA, LA
SMELL (TO)	OLER
SNACK	REFRIGERIO, EL
SNAIL	CARACOL, EL
SNAKE BITE	MORDEDURA DE SERPIENTE, LA
SNAKE	SERPIENTE, EL
SNEEZE	ESTORNUDO, EL
SNORKEL	SNÓRQUEL, EL
SNOW	NIEVE, LA
SNOWBALL	BOLA DE NIEVE, LA
SNOWBOARD	SNOWBOARD, LA
SNOWMAN	MUÑECO DE NIEVE, EL
SNOWMOBILE	MOTONIEVE, EL
SOAK	REMOJAR
SOAP	JABÓN, EL
SOCCER	FÚTBOL, EL
SOCKS	CALCETINES, LOS
SODA	REFRESCO, EL
SOFA	SOFÁ, EL
SOFT	SAUVE
SOME	ALGUNOS(AS)
SOMEDAY	ALGÚN DÍA
SON-IN-LAW	YERNO, EL
SON	HIJO, EL
SONG	CANCIÓN, LA
SOON	PRONTO
SORE THROAT	DOLOR DE GARGANTA, EL
SOUL	ALMA, EL
SOUR CREAM	CREMA ÁCIDA, LA
SOUR	AGRIO(A)
SOUTH	SUR
SOY MILK	LECHE DE SOYA, LA
SOY SAUCE	SALSA DE SOYA, LA
SPEAK (TO)	HABLAR
SPICY	PICANTE
SPIDER	ARAÑA, LA
SPILL (TO)	DERRAMAR
SPIN (TO)	GIRAR
SPINACH	ESPINACA, LA
SPLASH MAT	PLÁSTICO, EL
SPLASH, (TO)	SALPICA
SPOILED	MIMADO (A)
SPONGE	ESPONJA, LA

SPOON	CUCHARA, LA
SPORTS	DEPORTES, LOS
SPORTSCOAT	SACO, EL
SPRING	PRIMAVERA, LA
SPRINKLER	REGADOR, EL
SQUASH	CALABAZA, LA
SQUIRREL	ARDILLA, LA
STAIN REMOVER	QUITAMANCHAS, EL
STAIN	MANCHA, LA
STARCH	ALMIDÓN, EL
STARFISH	ESTRELLA MARINA, LA
STAR	ESTRELLA, LA
START (TO)	EMPEZAR
STATE	ESTADO, EL
STEAK	BISTEC, EL
STEAM (TO)	COCINA R AL VAPOR
STEP STOOL	BANQUITO, EL
STEPDAUGHTER	HIJASTRA, LA
STEPFATHER	PADRASTRO, EL
STEPMOTHER	MADRASTRA,LA
STEPSON	HIJASTRO,EL
STEREO	ESTÉREO, EL
STERILIZE (TO)	ESTERILÍZAR
STICK	PALO, EL
STICKER	ESTAMPA, LA
STING (INSECT BITE)	PIQUETE, EL
STOCKINGS	MEDIAS, LAS
STOMACH ACHE	DOLOR DE ESTÓMAGO, EL
STOMACH	ESTÓMAGO, EL
STOP (TO)	PARAR
STORE	TIENDA, LA
STORM	TORMENTA, LA
STORY	CUENTO, EL
STRAIGHT AHEAD	DERECHO
STRANGE	RARO (A)
STRAWBERRIES	FRESAS, LAS
STREAM	ARROYO, EL
STREET	CALLE, LA
STROLLER	CARRIOLA, LA
STRONG	FUERTE
STUFFED ANIMAL	PELUCHE, EL
SUGAR-FREE	SIN AZÚCAR
SUGAR	AZÚCAR, EL
SUIT	TRAJE, EL
SUMMER	VERANO, EL
SUN	SOL, EL
SUNBURN	QUEMADURA , LA
SUNDAY	DOMINGO, EL
SUNFLOWER SEED	SEMILLA DE GIRASOL, LA
SUNFLOWER	GIRASOL, EL
SUNGLASSES	LENTES DE SOL, LOS
SUNNY	SOLEADO(A)
SUNRISE	AMANECER, EL
SUNSCEEN	PROTECTOR SOLAR, EL
SUNSET	PUESTA DEL SOL, LA
SUNSTROKE	INSOLACIÓN, LA
SURPRISED	SORPRENDIDO (A)

SWAMP	PANTANO, EL
SWEATER	SUÉTER, EL
SWEATSHIRT	SUDADERA, LA
SWEEP (TO)	BARRER
SWEET POTATO	CAMOTE, EL
SWEET	DULCE
SWELLING	INFLAMACIÓN, LA
SWIMMING RING	LLANTITA, LA
SWIMMING	NATACIÓN, LA
SWIMSUIT	TRAJE DE BAÑO, EL
SWING	COLUMPIO, EL
SWOLLEN	INFLAMADO (A)
SYNAGOGUE	SINAGOGA, LA
SYRUP	JARÁBE, EL
T-SHIRT	CAMISETA, LA
TABLE	MESA, LA
TAILOR	SASTRE, EL
TAKE (TO)	TOMAR
TALCUM POWDER	TALCO, EL
TALL	ALTO (A)
TAP DANCING CLASS	CLASE DE TAP, LA
TAPE	CINTA, LA
TASTE (TO)	SABOREAR
TASTY	SABROSO(A)
TAXES	IMPUESTOS, LOS
TEA SET	JUEGO DE TÉ, EL
TEA	TÉ, EL
TEACHER	MAESTRO, EL
TEASPOON	CUCHARADITA, LA
TEDDY BEAR	OSITO DE PELUCHE, EL
TEENAGER	ADOLESCENTE, EL
TELEPHONE	TELÉFONO, EL
TELEVISION	TELEVISIÓN, LA
TELL (TO)	CONTAR
TENNIS SHOES	TENIS, LOS
TENNIS	TENIS, EL
THANK YOU	GRACIAS
THE	EL (MASC.) LA (FEM)
THEIR	SU
THEN	ENTONCES
THERE	ALLÍ
THERMOMETER	TERMÓMETRO, EL
THESE	ESTOS/ESTAS
THEY (FEM.)	ELLAS
THEY (MASC.)	ELLOS
THIGHS	MUSLOS, LOS
THIN	FLACO (A)
THING	COSA, LA
THINK, (TO)	PENSAR
THIS ONE	ÉSTE/ÉSTA
THROW AWAY (TO)	TIRAR
THUNDER	TRUENO, EL
THURSDAY	JUEVES, EL
THYME	TOMILLO, EL
TIDE	MAREA, LA
TIE	CORBATA, LA
TIGER	TIGRE, EL
TIME	TIEMPO, EL

TIRED	CANSADO (A)
TO BE	SER
TO THE LEFT	A LA IZQUIERDA
TO THE RIGHT	A LA DERECHA
TOAST	PAN TOSTADO, EL
TOASTER	TOSTADOR, EL
TODAY	HOY
TOE	DEDO DEL PIE, EL
TOFU	TOFU, EL
TOGETHER	JUNTOS(AS)
TOILET PAPER	PAPEL DE BAÑO, EL
TOILET	EXCUSADO, EL
TOMATO	JITOMATE, EL
TOMORROW	MAÑANA
TONGUE	LENGUA, LA
TONIGHT	HOY EN LA NOCHE
TONSILLITIS	AMIGDALITIS, EL
TOOTH	DIENTE, EL
TOOTHBRUSH	CEPILLO DE DIENTES, EL
TOOTHPASTE	PASTA DE DIENTES, LA
TORNADO	CICLÓN, EL
TOW TRUCK	GRÚA, LA
TOWEL	TOALLA, LA
TOWN	PUEBLO, EL
TOY	JUGUETE, LA
TRACTOR	TRACTOR, EL
TRAIN	TREN, EL
TRAINING POTTY	BASINICA, LA
TRANSPORTATION	TRANSPORTE, EL
TRASH BAG	BOLSA DE BASURA, LA
TRASH	BASURA, LA
TRAVEL (TO)	VIAJAR
TREE	ÁRBOL, EL
TRICYCLE	TRICICLO, EL
TRIPLETS	TRILLIZOS
TROMBONE	TROMBÓN, EL
TRUCK	CAMIÓN, EL
TRUMPET	TROMPETA, LA
TUESDAY	MARTES, EL
TULIP	TULIPÁN, EL
TUNA	ATÚN, EL
TURKEY	PAVO, EL
TURN OFF (TO)	APAGAR
TURN ON (TO)	PRENDER
TURTLE	TORTUGA, LA
TV	TELEVISIÓN, LA
TWEEZERS	PINZAS, LAS
TWICE	DOS VECES
TWINS	GEMELOS
U.S.A.	E.U.A.
UGLY	FEO (A)
ULCER	ULCERA, LA
UNCLE	TÍO, EL
UNDER	ABAJO DE
UNDERWEAR	CALZONES, LOS
UNICORN	UNICORNIO, EL
UNITED STATES OF AMERICA	
	ESTADOS UNIDOS, LOS

UNLOAD (TO)	DESCARGER
UNTIL	HASTA
UP	ARRIBA
UPSTAIRS	ARRIBA/PLANTA ALTA
URINE	ORINA, LA
VACATION	VACACIÓN, LA
VACUUM	ASPIRADORA, LA
VACUUM (TO)	ASPIRA R
VAGINA	VAGINA, LA
VALLEY	VALLE, EL
VANILLA	VAINILLA, LA
VASELINE	VASELINA, LA
VCR	VIDEOCASETERA, LA
VEGETABLES	VERDURAS, LAS
VEGETARIAN	VEGETARIANO, EL
VELCRO	VELCRO, EL
VELVET	TERCIOPELO, EL
VERY	MUY
VETERINARIAN	VETERINARIO, EL
VIDEOS	VIDEOS, LOS
VINEGAR	VINAGRE, EL
VIOLET	VIOLETA, LA
VIOLIN	VIOLÍN, EL
VIRGIN	VIRGEN, LA
VISITOR	VISITANTE, EL
VOLLEYBALL	VÓLIBOL, EL
VOMIT (TO)	VÓMITAR
VOMITING	VOMITANDO
WAFFLES	WAFLES, LOS
WAGON	VAGÓN, EL
WAIT (TO)	ESPERAR
WAKE UP (TO)	DESPERTAR
WALK (TO)	CAMINAR
WALL	PARED, LA
WALLET	CARTERA, LA
WALNUT	NUEZ DE CASTILLA, LA
WALRUS	MORSA, LA
WANT (TO)	QUERER
WARM	CALIENTITO (A)
WASH (TO)	LAVAR
WASHCLOTH	TOALLITA, LA
WASHER	LAVADORA, LA
WASP	AVISPA, LA
WATCH (TO)	MIRAR
WATER VALVE	VÁLVULA DE AGUA, LA
WATER WINGS	FLOTADORES, LOS
WATER	AGUA, EL
WATERCRESS	BERRO, EL
WATERMELON	SANDIA, LA
WAVES	OLAS, LAS
WAX PAPER	PAPEL DE CERA, EL
WE	NOSOTROS
WEATHER	TIEMPO, EL
WEDDING	BODA, LA
WEDNESDAY	MIERCOLES, EL
WEED (PLANT)	MALA HEIRBA, LA
WEEK	SEMANA, LA
WEEKEND	FIN DE SEMANA, EL
WEIGH ,(TO)	PESAR
WELCOME	BIENVENIDOS
WELL MANNERED	EDUCADO (A)
WELL	BIEN
WEST	OESTE
WET	MOJADO (A)
WHALE	BALLENA, LA
WHAT	¿QUÉ?
WHEELCHAIR	SILLA DE RUEDAS, LA
WHEN	¿CUÁNDO?
WHITE BEANS	HAICHULAS BLANCAS, LAS
WHITE BREAD	PAN BLANCO, EL
WHITE CAKE	PASTEL BLANCO, EL
WHITE	BLANCO(A)
WHITES (CLOTHES)	ROPA BLANCA, LA
WHO	¿QUIÉN?
WHY	POR QUÉ?
WIDOW	VIUDA, LA
WIDOWED	VIUDO (A)
WIFE	ESPOSA, LA
WILD ANIMALES	ANIMALS SALVAJES, LOS
WILD RICE	ARROZ SALVAJE, EL
WIND	VIENTO, EL
WINDOW	VENTANA, LA
WINDY	CON VIENTO
WINTER	INVIERNO, EL
WIPES	TOALLITAS HÚMEDAS, LAS
WISH (TO)	DESEAR
WITH	CON
WITHOUT	SIN
WOLF	LOBO, EL
WOMAN	MUJER, LA
WOODPECKER	PICAPOSTE, EL
WOOL	LANA, LA
WORK	TRABAJO, EL
WORK (TO)	TRABAJAR
WORKING VISA	VISA DE TRABAJO, LA
WORM	GUSANO, EL
WORRIED	PREOCUPADO (A)
WORRY (TO)	PREOCUPARSE
WOUND	HERIDA, LA
WRIST	MUÑECA, LA
WRITE (TO)	ESCRIBIR
WRITER	ESCRITOR, EL
YAM	CAMOTE, EL
YARD	JARDIN, EL
YEAR	AÑO, EL
YELL (TO)	GRITAR
YELLOW	AMARILLO(A)
YES	SI
YESTERDAY	AYER
YOGURT	YOGHOURT, EL
YOLK	YEMA, LA
YOU (FAMILIAR)	TÚ
YOU (FORMAL)	USTED
YOU (PL.)	USTEDES
YOUNG BOY	MUCHACHO, EL
YOUNG GIRL	MUCHACHA, LA

YOUNG PERSON	JÓVEN, EL
YOUNG	JÓVEN
YOU'RE WELCOME	DE NADA
ZEBRA	CEBRA, LA
ZIPPER	CIERRE, EL
ZOO	ZOOLÓGICO, EL
ZUCCHINI	CALABAZA VERDE, LA

ESPAÑOL

A

INGLÉS

A la persona cuyo idioma nativo es el español:

Cuidar niños es una actividad sumamente satisfactoria – con o sin barreras de lenguaje, pero llena de retos todos los días. Mi objetivo con este libro es ayudar en el proceso de comunicación, ofreciendo frases y palabras simples traducidas tanto para los padres, como para la gente que se dedica a cuidar niños.

Las primeras páginas contienen información para caso de emergencias. Favor de preguntar a su empleador si hay algo que usted no entiende en estas páginas, las cuales son sumamente importantes. A continuación encontrará capítulos divididos por temas y perspectivas. Los primeros capítulos se cubren desde el punto de vista de la persona que habla en inglés. Cap. 1 – 11 (inglés a español) Posteriormente, se cubren capítulos desde el punto de vista de la persona que habla en español. Cap. 1 – 9 (español a inglés) También puede encontrar frases y palabras útiles en la primera parte del libro, tales como información acerca de precauciones alimenticias en el capítulo 4 e informacion acerca de seguridad en el capitulo 11. Así es que por favor, lea estos capítulos también.

El glosario es un gran recurso para encontrar todo típo de palabras. Por ejemplo, cuando salga al jardín, la página 189 le ofrecerá una serie de palabras, desde tierra hasta mariposa. Finalmente, la sección de vocabulario hasta el final del libro, enlista todas las palabras que se usan en el libro, con el fin de una referencia fácil.

Esperamos que le guste el libro!

1

introducción
introduction

introducción

adios	good-bye
apartamento, el	apartment
autobus, el	bus
bebé, el	baby
bienvenidos	welcome
buenas noches	good evening
buenas tardes	good afternoon
buenos días	good morning
casa, la	house
ciudad, la	city
coche, el	car
entrevista, la	interview
esposa, la	wife
esposo, el	husband
estado, el	state
familia, la	family
gracias	thank you
hija, la	daughter
hijo, el	son
hola	hello
mascota(s), la(s)	pet(s)
niñera, la	nanny
niño/niña, el/la	child
niños, los	children
nombre, el	name
país, el	country
parada del autobus, la	bus stop
por favor	please
profesión, la	profession
trabajo, el	work
transporte, el	transportation
tren, el	train
la colonia, la	neighborhood
vecino, el	neighbor

el primer encuentro
the first encounter

Hola	***Hello***
Mi nombre es__.	*My name is__.*
Mucho gusto.	***Nice to meet you.***
¿Como se llama usted?	*What is your name?*

acerca de su familia
about your family

¿Cuantos hijos tiene?	***How many children do you have?***
¿Cómo… – se llama? – se llaman?	*What…* *– is his/her name?* *– are their names?*
¿Cuántos años… – tiene? – tienen?	***How old…*** ***– is he/she?*** ***– are they?***
¿A cuántos niños estaría cuidando?	*How many children would I be watching.*
¿Están sus hijos en la escuela?	***Are your children in school?***
¿Cuánto tiempo tiene viviendo aquí?	*How long have you lived here?*
¿Tiene mascotas?	***Do you have any pets?***
¿Trabajan afuera de la casa los dos papás?	*Do both parents work out of the house?*
¿Usted estaría en la casa durante el día?	***Would you be home during the day?***

acerca de mí
about me

Mi dirección es __ .	***My address is __ .***
Mi número de teléfono es __ .	*My phone number is __ .*
Vivo en __ .	***I live in __ .***
Vivo con __ .	*I live with __ .*
Soy /No soy casado(a).	***I am/am not married.***
Tengo __ años.	*I am __ years old.*
He trabajado de niñera por __ años.	***I have worked as a babysitter/ nanny for __ years.***
Puedo/No puedo… – leer – escribir …en inglés.	*I can/cannot …* *– read* *– write* *... in English.*
Yo soy de __ .	***I come from __ .***

Tengo una licenciatura en __ en mi país.	*I have a degree in __ from my country.*
He estado en los Estados Unidos por __ años/meses.	***I have been in the United States for __ years/months.***
Pienso quedarme en los Estados Unidos por __ años/meses.	*I plan to stay in the United States for __ years/ months.*

acerca de mi familia
about my family

Él/Ella es mi...	***This is my...***
– esposo.	***– husband.***
– esposa.	***– wife.***
– pareja.	***– partner.***
– hijo.	***– son.***
– hija.	***– daughter.***
– p 92.	***– p 184.***
Su nombre es__.	*His/Her name is__.*
Yo soy/Mi esposo(a) es <u>p 94.</u>	***I am/My spouse is <u>p 186</u>.***
Tengo......	*I have...*
– un niño/una niña.	*– a boy/a girl.*
– dos niños.	*– two children.*
– tres niños.	*– three children.*
El nombre de ...	***My...***
– nuestro niño	***– son's***
– nuestra niña	***– daughter's***
...es __ .	***...name is __ .***
Él/Ella tiene…	*He/She is…*
– <u>p 187</u> años.	*– <u>p 95</u> years old.*
– <u>p 187</u> meses.	*– <u>p 95</u> months old.*
Él/Ella/Ellos/Ellas vive...	***He/she/they live...***
– conmigo.	***– with me.***
– con __ en __ .	***– with __ in __ .***
Él/Ella está...	*He/she is…*
– en la escuela.	*– in school.*
– conmigo durante el día.	*– with me during the day.*
– en la casa.	*– at home.*
– en la Universidad.	*– in college.*
– grande.	*– grown up.*

2

descripción del trabajo
employment details

[quick look]

descripción del trabajo

....

año, el	year
comida(s), la(s)	meal(s)
compensación, la	compensation
contratar	(to) hire
contrato, el	contract
fin de semana, el	weekend
horas extras	extra hours
horas, las	hours
impuestos, los	taxes
lavado de ropa, el	laundry
licencia de manejar, la	driver's licence
limpieza de casa, la	house cleaning
mañana, la	morning
manejar	(to) drive
medio tempo	part-time
mes, el	month
noche, la	night
pasaporte, el	passport
por hora	hourly
pregunta(s), la(s)	question(s)
residente legal, el	legal resident
salario, el	salary
seguro medico, el	health insurance
semana, la	week
tarde, la	afternoon
tiempo completo	full-time
trabajo, el	work
transporte, el	transportation
visa de trabajo, la	working visa
lunes, el	Monday
martes, el	Tuesday
miércoles, el	Wednesday
jueves, el	Thursday
viernes, el	Friday
sábado, el	Saturday
domingo, el	Sunday

bilingual babycare

horas
hours

¿Qué tipo de niñera está buscando...	*What type of babysitter are you looking for...*
– de tiempo completo?	*– full time?*
– de medio tiempo?	*– part time?*
– de vivir en casa?	*– live-in?*
– de vivir fuera de la casa?	*– live-out?*
¿Cuántos días de la semana quiere que trabaje?	*How many days per week would you like me to work?*
¿Cúal sería el horario de trabajo?	***What are the hours on those days?***
¿A qué hora...	*What time do you...*
– se va a trabajar?	*– go to work?*
– llega de trabajar?	*– come home from work?*
También estoy disponible para trabajar...	***I am also available to work...***
– los fines de semana.	***– on weekends.***
– en las noches.	***– in the evenings.***
Yoy a tener que irme a las __ am/pm el __ .	*I would need to leave by __ (time) on __ (day)*
Podría llegar aquí a las __ .	***I could get here by __ .***

compensación
wages

Me gustaría ganar $____...	***I would like to be paid $ __ ...***
– por hora.	***– per hour.***
– por semana.	***– per week.***
– por mes.	***– per month.***
– por quedarme a dormir en la noche.	***– per overnight stay.***
Me gustaría que me pagara...	*I would like to receive my pay...*
– por día.	*– daily.*
– por semana.	*– weekly.*
– por mes.	*– monthly.*
Me gustaria que me pagara...	***I would like to be paid...***
– en efectivo.	***– in cash.***
– en cheque.	***– by check.***
– con un depósito directo a mi cuenta del banco.	***– by direct deposit to my bank account.***
Me gustaría que mi sueldo...	*I would like my salary to...*
– incluyera los impuestos.	*– include taxes.*
– excluyera los impuestos.	*– exclude taxes.*
Si no piensa pagarme cuando estén de vacaciones, por favor avíseme para que pueda buscar otro trabajo.	***If you do not plan on paying me while you are on vacation, please tell me so I can find other work.***
Me gustaría que me pagara aún cuando estén de vacaciones.	I would like to get paid when you are on vacation.

beneficios
benefits

¿Cúantos...	*How many...*
– días por estar enfermo(a)	*– sick days*
– días de vacaiones	*– vacation days*
– de maternidad	*– maternity leave days*
...tendría?	*...will I receive?*
¿Mis prestaciones incluyerían…	*Will you provide me with…*
– seguro médico?	*– healthcare?*
– hospedaje?	*– housing?*
– un teléfono celular?	*– a cell phone?*
– comidas?	*– meals?*
– un coche?	*– a car?*
– un lugar de estacionnamiento?	*– a parking space?*
– un pase para el camión/metro?	*– bus/subway pass?*

transporte
transportation

Voy a venir a trabajar...	***I will come to work...***
– en coche.	***– by car.***
– en autobús.	***– by bus.***
– en tren.	***– by train.***
Tengo/No tengo coche.	*I do/don't have a car.*
Me dará un aventón...	***I can get a ride from...***
– un(a) amigo(a).	***– a friend.***
– mi esposo(a).	***– my spouse.***
¿Donde está la parada de autobús más cercana?	*Where is the nearest bus stop?*
¿Me puede recoger en la parada del autobús?	***Can you pick me up at the bus stop?***

la parte legal
cuestiones legales

Soy/No soy ciudadano(a) de los Estados Unídos.	***I am/am not a US citizen.***
Aquí está mi…	*Here is my…*
– tarjeta de seguro social.	*– social security card.*
– licencia de manejar.	*– driver's license.*
– pasaporte.	*– passport.*
– visa de trabajo.	*– work visa.*
¿Me puede ayudar a tramitar una visa de trabajo?	***Will you help me get a work visa?***

general
general

¿A cuántos niños estaría cuidando?	***How many children will I be watching?***

¿Qué otras responsabilidades tendría?

What else would you expect me to do?

Prefiero no tener que...
 – hacer la limpieza.
 – lavar la ropa.
 – hacer las compras.
 – preparar las comidas.
 – manejar con los niños en mi coche.

I would prefer not to...
 – do housecleaning.
 – do laundry.
 – go shopping.
 – prepare meals.
 – drive children in my car.

¿Estaría manejando con sus niños?

Will I be driving your children?

¿Voy a poder llevar los niños conmigo...
 – en el autobús
 – en el metro
 – en un taxi
 ...para ir a sus actividades?

Will I be able to take the children...

– on a bus
– on a subway
– in a taxi
...to go to their activities?

¿Está bien si traigo a mi hijo(a) conmigo a trabajar algunos días?

Is it O.K. if I bring my child to work with me on some days?

¿Estará trabajando en la casa?

Do you work from home?

¿Me va a dar una llave de la casa?

Will you give me a door key?

¿Tiene un sistema de alarma de la casa?

Do you have an alarm system?

¿Quiere que abre la puerta/conteste el teléfono cuando usted no está?

Should I answer the door /phone when you are gone?

Voy a traer mi propia comida.

I will bring my own food.

¿Puedo traer visitas a la casa?

May I have visitors in the house?

¿Ha tenido una niñera trabajando con usted antes?

Have you had a babysitter/nanny before?

3

actividades
activities

actividades

. . . .

arenero, el	sandbox
barco, el	boat
bicicleta, la	bicycle
caminar	(to) walk
caricaturas, las	cartoons
carriola, la	stroller
columpio, el	swing
compartir	(to) share
crayolas, las	crayons
cuento, el	story
dibujar	(to) draw
disfráz, el	costume
divertirse	(to have) fun
escalar	(to) climb
estampa, la	sticker
gatear	(to) crawl
gises, los	chalk
globo, el	balloon
hacer	(to) make
juegos del parque, los	playground
jugar	(to) play
juguetes, los	toys
leer	(to) read
libro para colorear, el	coloring book
lodoso(a)	muddy
muñeca, la	doll
papel, el	paper
patineta, la	scooter/ skateboard
pegamento, el	glue
película, la	movie
pelota, la	ball
plastilina, la	clay/play doh
plumones, los	markers
resbaladía, la	slide
rompecabezas, el	puzzle
ruido, el	noise
tijeras, las	scissors
tiradero, el	mess

actividades generales
general activities

Hoy él/ella aprendió a...	***Today he/she learned to...***
– **voltearse.**	***– rolled over.***
– **gatear.**	***– crawled.***
– **caminar.**	***– walked.***
– **hablar.**	***– spoke.***
– **sonreir.**	***– smiled.***
– **reirse.**	***– laughed.***

Por favor enséñeme como…
– abrir
– cerrar
– abrochar los cinturones de
– atorar las ruedas de
– poner la cubierta del sol a
…la carriola.

Please show me how to…
– open
– close
– fasten the seat belts on
– lock the wheels on
– put the sun cover on
...the stroller.

Hoy fuimos...	***Today we went to...***
– **al parque.**	***– the park.***
– **al zoológico.**	***– the zoo.***
– **p 199**.	***– p 107.***

¿Dondé está...
– el parque?
– la biblioteca?
– el protector solar?
– la carriola?
– __ ?

Where is…
– the park?
– the library?
– the sunscreen?
– the stroller?
– __ ?

Pienso llevar a los niños...	***I plan on going to...***
– **al parque.**	***– the park.***
– **al zoológico.**	***– the zoo.***
– **a la casa de un amigo.**	***– a friend's house.***

¿Qué cosas le gustaría que hiciera con los niños?

What types of things would you like me to do with the children?

¿Les gusta...	***Do they like to...***
– **leer?**	***– read?***
– **jugar afuera?**	***– play outside?***
– **ir al parque?**	***– go to the park?***
– **ir la biblioteca?**	***– go to the library?***
– **ir al zoológico?**	***– go to the zoo?***
– **jugar juegos de mesa?**	***– play board games?***
– **jugar con otros niños?**	***– play with other children?***

¿A qué hora va a llegar a la casa hoy?

When will you be home today?

¿Puedo llevar a sus hijos en mi coche?

May I take the children in my car?

¿A qué hora quiere que…
– salgamos?
– regresemos?

What time would you like us to….
– leave?
– come back?

Regresarémos a la casa…	*We will be home…*
– antes del almuerzo.	*– before lunch.*
– para la hora de la siesta.	*– for nap time.*
– a las <u>p 187</u> (am/pm).	*– by <u>p 95</u> (am/pm).*

Hoy nos vamos a quedar en la casa porque…	We will stay in the house today since it is…
– hace demasiado calor.	– too hot.
– hace demasiado frío.	– too cold.
– hay demasiado viento.	– too windy.
– va a llover.	– supposed to rain.
– <u>p 191.</u>	– <u>p 99</u>.

A él/ella le invitaron a…	*He/she has been invited to…*
– una fiesta de cumpleaños.	*– a birthday party.*
– la casa de un amigo.	*– a friends house.*
– a jugar con un grupo de niños.	*– a playgroup.*

¿Qué juguetes/juegos le gustan a él/ella? — *What toys/games does he/she like?*

Por favor llamame a mi teléfono celular si me necesitas. — *Please call me on my cell phone if you need me.*

El número de mi teléfono celular es __ . — *My cell phone number is __ .*

¿Va a llevar su teléfono celular consigo? — *Will you have your cell phone with you?*

¿Cuál es el número de su teléfono celular? — *What is your cell phone number?*

¿Con qué juguete quieres jugar ahora? — *What toy do you want to play with now?*

¿Quieres jugar un juego? — *Do you want to play a game?*

parques y paseos
parks & playgrounds

A él/ella le encanta…	*He/She loves…*
– la resbaladilla.	*– the slide.*
– el columpio.	*– the swing.*
– escalar.	*– to climb.*
– jugar en la arena.	*– to play in the sand.*

¿Puede él/ella quitarse los zapatos…	Can he/she take his/her shoes off…
– en el jardín?	– in the yard?
– en el parque?	– at the park?

¿Podemos llevarnos…	*Can we take…*
– los juguetes	*– the toys*
– la bicicleta	*– the bicycle*
– el perro	*– the dog*
…con nosotros?	*…with us?*

A él/ella le gustó/no le gusto	He/she did/did not like…
– los columpios.	– the swings.
– la resbaladilla.	– the slide.
– escalar.	– climbing.
– jugar con otros niños.	– playing with other kids.

clases y actividades
classes and activities

¿Qué día/A qué hora tiene clases?	*What day/time does he/she have classes?*
¿Dónde está la clase?	*Where is the class?*
¿Donde está/están...	*Where is/are the...*
– los zapatos para bailar?	*– dance shoes?*
– la ropa de gimnasia?	*– gym clothes?*
– el traje de baño?	*– swim suit?*
Necesitamos...	*We need to...*
– registrarlo/la en	*– register*
– pagar	*– pay*
... la clase.	*... for the class.*
¿Cómo nos vamos a ir?	*How should we get there?*
¿A que horas empieza...	*What time is the ...*
– jugar con un sus amigos?	*– playgroup?*
– la clase de gimnasia?	*– gym class?*
– la clase de baile?	*– dance class?*
– la clase de arte?	*– art class?*
– la clase de natación?	*– swim class?*
	...start?

arte y manualidades
arts & crafts

¿Dónde quiere que hagamos proyectos de arte y manualidades?	*Where should we do arts & crafts projects?*
– adentro?	*– inside?*
– afuera?	*– outside?*
– en la mesa?	*– on the table?*
¿Usa ropa especial para hacer actividades manuales?	*Do you use special arts & crafts attire?*
– mandíl?	*– apron?*
– camisas?	*– shirts?*
– pantalones?	*– pants?*
– zapatos?	*– shoes?*
¿Hay algo para poner encima de/debajo de la mesa?	*Is there something to put on/under the table?*
A él/ella le gusta...	*He/She likes to...*
– dibujar.	*– draw.*
– pintar.	*– paint.*
– jugar con estampas.	*– play with stickers.*
– jugar con cuentas.	*– play with beads.*
¿Donde está/están...	*Where is/are.....*
– el papel?	*– the paper?*
– las pinturas?	*– the paint?*
– las crayolas?	*– the crayons?*
– el pegamento?	*– the glue?*
– la cinta?	*– the tape?*
– los plumones lavables?	*– the washable markers?*

¿Dónde quiere que usemos las pinturas?	*Where should we use the paints?*
La crayola es...	***The crayon is...***
– roja.	***– red.***
– azul.	***– blue.***
– amarilla.	***– yellow.***
– verde.	***– green.***
Necesitamos más __ .	*We need more __ .*
¿Quieres pintar?	***Do you want to paint?***

libros
books

¿Cuáles son sus libros favoritos?	***What are his/her favorite books?***
¿Dónde están los libros?	*Where are the books?*
¿Tiene libros en español?	***Do you have any Spanish books?***
Hoy le leí un libro...	*I read him/her a book...*
– en la mañana.	*– this morning.*
– en la tarde.	*– this afternoon.*
– antes de la siesta.	*– before nap time.*
– p 187.	*– p 95.*
¿Cuándo le lee libros normalmente?	***When do you usually read books to him/her?***
– en la mañana?	***– in the morning?***
– en la tarde?	***– in the afternoon?***
– antes de su siesta?	***– before nap?***
– antes de dormirse en la noche?	***– before bed?***
A él/ella le gusta leer estos libros.	*He/She likes to read these books.*
¿Podemos conseguirle una tarjeta para sacar libros de la biblioteca?	***Can we get him/her a library card?***
Vamos a ir a la biblioteca a las p 187 para la hora de la lectura.	*We are going to the library at p 95 for reading hour.*
¿Quieres leer un libro?	***Do you want to read a book?***
¿Qué libro quieres leer?	*What book do you want to read?*

televisión & videos
tv & videos

¿Cuándo puede ver la televisión/los videos?	***When can he/she watch TV/videos?***
¿Qué programas/videos/DVDs puede ver?	*Which TV shows/videos/DVDs can he/she watch?*
¿Cuántos minutos/Cuántas horas al día puede ver la televión?	***How many minutes/hours per day can he/she watch tv?***
¿Podemos sacar más películas	*Can we get more movies from...*

de...
– la tienda de videos?
– la biblioteca?

A él/ella no le gusta este programa/video/DVD.

Hoy vimos __ .

¿Cómo prendo...
– la televisión?
– el DVD?
– la videocasetera?

¿Donde está la tienda de videos?

¿Quieres ver la televisión/un video/un DVD?

¿Qué video/DVD quieres ver?

– the video rental store?
– the library?

He/she does not like this tv show/video/DVD.

Today we watched __ .

How do I turn on the...
– TV?
– DVD player?
– Video player?

Where is the video store located?

Do you want to watch a video/DVS?

Which video/dvd do you want to watch?

4

comida
food

comida

··

ahogarse	(to) choke
alergia, la	allergy
almuerzo, el	lunch
babero, el	bib
biberón, el	bottle
calentar	(to) heat up
caliente	hot
calientito(a)	warm
cena, la	dinner
chupón, el	nipple
comida, la	food
congelar	(to) freeze
cuchara, la	spoon
cuchillo, el	knife
derramar	(to) spill
desayuno, el	breakfast
dolor de estómago, el	stomach ache
esterilizar	(to) sterilize
fecha de vencimiento, la	expiration date
fruta, la	fruit
gas, el	gas
gotear	(to) leak
gripe, la	cold
hervir	(to) boil
jugo de cajita, el	juice box
lavaplatos, el	dishwasher
leche materna, la	breastmilk
leche, la	milk
lonchera, la	lunchbox
moho, el	mold
podrido(a)	rotten
refrigerar	(to) refrigerate
refrigerio, un	snack
repetir	(to) burp
servilleta, la	napkin
silla para comer del bebé, la	highchair
taza, la	cup
tenedor, el	fork
vaso entrenador, el	sippy cup

líquidos
liquids

BIBERONES

Hoy él/ella tomó __
onzas/biberones.

Tomó un biberón a las __ am/pm.

A él/ella no le gustó __ .

¿Dónde están...
– los biberones?
– los vasos entrenadores?
– los chupones?

¿Cómo quiere que caliente...

– la leche materna?
– la leche?
– __ ?

¿A qué horas quiere que le de el biberón?

¿Qué le gusta tomar?

¿Está bien si le doy...
– agua de la llave?
– refresco?
– jugo?
– un licuado de frutas?

¿Dónde quiere que le de el biberón?

¿Cómo quiere que lave los biberones/chupones?
– en agua hervida?
– en la lavaplatos?
– en el esterilizador de botellas?
– a mano?

¿Cada cuándo quiere que esterilice los biberones?

BOTTLES

Today he/she drank __
ounces/bottles.

He/she had a bottle at __ am/pm.

He/she did not like __ .

Where are...
– the bottles?
– the sippy cups?
– the nipples?

How would you like me to heat...
– the breast milk?
– the milk?
– __ ?

When would you like me to give him/her the bottle?

What does he/she like to drink?

Is it OK to give him/her...
– tap water?
– soda?
– juice?
– a smoothie?

Where would you like me to give him/her the bottle?

How should I clean the bottles/pacifiers?
– in boiling water?
– dishwasher?
– bottle sterilizer?
– by hand?

How often should I sterilize the bottles?

solidos
solids

Hoy él/ella comió __ .

Comió la última vez a las __ .

¿Qué quiere que le dé de comer para...
– el desayuno?
– la comida?
– la cena?
– un refrigerio?

Today he/she ate __ .

He/she last ate at __ .

What would you like me to feed him/her for...
– breakfast?
– lunch?
– dinner?
– snack?

¿Qué...	*Which...*
– platos	*– plates*
– cucharas	*– spoons*
– tenedores	*– forks*
– baberos	*– bibs*
– vasos entrenadores	*– sippy cups*
...quiere que use?	*...would you like me to use?*

¿Hay algo en particular que quiere/no quiere que coma?

Is there anything in particular you want/do not want him/her to eat?

¿Es alérgico(a) a alguna comida?

Does he/she have any food allergies?

¿A qué hora quiere que coma...

At what time would you like him/her to eat...

- **el desayuno?**
- **la comida?**
- **la cena?**

- *breakfast?*
- *lunch?*
- *dinner?*

¿Puedo calentar la comida...
– en el microondas?
– en el horno?
– en la estufa?

Can I heat the food...
– in the microwave?
– in the oven?
– on the stove?

¿Él/Ella debe de comer en...
– la cocina?
– la mesa?
– la silla para comer del bebé?

Should he/she eat...
– in the kitchen?
– at the table?
– in the highchair?

compras
shopping

¿Quiere que vaya a comprar la comida?

Do you want me to shop for food?

¿A qué tienda debería de ir?

Which store should I go to?

¿Quiere que compre...
– leche entera?
– leche semi-descremada?
– leche descremada?
– leche orgánica?

Do you want me to buy?
– whole milk?
– low fat milk?
– non fat milk?
– organic milk?

¿Necesitamos comprar más __ .

We need to buy more __ .

¿Voy a necesitar $ __ para comprar estas cosas.

I will need $ __ to buy these items.

5

sueño
sleep

sueño

....

abrazar	(to) cuddle/hug
acostarse	(to put to) sleep
agitado(a)	restless
almohada, la	pillow
armario, el	armoire
bacinete, el	bassinet
cama, la	bed
cambiador, el	changing table
chupón, el	pacifier
closet, el	closet
colcha, la	bedspread
colchón, el	mattress
cortina, la	curtain
covija, la	blanket
cuna, la	crib
despertar	(to) wake up
despierto(a)	awake
dormido(a)	(to) asleep
edredón, el	comforter/quilt
funda, la	pillowcase
librero, el	bookshelf
llorando	crying
llorar	(to) cry
luz, la	light
mesedora, la	rocking chair
mesita de noche, la	nightstand
monitor, el	monitor
oscuro	dark
pajama, la	pajamas
pesadilla, la	nightmare
quedarse dormido(a)	(to) fall asleep
recámara, la	bedroom
sábana de la cuna, la	cribsheet
sábana, la	sheet
siesta, la	nap
sueño, el	dream

la hora de dormir
naps & bedtime

Él/Ella se durmió __ horas/minutos hoy.

He/she slept for __ hours/minutes today.

¿A qué hora normalmente …
– toma su siesta?
– se acuesta en la noche?
– se despierta?

What time does he/she usually…
– take a nap?
– go to bed at night?
– wake up?

¿A qué hora quiere que lo/la acueste?

When should I put him(her) to sleep?

¿A qué hora quiere que lo/la despierte?

When should I wake him(her)?

Él/Ella es/no es bueno(a) para dormir.

He/She is/is not a good sleeper.

¿Cuánto tiempo lo/la dejo dormir?

How long should I let him/her sleep?

¿Él/Ella necesita una cobija o un juguete para quedarse dormido(a)?

Does he/she need a blanket or toy to fall asleep?

¿Quiere que lo/la bañe antes de su siesta?

Do you want me to bathe him/her before naptime?

¿Puedo dejar que se duerma…
– en el coche?
– en la carriola?
– en el columpio?
– en el parque?

Can I let him/her fall asleep…
– in the car?
– in the stroller?
– in the swing?
– at the park?

¿No le importa si leo/veo la televisión mientras él/ella se duerme?

Do you mind if I read/watch tv while he/she naps?

Voy a lavar la ropa mientras él/ella se duerme.

I will do the laundry while he/she naps.

¿Quiere que lo/la levante de inmediato cuando llora, o quiere que lo/la deje un ratito para ver si se vuelve a dormir?

Do you want me to pick him/her up right away when she cries or do you want me to wait a little bit to see if he/she goes back to sleep?

¿Cómo bajo el barandal de la cuna?

How do I lower the crib railing?

¿Dónde está el monitor del bebé?

Where is the baby monitor?

A él/ella le gusta dormir boca abajo. Está bien con usted?

He/she likes to sleep on her stomach, is this OK with you?

limpieza
cleaning

¿Cada cuando quiere que cambie las sábanas?	*How often should I change the sheets?*
¿Dónde están las sabanas limpias?	*Where are the clean sheets?*
Él/Ella ensució las sábanas hoy.	*He/she soiled her sheets today.*
¿Puedo poner…	*Can…*
– las fundas	*– the pillowcase*
– el edredón	*– comforter*
– las sábanas de la cuna	*– crib sheets*
…en la lavadora?	*…go in the washing machine?*
¿Debería de lavar esto a mano?	*Should I wash this by hand?*

bilingual babyca

6

vistiéndose
getting dressed

vistiéndose

....

abrigo, el	overcoat
traje de baño, el	bathing suit
blusa, la	blouse
botas, las	boots
calcetines, los	socks
calzones, los	panties/underwear
camisa, la	shirt
camiseta, la	t-shirt
chamarra, la	jacket
falda, la	skirt
impermeable, el	raincoat
medias, las	stockings
pantalones, los	pants
pantuflas, las	slippers
ropa, la	clothes
vestido, el	dress
saco, el	sportscoat
shorts, los	shorts
sombrero, el	hat
suéter, el	sweater
sudadera, la	sweatshirt
tenis, los	tennis shoes
traje, el	suit
zapatos, los	shoes

general
general

¿Qué ropa debería de usar él/ella hoy?	*What should he/she wear today?*
¿Dónde está… – un sombrero? – una chamarra? – un suéter? – p 200?	*Where is…* *– a hat?* *– a jacket?* *– a sweater?* *– p 108?*

| ¿Quiere que lo/la vista en…

– ropa para jugar
– ropa de vestir
– p 200
…hoy? | *Do you want me to dress him/her…*
– in play clothes
– in nice clothes
– in p 108
…today? |

Él/Ella quiere ponerse… — *He/She wants to wear…*

A él/ella gusta vestirse sólo(a).	*He/She likes to dress himself/herself.*

| Este es su…
– pantalón favorito.
– camisa favorita.
– chamarra favorita.
– p 200. | *This is his/her favorite…*
– pair of pants.
– shirt.
– jacket.
– p 108. |

¿Dónde pongo la ropa que ya no le queda?	*Where should I put the clothes that are too small?*

outdoors
al aire libre

| ¿Dónde?…
– está la ropa para la lluvia.
– están las botas de hule.
– están las botas para la nieve.
– están los guantes. | *Where …*
– are the rain clothes?
– are the rubber boots?
– are the snow boots?
– are the gloves? |

Vamos a llevar esta chamarra al parque. — *We will take this jacket to the park.*

¿Dónde pongo la ropa mojada/lodosa?	*Where should I put wet/muddy clothes?*

¿Tiene un paraguas? — *Do you have an umbrella?*

| Tienes que ponerte…
– un traje de baño.
– un rompevientos.
– un suéter.
– p 200. | *You need to wear*
– a bathing suit.
– a wind breaker.
– a sweater.
– p 108. |

lavando ropa
laundry

¿Quiere que lave esta ropa...
– en la lavadora?
– a mano?
– inmediatamente?

P 200 está sucio(a).

¿Cómo quiere que lave esto?

Por favor enséñeme como usar la lavadora/la secadora.

¿Cuanto le pongo de detergente?

¿Le pone algo especial para las manchas?

¿Dónde está...
– el detergente?
– el suavizante de ropa?
– el líquido para las manchas?
– el blanqueador?

¿Dónde debo de poner a remojar la ropa con popó antes de ponerla en la lavadora?

¿Quiere que guarde la ropa doblada?

¿Qué ropa no debo de meter en la secadora?

Should I wash these clothes...
– in the washer?
– by hand?
– immediately?

The p 108 is dirty.

How should I wash this?

Please show me how to use the washing machine/dryer.

How much detergent should I use?

Do you add anything for tough stains?

Where is...
– the detergent?
– the fabric softener?
– the stain remover?
– the bleach?

Where should I soak soiled clothes before putting them in the wash?

Do you want me to put the folded clothes away?

Which clothes don't go in the dryer?

7

la hora del baño
bath time

la hora del baño

· ·

acondicionador, el	conditioner
agua, el	water
arreglarse	(to) groom
bañera, la	infant tub
baño de burbujas, el	bubble bath
baño, el	bath
caliente	hot
cepillo, el	brush
champú, el	shampoo
cinta, la	headband
cortina de baño, la	shower curtain
crema, la	lotion
espejo, el	mirror
esponja, la	sponge
frío(a)	cold
jabón, el	soap
la llave	faucet
lavabo, el	sink
listón de pelo, el	ribbon
mojado(a)	wet
pasta de dientes, la	toothpaste
peine, el	comb
regadera, la	shower
resbaloso(a)	slippery
salpicando	splashing
salpicar	(to) splash
secadora para el pelo, la	hairdryer
seco(a)	dry
tina, la	bathtub
toalla, la	towel
toallita, la	washcloth

general
general

¿Cuándo quiere que lo/la bañe?	**When should I bathe him/her?**

¿Donde está…
– el jabón?
– el champú?
– el acondicionador?
– la crema?

Where is…
– the soap?
– the shampoo?
– the conditioner?
– the lotion?

¿Le pongo agua…
– calientita?
– fresca?

Should I make the water…
– warm.
– cool.

¿Qué tina debo de usar?

Which tub should I use?

A él/ella le encanta estar desnudo(a).

He/she loves to be naked.

A él/ella no le gusta…
– mojarse el pelo.
– el champú.
– la coladera.
– el agua.
– que el jabón le entre a los ojos.

He/She doesn't like…
– getting his/her hair wet.
– shampoo.
– the drain.
– water.
– getting soap in his/her eyes.

Él/ella tiene la piel sensible.

He/She has sensitive skin.

¿Qué productos de limpieza debo de usar para limpiar la tina?

Which product should I use to clean the tub.

Le entró jabón a sus ojos hoy.

He/she got soap in her/his eyes today.

No…
– salpiques en la tina.
– tomes el agua de la tina.

Do not…
– splash in the tub.
– drink the bath water.

8

pañales y entrenamiento para usar el excusado
diapers & potties

pañales

....

accidente, el	accident
banquito, el	step stool
basinica, la	training potty
bolitas de algodón, las	cotton balls
bote de pañales, el	diaper pail
botiquín, el	medicine cabinet
calzón de hule, el	diaper cover
calzones entrenadores, los	pull-ups
cambiador, el	changing table
cambiar	(to) change
detergente, el	detergent
estampa, la	sticker
excusado, el	toilet
lavabo, el	sink
limpiar	(to) clean up
mojado(a)	wet
oler	(to) smell
olor desagradable	bad odor
orina, la	urine
pañal de tela, el	cloth diaper
pañal, el	diaper
papel de baño, el	toilet paper
piel, la	skin
pomado, la	ointment
popó, la	poop
premio, el	reward
repartidor, el	delivery person
rosadura, la	rash
seco(a)	dry
seguros, los	pins
servicio a domicilio, el	delivery service
talco, el	talcum powder
toallitas húmedas, las	wipes
Velcro, el	Velcro

pañales
diapers

¿Dónde tiro los pañales con…
 – **popó?**
 – **pipí?**

Where should I dispose of…
 – *poopie diapers?*
 – *pee pee diapers?*

Él/Ella está llorando. Voy a cambiar su pañal.

He/she is crying. I will change his/her diaper.

Necesitamos más…
 – **pañales.**
 – **toallitas húmedas.**
 – **pomada para rosaduras.**
 – **bolitas de algodón.**
 – **pañuelos desechables.**

We need more…
 – *diapers.*
 – *wipes.*
 – *diaper rash ointment.*
 – *cotton balls.*
 – *tissue.*

¿Podría comprar más panales hoy?

Could you buy more diapers today?

Estos pañales lo/la están rosando.

These diapers are giving him/her a rash.

¿Quiere que cambie la bolsa del bote de pañales…
 – ahora?
 – hoy?
 – todos los días?

Do you want me to change the bag in the diaper pail…
 – *now?*
 – *today?*
 – *everyday?*

PAÑALES DE TELA

¿Cuándo viene el servicio a recoger los pañales sucios?

CLOTH DIAPERS

When does the service pick up the soiled diapers?

¿Dónde guarda…
 – los pañales limpios?
 – los pañales sucios?
 – los calzones de hule?

Where do you keep…
 – *clean diapers?*
 – *dirty diapers?*
 – *diaper covers?*

¿Dónde debo de poner la bolsa del servicio a domicilio?

Where should I put the bag for the delivery service?

¿Dónde quiere que ponga los pañales sucios cuando no estemos?

Where should I put soiled diapers while we are out?

¿Cada cuando quiere que cambie su pañal de tela?

How often should I change the cloth diapers.

No estoy acostumbrado(a) a los pañales de tela.

I am not used to cloth diapers.

He usado pañales de tela antes. *I have used cloth diapers before.*

entrenamiento para usar el excusado
potty training

Creo que él/ella está listo(a) para empezar a usar el excusado.

I think he/she is ready to start using the potty.

¿Recibe un premio cuando usa el excusado, tal como…
– una estampa?
– un dulce?
– una estrella?

Does he/she get a reward for going in the potty, like a…
– sticker?
– treat?
– star?

A él/ella le gusta…
– la basinica.
– jalarle al excusado.
– jugar con el papel de baño.
– la sillita que va encima del excusado.

He/She likes…
– the small potty.
– flushing the toilet.
– playing with toilet paper.
– the potty seat.

¿Dónde está…
– el video
– el libro
…que les enseña como usar el excusado?

Where is…
– the video
– the book
…that teaches them how to use the potty?

¿Se pueden echar estas toallitas al excusado?

Are these flushable wipes?

Él/Ella tiene miedo…
– de caerse en el excusado.
– del ruido que hace cuando le jalas al excusado.

He/She is afraid of…
– falling in the toilet.
– the sound of flushing.

hygiene
higiene

Creo que él/ella tiene popó.

I think he/she has a dirty diaper.

Él/Ella…
– está rosado(a).
– tiene una infección de las vías urinarias.

He/She has…
– a diaper rash.
– a urinary tract infection.

¿Dónde está la pomada para las rosaduras?

Where is the diaper rash cream?

Por favor lávate las manos después de ir al baño.

Please wash your hands after using the potty.

¿Dónde están los calzones limpios?

Where are the clean underwear?

9

salud y seguridad
health & safety

salud y seguridad

accidente, el	accident
ahogarse	(to) choke/ (to) drown
alergia, la	allergy
ampolla, la	blister
antihistaminico, el	antihistamine
ataque, el	seizure
caja de primeros auxilio, las	first aid kit
comezón, la	itch
congelamiento, el	frostbite
contagioso(a)	contagious
curita, la	band-aid
deshidratación, la	dehydration
dolor de estómago, el	stomach ache
dolor de garganta, el	sore throat
estornudar	(to) sneeze
extinguidor, el	fire extinguisher
fiebre, la	fever
fractura, la	fracture
hemorragia, la	nosebleed
infectado(a)	infected
inflamado(a)	swollen
insolación, la	heatstroke
intoxicación, la	poisoning
jarabe para la tos, el	cough syrup
mordedura, la	bite
moretón, el	bruise
piquete, el	sting (insect bite)
quemado(a)	burned
quemadura de sol, la	sunburn
quemadura, la	burn
rasguño, el	scratch
repelente, el	insect repellent
roto(a)	broken
sangrar	(to) bleed
sangre, la	blood
toser	(to) cough
vomitar	(to) vomit

seguridad general
general safety

¿Dónde está/están...	*Where is/are...*
– el casco?	*– the helmet?*
– las muñequeras?	*– the wrist pads?*
– las codilleras?	*– the elbow pads?*
– las rodilleras?	*– the knee pads?*

¿Cómo funciona el sistema de alarma? — *How does the alarm system work?*

¿Cómo cierro las puertas/las ventanas con seguro? — *How do I lock the doors/windows?*

¿Qué hago si le da una reacción alérgica? — *What should I do if he/she has an allergic reaction?*

Enséñeme como se usa el EpiPen, por favor. — *Please show me how to use the EpiPen.*

Enséñeme cómo se pone el asiento del coche, por favor. — *Please show me how to install the carseat.*

Por favor enséñeme como se ajusta el cinturón...	*Please show me how to fasten the seat belt...*
– de la silla para comer.	*– on the high chair.*
– del columpio.	*– on the swing.*
– __ .	*– __ .*

¿Tiene cubiertas de plástico para los enchufes eléctricos? — *Do you have plastic covers for the electical outlets?*

Creo que estas plantas son venenosas. — *I think these plants are poisonous.*

Él/Ella sabe cómo abrir las puertas. — *He/She knows how to open the doors.*

enfermedades
illness

Él/Ella no se siente bien el día de hoy. — *He/She does not feel well today.*

Creo que él/ella...	*I think he/she...*
– tiene fiebre.	*– has a fever.*
– tiene dolor de estómago.	*– has a stomach ache.*
– tiene gripe/influenza.	*– has a cold/the flu.*
– tiene <u>p 202</u>.	*– has <u>p 111.</u>*

Creo que le están saliendo los dientes. — *I think he/she is teething.*

¿Le puedo dar medicina cuando usted no esté aquí? — *Can I give him/her medicine while you are gone?*

¿Qué dosis de medicina le debo de dar? — *How much medicine should I give him/her.*

¿Cada cuándo se la debo de dar? — *How often should I give it to him/her?*

Creo que él/ella es contagioso(a). — *I think he/she is contagious.*

¿Dónde está la medicina?	*Where is the medicine?*
Él/Ella vomitó...	*He/She vomited...*
– hoy.	*– today.*
– p 187 veces hoy.	*– p 95 times today.*
– a las p 187 .	*– at p 95 .*
Él/Ella tuvo diarrea...	*He/She had diarrea...*
– hoy.	*– today.*
– __ veces hoy.	*– __ times today.*
Su popó era...	*His/Her poop was...*
– normal.	*– normal.*
– medio verde.	*– greenish.*
– aguada.	*– runny.*
– apestosa	*– smelly.*
El moco es...	*The mucus es...*
– verde.	*– green.*
– amarillo.	*– yellow.*
– claro.	*– clear.*
– con sangre.	*– bloody.*
¿Dónde está el termómetro?	*Where is the thermometer?*
Su temperatura es __ .	*His/her temperature is __ .*
Su temperatura fue de __ grados a las __ .	*His/her temperature was __ at __ .*

accidents
accidentes

Él/Ella se cayó y se lastimó su...	*He/She fell and hurt his/her...*
– cabeza.	*– head.*
– rodilla.	*– knee.*
– codo.	*– elbow.*
– p 203.	*– p 112*
¿Donde está/están...	*Where is/are...*
– las curitas especiales?	*– the special Band-Aids?*
– la pomada antibiótica?	*– the antibiotic cream?*
– el desinfectante?	*– the disinfectant?*
– p 203?	*– p 111?*
Él/Ella estaba llorando, pero ahora está bien.	*He/she was crying, but is O.K. now.*
__ ...	*__ ...*
– lo/la pegó	*– hit*
– lo/la mordió	*– bit*
– lo/la pateó	*– kicked*
– lo/la chupó	*– licked*
– lo/la pegó	*– punched*
...hoy.	*...him/her today.*

mordeduras y piquetes
bites & stings

A él/ella lo/la mordió...	*He/She was bitten by a...*
– un perro.	*– dog.*
– una vívora.	*– snake.*
– p 190.	*– p 98.*
A él/ella le picó…	*He/She was stung by a…*
– un mosquito.	*– mosquito.*
– una abeja.	*– bee.*
– un abispa.	*– wasp.*
– un abispón.	*– hornet.*
– una hormiga.	*– ant.*
– p 190.	*– p 98.*
Él/Ella tiene piquetes por todo…	*He/She has bites all over his/her…*
– sus brazos.	*– arms.*
– sus piernas.	*– legs.*
– sus hombros.	*– shoulders.*
– su espalda.	*– back.*
– su cara.	*– face.*
– p 203.	*– p 112.*
¿Dónde está…	*Where is…*
– la pomada para quitar la comezón?	*– the anti – itch ointment?*
– el repelente de mosquitos?	*– the mosquito repellent?*
No vi que fue lo que le picó.	*I did not see what stung/bit him/her.*

G

glosario
glossary

PALABRAS BÁSICAS
BABY BASICS

personas importantes
special people

BEBÉ, EL – *BABY*
GEMELOS, LOS – *TWINS*
HERMANA CHICA, LA – *LITTLE SISTER*
HERMANA GRANDE, LA – *BIG SISTER*
HERMANO CHICO, EL – *LITTLE BROTHER*

HERMANO GRANDE, EL – *BIG BROTHER*
NIIÑERA, LA – *BABYSITTER/ NANNY*
NIÑO/LA NIÑA, LA – *CHILD*
NIÑOS, LOS – *CHILDREN*
PREMATUROS – *PREMATURE*
TRILLIZOS – *TRIPLETS*

equipo y juguetes
equipment & toys

ASSIENTO DEL COCHE, EL – *CAR SEAT*
BABERO, EL – *BIB*
BAMBINETE, EL – *BASSINET*
BICILETA, LA – *BICYCLE*
CABALLITO BALANCÍN, EL – *ROCKING HORSE*
CAMBIADOR, EL – *CHANGING TABLE*
CARRIOLA, LA – *STROLLER*
CINTRUÓN, EL – *SAFETY STRAP*
COLUMPIO, EL – *SWING*
CUNA PORTÁTIL, LA – *PORTABLE*

CRIB
CUNA, LA – *CRIB*
HEBILLA, LA – *BUCKLE*
KANGURERO, EL – *FRONT PACK/SLING*
MOCHILA, LA – *BACKPACK*
BURBUJAS, LAS – *BUBBLES*
ROTO – *BROKEN*
RUEDA, LA – *WHEEL*
SILLA PARA COMER DEL BEBÉ, LA – *HIGHCHAIR*
TRICÍCLO, EL – *TRICYCLE*

consuelo
comfort

ABRAZO, EL – *HUG*
BESO, EL – *KISS*
BIBERÓN, EL – *BOTTLE*
CANCIÓN PARA BEBÉS, LA – *LULLABY*
CANTAR UNA CANCIÓN – *SING A SONG*
CHUPÓN, EL – *PACIFIER/NIPPLE*
COBIJA, LA – *BLANKET*

DAR UN BIBERÓN – *GIVE A BOTTLE*
LECHE MATERNA, LA – *BREASTMILK*
MECEDORA, LA – *ROCKING CHAIR*
REFRIGERIO, EL – *SNACK*
TIEMPO PARA DESCANSAR, EL – *QUIET TIME*
VASO ENTRENADOR, EL – *SIPPY CUP*

pañales
diapers

BASINICA, LA – *TRAINING POTTY*
BOTE DE PAÑALES, EL – *DIAPER PAIL*
CALZONES ENTRENADORES, LOS – *PULL-UPS*
CAMBIAR – *CHANGE (TO)*

EXUSADO, EL – *TOILET*
ORINA, LA – *URINE*
PAÑAL, EL – *DIAPER*
ROSADURA, LA – *RASH*
SECO(A) – *DRY*
TOALLITAS HÚMEDAS, LAS – *WIPES*

cosas que hacen los ninos
things babies do

ABRAZAR – *CUDDLE (TO)*
CAERSE – *FALL (TO)*

CAMINAR – *WALK (TO)*

continuará...

CHUPARSE EL DEDO – *SUCK HIS/HER THUMB (TO)*
DECIR UNA PALABRA – *SAY A WORD (TO)*
DORMIRSE – *SLEEP (TO)*
ESTAR CONSADO(A) – *TIRED (TO BE)*
GATEAR – *CRAWL (TO)*
GRITAR – *SCREAM (TO)*
HABLAR – *TALK (TO)*
HACER UN BERRINCHE – *THROW A TANTRUM (TO)*
LLORAR – *CRY (TO)*
REIRSE – *LAUGH (TO)*
REPITER – *BURP (TO)*
SONREÍR – *SMILE (TO)*
TENER HAMBRE – *HUNGRY (TO BE)*
TOMAR UN PASO – *TAKE A STEP (TO)*
TOMAR UNA SIESTA – *TAKE A NAP (TO)*
VOLTEARSE – *ROLL OVER (TO)*

FRASES COMUNES
EVERYDAY PHRASES

expresiones comunes
expressions

¿CÓMO ESTÁ? – *HOW ARE YOU?*
¿CÓMO LE VA? – *HOW'S IT GOING?*
¿PUEDO AYUDARLE? – *CAN I HELP YOU?*
¿QUÉ PASA? – *WHAT'S HAPPENING*
¿QUÉ PASO? – *WHAT HAPPENED?*
¿SE PUEDE PASAR? – *MAY I ENTER?*
ADIOS – *GOOD-BYE*
AYUDA – *HELP*
BIENVENIDOS – *WELCOME*
BUENA IDEA – *GREAT IDEA*
BUENA SUERTA – *GOOD LUCK*
BUENAS NOCHES – *GOOD EVENING*
BUENAS TARDES – *GOOD AFTERNOON*
BUENOS DÍAS – *GOOD MORNING*
CUIDADO – *CAREFUL*
DE NADA – *YOU'RE WELCOME*
FELICIDADES – *CONGRATULATIONS*
FELIZ CUMPLEAÑOS – *HAPPY BIRTHDAY*
GRACIAS – *THANK YOU*
HOLA – *HELLO*
LO SIENTO – *I'M SORRY*
MÁS O MENOS – *MORE OR LESS*
MUCHAS GRACIAS – *THANK YOU VERY MUCH*
NO SÉ – *I DON'T KNOW*
NO SE PREOCUPE – *DON'T WORRY*
PÁSE/ADELANTE – *COME IN*
PERDÓN – *EXCUSE ME*
POR EJEMPLO – *FOR EXAMPLE*
POR FAVOR – *PLEASE*
QUÉ BIEN – *THAT'S GREAT!*
QUÉ LÁSTIMA – *THAT'S TOO BAD*
QUE SE DIVIERTA – *HAVE FUN*
QUÉ TENGA BUEN DÍA – *HAVE A NICE DAY*
QUIZÁS – *MAYBE*
SALUD – *BLESS YOU (AFTER A SNEEZE)*
VÁMONOS – *LET'S GO*
VENGA – *COME HERE*

preguntas
questions

¿A QUÉ DISTANCIA? – *HOW FAR?*
¿CÓMO? – *HOW?*
¿CUÁNDO? – *WHEN?*
¿CUÁNTO TIEMPO? – *HOW LONG?*
¿CUÁNTO? – *HOW MANY?*
¿CUÁNTO? – *HOW MUCH?*
¿POR QUÉ? – *WHY?*
¿QUÉ? – *WHAT?*
¿QUIÉN? – *WHO?*

¿donde está?
where is it?

A LA DERECHA – *TO THE RIGHT*
A LA IZQUIERDA – *TO THE LEFT*
ABAJO – *DOWN*
ABAJO DE – *UNDER*
ADENTRO DE – *INSIDE*
AFUERA DE – *OUTSIDE*
AL LADO DE – *NEXT TO*
ALLÁ – *OVER THERE*
ALLÍ – *THERE*
AQUÍ – *HERE*
ARRIBA – *UP*
ARRIBA DE – *ABOVE*
CERCA DE – *NEAR*
DERECHO – *STRAIGHT AHEAD*
DETRÁS DE – *BEHIND*
EN FRENTE DE – *IN FRONT OF*
ENCIMA DE – *ON TOP OF*
ENTRE – *BETWEEN*

continuará...

ESPAÑOL glosario

ESTE – *EAST*
NORTE – *NORTH*

OESTE – *WEST*
SUR – *SOUTH*

lugares para vivir
places to live

APARTAMENTO, EL – *APARTMENT*
CASA, LA – *HOUSE*
CIUDAD, LA – *CITY*
CONDADO, EL – *COUNTY*
CONDOMINIO, EL – *CONDO*

E.U.A. – *U.S.A.*
ESTADO, EL – *STATE*
ESTADOS UNIDOS, LOS – *UNITED STATES OF AMERICA*
PAÍS, EL – *COUNTRY*

palabras comunes
common words

A – *AT*
ANTES DE – *BEFORE*
AUNQUE – *ALTHOUGH*
CADA UNO – *EACH*
CON – *WITH*
DE – *FROM*
ENTONCES – *THEN*
ÉSE/ÉSA – *THAT ONE*
ÉSTE/ÉSTA – *THIS ONE*
ESTOS/ESTAS – *THESE*
MUY – *VERY*

NO – *NO*
OTRA VEZ – *AGAIN*
PARA – *FOR*
PORQUE – *BECAUSE*
SI – *IF/YES*
SIN – *WITHOUT*
SÓLO/SOLAMENTE – *ONLY*
TODOS – *ALL*
UN, UNA – *A, AN*
Y – *AND*

PERSONAS
PEOPLE

pronombres
pronouns

ÉL – *HE*
ELLA – *SHE*
ELLAS – *THEY (FEM.)*
ELLOS – *THEY (MASC.)*
NOSOTROS – *WE*

TÚ – *YOU (FAMILIAR)*
USTED – *YOU (FORMAL)*
USTEDES – *YOU (PL.)*
YO – *I*

familia
family

ÉL/ELLA ES MI __   *HE/SHE IS MY __*
. . . .

ABUELA – *GRANDMOTHER*
ABUELO – *GRANDFATHER*
CUÑADA – *SISTER-IN-LAW*
CUÑADO – *BROTHER-IN-LAW*
ESPOSA – *WIFE*
ESPOSO – *HUSBAND*
HERMANA – *SISTER*
HERMANO – *BROTHER*
HIJA – *DAUGHTER*
HIJASTRA – *STEPDAUGHTER*
HIJASTRO – *STEPSON*
HIJO – *SON*
MADRASTRA – *STEPMOTHER*
MADRE – *MOTHER*
NIETA – *GRANDDAUGHTER*
NIETO – *GRANDSON*
NOVIO(A) – *FIANCEE*

NOVIA – *GIRLFRIEND*
NOVIO – *BOYFRIEND*
NUERA – *DAUGHTER-IN-LAW*
PADRASTRO – *STEPFATHER*
PADRE – *FATHER*
PAPÁS/PADRES – *PARENTS*
PARIENTES – *RELATIVES*
PRIMA – *COUSIN (FEMALE)*
PRIMO – *COUSIN (MALE)*
SOBRINA – *NIECE*
SOBRINO – *NEPHEW*
SUEGRA – *MOTHER-IN-LAW*
SUEGRO – *FATHER-IN-LAW*
TÍA – *AUNT*
TÍO – *UNCLE*
YERNO – *SON-IN-LAW*

bilingual babycare

típos de personas
types of people

ADOLESCENTE, UN – *TEENAGER*
AMIGO(A), UN(A) – *FRIEND*
BEBÉ, UN(A) – *BABY*
CONOCIDO(A), UN(A) – *ACQUAINTANCE*
HOMBRE, UN – *MAN*
JÓVEN, UN – *YOUNG PERSON*
MUCHACHA, UNA – *YOUNG GIRL*

MUCHACHO, UN – *YOUNG BOY*
MUJER, UNA – *WOMAN*
NIÑA, UNA – *LITTLE GIRL*
NIÑO, UN – *LITTLE BOY*
PERSONA MAYOR, UNA – *OLDER PERSON*
PERSONA, UNA – *PERSON*
SEÑORITA, UNA – *SINGLE WOMAN*

características físicas
physical attributes

ÉL/LA BEBÉ ES __. *THE BABY IS __.*
ÉL/ELLA NO ES __. *HE/SHE IS NOT __.*
YO SOY __. *I AM __*
¿ERES __ ? *ARE YOU __ ?*

. . . .

ALTO(A) – *TALL*
BAJO(A) – *SHORT*
BONITO(A) – *PRETTY*
CALVO(A) – *BALD*
CLARO(A) – *FAIR*
FEO(A) – *UGLY*
FLACO(A) – *THIN*
GORDO(A) – *FAT*

GRANDE – *BIG*
GUAPO(A) – *GOOD LOOKING*
JÓVEN – *YOUNG*
MORENO(A) – *DARK*
PELIRROJO(A) – *RED HEAD*
PEQUEÑO(A) – *SMALL*
RUBIO(A) – *BLOND*
VIEJO(A) – *OLD*

palabras descriptivas (ser)
descriptions

ÉLBEBÉ ES __ *THE BABY IS __*
ÉL/ELLA NO ES __ *HE/SHE IS NOT __*
YO SOY __ *I AM __*
¿ERES __ ? *ARE YOU __ ?*

. . . .

AGRADABLE – *PLEASANT*
AGRESIVO(A) – *AGGRESSIVE*
AMABLE – *FRIENDLY*
CASADO(A) – *MARRIED*
CORTÉS – *POLITE*
CREATIVO(A) – *CREATIVE*
DIFÍCIL – *DIFFICULT*
DIVORCIADO(A) – *DIVORCED*
EDUCADO(A) – *WELL MANNERED*
FÁCIL – *EASY*
FAMOSO(A) – *FAMOUS*
FUERTE – *STRONG*
GEMELO(A), UN(A) – *TWIN (A)*
INTELIGENTE – *INTELLIGENT*
LENTO(A) – *SLOW*
MADURO(A) – *MATURE*

MALDITO(A) – *MEAN*
MALO(A) – *BAD*
NUEVO(A) – *NEW*
OCCURENTE – *IMAGINATIVE*
PACIENTE – *PATIENT*
POBRE – *POOR*
PUNTUAL – *PUNCTUAL*
RÁPIDO(A) – *FAST*
RARO(A) – *STRANGE*
RICO(A) – *RICH*
SIMPÁTICO(A) – *NICE*
SOLTERO(A) – *SINGLE*
TÍMIDO(A) – *SHY*
TONTO(A) – *DUMB*
VALIENTE – *BRAVE*
VIUDO(A) – *WIDOWED*

palabras descriptivas (estar)
descriptions

EL BEBÉ ESTÁ __. *THE BABY IS __.*
ÉL/ELLA NO ESTÁ __. *HE/SHE IS NOT __.*
YO ESTOY __. *I AM __.*
¿ESTÁS __ ? *ARE YOU __ ?*

continuará...

. . . .

ABURRIDO(A) – *BORED*
BIEN – *WELL*
CALLADO(A) – *QUIET*
CANSADO(A) – *TIRED*
CELOSO(A) – *JEALOUS*
CHISTOSO(A) – *FUNNY*
CONTENTO(A)/FELÍZ – *HAPPY*
DE MAL HUMOR – *GRUMPY*
DEPRIMIDA(A) – *DEPRESSED*
DISPONIBLE – *AVAILABLE*
EMOCIONADO(A) – *EXCITED*
ENFERMO(A) – *SICK*

INTERESADO(A) – *INTERESTED*
MIMADO(A) – *SPOILED*
MOJADO(A) – *WET*
NERVIOSO(A) – *NERVOUS*
OCUPADO(A) – *BUSY*
PEREZOSO(A) – *LAZY*
PREOCUPADO(A) – *WORRIED*
PRESIONADO(A) – *PRESSURED*
QUIETO(A) – *CALM*
SECO(A) – *DRY*
SORPRENDIDO(A) – *SURPRISED*
TRISTE – *SAD*

profesiones
careers

YO SOY __. *I AM __.*
MI ESPOSO/ESPOSA/PAREJA ES __. *MY HUSBAND/WIFE/PARTNER IS __.*
. . . .

ABOGADO(A), UN(A) – *LAWYER*
ACTOR, UN – *ACTOR*
AMA DE CASA, UNA – *HOMEMAKER*
ARQUITECTO(A), UN(A) – *ARCHITECT*
ARTISTA, UN(A) – *ARTIST*
AUTOR(A), UN(A) – *AUTHOR*
BANQUERO(A), UN(A) – *BANKER*
BOMBERO(A), UN(A) – *FIREMAN*
CARPINTERO(A), UN(A) – *CARPENTER*
COCINERO(A), UN(A) – *CHEF*
DENTISTA, UN(A) – *DENTIST*
DOCTOR(A), UN(A) – *DOCTOR*
EMPLEADO(A), UN(A) – *EMPLOYEE*
EMPRENDEDOR(A), UN(A) – *ENTREPRENEUR*
EMPRESARIO(A), UN(A) – *BUSINESSMAN*
ENFERMERO(A), UN(A) – *NURSE*
ESCRITOR(A), UN(A) – *WRITER*
GERENTE(A), UN(A) – *MANAGER*
GRANJERO(A), UN(A) – *FARMER*

JARDINERO(A), UN(A) – *GARDENE*
JEFE(A), UN(A) – *BOSS*
MAESTRO(A), UN(A) – *TEACHER*
MECANICO(A), UN(A) – *MECHANIC*
MÚSICO, UN – *MUSICIAN*
PANADERO(A), UN(A) – *BAKER*
PARAMÉDICO(A), UN(A) – *PARAMEDIC*
PARTERA, UNA – *MIDWIFE*
PEDIATRA, UN(A) – *PEDIATRICIAN*
PERIODISTA, UN(A) – *JOURNALIS*
PLOMERO(A), UN(A) – *PLUMBER*
POLICÍA, UN(A) – *POLICEMAN*
PRESIDENTE, UN – *PRESIDENT*
PROFESIONAL INDEPENDIENTE, UN(A) – *FREELANCER*
PSICÓLOGO(A), UN(A) – *PSYCHOLOGIST*
SACERDOTE, UN – *PRIEST*
SASTRE, UN(A) – *TAILOR*
VETERINARIO(A), UN(A) – *VETERINARIAN*

la religión
religion

ALMA, EL – *SOUL*
BIBLIA, LA – *BIBLE*
CAPILLA, LA – *CHAPEL*
CATEDRAL, LA – *CATHEDRAL*
CIELO, EL – *HEAVEN*
CRUZ, LA – *CROSS*
DIABLO, EL – *DEVIL*
DIOS – *GOD*

IGLESIA, LA – *CHURCH*
INFIERNO, EL – *HELL*
MISA, LA – *MASS*
SACERDOTE, EL – *PRIEST*
SANTOS, LOS – *SAINTS*
SINAGOGA, LA – *SYNAGOGUE*
VIRGEN, LA – *VIRGIN (THE)*

. . . .

YO SOY __. *I AM __.*
. . . .

AGNÓSTICO(A) – *AGNOSTIC*
ATEO(A) – *ATHEIST*
CATÓLICO(A) – *CATHOLIC*
CRISTIANO(A) – *CHRISTIAN*

JUDÍO(A) – *JEWISH*
MORMÓN(A) – *MORMON*
MUSULMÁN(A) – *MUSLEM*
PROTESTANTE – *PROTESTANT*

TIEMPOS, DÍGITOS Y DÍAS
TIME, DIGITS & DAYS

números
numbers

1 – ONE	25 – TWENTYFIVE
2 – TWO	26 – TWENTYSIX
3 – THREE	27 – TWENTYSEVEN
4 – FOUR	28 – TWENTYEIGHT
5 – FIVE	29 – TWENTYNINE
6 – SIX	30 – THIRTY
7 – SEVEN	40 – FOURTY
8 – EIGHT	50 – FIFTY
9 – NINE	60 – SIXTY
10 – TEN	70 – SEVENTY
11 – ELEVEN	80 – EIGHTY
12 – TWELVE	90 – NINETY
13 – THIRTEEN	100 – ONEHUNDRED
14 – FOURTEEN	200 – TWOHUNDRED
15 – FIFTEEN	300 – THREEHUNDRED
16 – SIXTEEN	400 – FOURHUNDRED
17 – SEVENTEEN	500 – FIVEHUNDRED
18 – EIGHTEEN	600 – SIXHUNDRED
19 – NINETEEN	700 – SEVENHUNDRED
20 – TWENTY	800 – EIGHTHUNDRED
21 – TWENTYONE	900 – NINEHUNDRED
22 – TWENTYTWO	1,000 – ONETHOUSAND
23 – TWENTYTHREE	MILLION – MILLION
24 – TWENTYFOUR	

horas del día
hours of the day

ES CUARTO PARA LAS DOS – IT IS A QUARTER TO TWO
SON CINCO PARA LAS DOS – IT IS FIVE TO TWO
SON LAS DOS – IT IS TWO O'CLOCK
SON LAS DOS Y CINCO – IT IS FIVE PAST TWO
SON LAS DOS Y MEDIA – IT IS TWO THIRTY
SON LOS DOS Y CUARTO – IT IS QUARTER AFTER TWO

días de la semana
days of the week

LUNES – MONDAY	VIERNES – FRIDAY
MARTES – TUESDAY	SABADO – SATURDAY
MIÉRCOLES – WEDNESDAY	DOMINGO – SUNDAY
JUEVES – THURSDAY	

meses del ano
months of the year

ENERO – JANUARY	JULIO – JULY
FEBRERO – FEBRUARY	AGOSTO – AUGUST
MARZO – MARCH	SEPTIEMBRE – SEPTEMBER
ABRIL – APRIL	OCTUBRE – OCTOBER
MAYO – MAY	NOVIEMBRE – NOVEMBER
JUNIO – JUNE	DICIEMBRE – DECEMBER

ESPAÑOL glosario

palabras relacionadas con el tiempo
time related words

AHORA – *NOW*	MEDIA NOCHE – *MIDNIGHT*
AHORITA – *RIGHT NOW*	MEDIODÍA, EL – *NOON*
ALGÚN DÍA – *SOMEDAY*	MES – *MONTH*
AMANECER, EL – *SUNRISE*	MES PASADO, EL – *LAST MONTH*
AÑO, EL – *YEAR*	MIENTRAS – *DURING*
ANOCHE – *LAST NIGHT*	NOCHE, LA – *EVENING, NIGHT*
ANOCHECER, EL – *DUSK*	NUNCA – *NEVER*
ANTES DE – *BEFORE*	OTRA VEZ – *AGAIN*
AYER – *YESTERDAY*	PASADO MAÑANA – *DAY AFTER*
CADA DÍA – *EACH DAY*	*TOMORROW*
CADA VEZ – *EVERY TIME*	PRIMERO – *FIRST*
DESPUES DE – *AFTER*	PRONTO – *SOON*
DESPUÉS DE – *AFTERWARDS*	PRÓXIMA VEZ, LA – *NEXT TIME*
DIARIO – *DAILY*	PRÓXIMO MES, EL – *NEXT MONTH*
DOS VECES – *TWICE*	PRÓXIMO(A), EL(LA) – *NEXT ONE*
ENTONCES – *THEN*	PUESTA DEL SOL, LA – *SUNSET*
FIN DE SEMANA, EL – *WEEKEND*	SEMANA PASADA, LA – *LAST WEEK*
HASTA – *UNTIL*	SIEMPRE – *ALWAYS*
HOY – *TODAY*	TARDE – *LATE*
HOY EN LA NOCHE – *TONIGHT*	TARDE, LA – *AFTERNOON*
LUEGO – *LATER*	TEMPRANO – *EARLY*
MAÑANA – *TOMORROW*	TIEMPO – *TIME*
MAÑANA POR LA MAÑANA –	ÚLTIMO(A), EL(LA) – *LAST*
TOMORROW MORNING	UNA VEZ – *ONCE*
MAÑANA, LA – *MORNING*	YA – *ALREADY*

medidas
measurements

CENTÍMETRO, UN – *CENTIMETER*	MILÍMETRO, UN – *MILLIMETER*
GRAMO, UN – *GRAM*	MILLA, UNA – *MILE*
KILO, UN – *KILO*	ONZA, UNA – *OUNCE*
LIBRA, UNA – *POUND*	PIE, UN – *FOOT*
LITRO, UN – *LITER*	PULGADA, UNA – *INCH*
METRO, UN – *METER*	YARDA, UNA – *YARD*

palabras cuantitativas
quantative words

ALGUNOS(AS) – *SOME*	MUCHO – *A LOT*
AMBOS – *BOTH*	MUCHOS(AS) – *MANY*
CADA UNO – *EACH*	NADA – *NOTHING*
CASI – *ALMOST*	NADIE – *NO ONE*
CUALQUIER(A) – *ANY*	NINGUNO(A) – *NONE*
CUARTO, UN – *QUARTER*	OTRO(A) – *ANOTHER*
DEMASIADO(A) – *TOO MUCH*	POCO, UN – *A LITTLE*
DOBLE, EL – *DOUBLE*	SUFICIENTE – *ENOUGH*
DOCENA, UNA – *A DOZEN*	TODO – *ALL*
JUNTOS(AS) – *TOGETHER*	VARIOS(AS) – *SEVERAL*
LO DEMÁS – *REST OF*	
MÁS – *MORE*	
MISMO(A), EL(LA) – *SAME*	
MITAD, LA – *HALF*	
MUCHAS VECES – *MANY TIMES*	

temporadas del año y días festivos
seasons & holidays

4 DE JULIO, EL – *JULY 4TH*
AÑO NUEVO, EL – *NEW YEARS DAY*
CINCO DE MAYO, EL – *MAY 5TH*
DÍA DE ACCIÓN DE GRACIAS, EL – *THANKSGIVING*
DÍA DE LA RAZA, EL – *COLUMBUS DAY*
DÍA DE LOS CAÍDOS, EL – *MEMORIAL DAY*
DÍA DE LOS MUERTOS, EL – *DAY OF THE DEAD*
DÍA DE LOS NOVIOS/SAN VALENTÍN, EL – *VALENTINES DAY*
DÍA DE LOS SANTOS REYES, EL – *JANUARY 6*
DÍA DE MARTIN LUTHER KING, EL – *MARTIN LUTHER KING DAY*
DÍA DE SAN PATRICIO, EL – *ST. PATRICK'S DAY*
DÍA DEL TRABAJO, EL – *LABOR DAY*
FELIZ AÑO NUEVO – *HAPPY NEW YEAR*
FELIZ NAVIDAD – *MERRY CHRISTMAS*
HALLOWEEN, EL – *HALLOWEEN*
HANUKAH, LA – *HANUKAH*
INVIERNO, EL – *WINTER*
KWANZAA, LA – *KWANZAA*
MIÉRCOLES DE CENIZA, EL – *ASH WEDNESDAY*
NAVIDAD, LA – *CHRISTMAS*
OTOÑO, EL – *FALL*
PASCUA, LA – *EASTER*
PASSOVER, EL – *PASSOVER*
PRIMAVERA, LA – *SPRING*
RAMADÁN, EL – *RAMADAN*
ROSH HASHANA, EL – *ROSH HASHANA*
VACACIÓN, LA – *VACATION*
VACACIONES DE PRIMAVERA, LAS – *SPRING BREAK*
VERANO, EL – *SUMMER*
VIERNES SANTO, EL – *GOOD FRIDAY*
YOM KIPPUR, EL – *YOM KIPPUR*

NATURALEZA
NATURE

jardín
garden

ÁRBOL, EL – *TREE*
ARBUSTO, EL – *BUSH*
ARENA, LA – *SAND*
BANCA, LA – *BENCH*
CACTUS, EL – *CACTUS*
CAPULLO, EL – *BUD*
DIENTE DE LEÓN, EL – *DANDELION*
FLOR, LA – *FLOWER*
GRAVA, LA – *GRAVEL*
HAMACA, LA – *HAMMOCK*
HELECHO, EL – *FERN*
HIEDRA, LA – *IVY*
HOJA, LA – *LEAF*
LODO, EL – *MUD*
MALA HEIRBA, LA – *WEED*
PALO, EL – *STICK*
PASTO, EL – *GRASS/LAWN*
PATIO, EL – *PATIO*
PIEDRA, LA – *ROCK*
PLANTA, LA – *PLANT*
POLVO, EL – *DUST*
RAÍZ, LA – *ROOT*
RAMA, LA – *BRANCH*
SEMILLA, LA – *SEED*
SOMBRA, LA – *SHADE*
SUELO, EL – *GROUND*
TIERRA, LA – *DIRT*

flores
flowers

AMAPOLA, LA – *POPPY*
GERANIO, EL – *GERANIUM*
GIRASOL, EL – *SUNFLOWER*
LAVANDA, LA – *LAVENDER*
LILA, LA – *LILAC*
MARGARITA, LA – *DAISY*
PETUNIA, LA – *PETUNIA*
ROSA, LA – *ROSE*
TULIPÁN, EL – *TULIP*
VIOLETA, LA – *VIOLET*

insectos
bugs & crawlers

ABEJA, LA – *BEE*
ARAÑA, LA – *SPIDER*
AVISPA, LA – *WASP*
AVISPÓN, EL – *HORNET*
BICHO, EL – *BUG*
CARACOL, EL – *SNAIL*
ESCARABAJO, EL – *BEETLE*
ESCARABAJO, EL – *ROLY-POLY*
ESCORPIÓN, EL – *SCORPION*
GRILLO, EL – *CRICKET*
GUSANO, EL – *WORM*

HORMIGA, LA – *ANT*
LIBÉLULA, LA – *DRAGONFLY*
MARIPOSA, LA – *BUTTERFLY*
MARIQUITA, LA – *LADYBUG*
MOSCA, LA – *FLY*
MOSQUITO, EL – *MOSQUITO*
ORUGA, LA – *CATEPILLAR*
POLILLA, LA – *MOTH*
PULGA, LA – *FLEA*
SALTAMONTES, EL – *GRASSHOPP*

mascotas
pets

BORREGO, EL – *SHEEP*
BURRO, EL – *DONKEY*
CABALLO, EL – *HORSE*
CACHORRO, EL – *PUPPY*
CANARIO, EL – *CANARY*
CANGREJO, EL – *CRAB*
CHIVO, EL – *GOAT*
COCHINO, EL – *PIG*
CONEJO, EL – *RABBIT*
CORDERO, EL – *LAMB*
GANSO, EL – *GOOSE*
GATITO, EL – *KITTEN*

GATO, EL – *CAT*
HÁMSTER, EL – *HAMSTER*
PATO, EL – *DUCK*
PERÍCO, EL – *PARAKEET*
PERÍCO, EL – *PARROT*
PERRO, EL – *DOG*
PEZ, EL – *FISH*
POLLO, EL – *CHICKEN*
RATÓN, EL – *MOUSE*
SAPO, EL – *FROG*
VACA, LA – *COW*

animales salvajes
wild animals

AGUILA, EL – *EAGLE*
ARDILLA, LA – *SQUIRREL*
BÚHO, EL – *OWL*
CAIMÁN, EL – *ALLIGATOR*
CAMELLO, EL – *CAMEL*
CANGURO, EL – *KANGAROO*
CASTOR, EL – *BEAVER*
CEBRA, EL – *ZEBRA*
CHANGO, EL – *MONKEY*
COCODRILO, EL – *CROCODILE*
COYOTE, EL – *COYOTE*
CUERVO, EL – *CROW*
DINOSAURIO, EL – *DINOSAUR*
ELEFANTE, EL – *ELEPHANT*
HALCÓN, EL – *HAWK*
HIPOPOTAMO, EL – *HIPPO*

JIRAFA, LA – *GIRAFFE*
LAGARTO, EL – *LIZARD*
LEÓN, EL – *LION*
LOBO, EL – *WOLF*
MAPACHE, EL – *RACCOON*
OSO, EL – *BEAR*
PÁJARO, EL – *BIRD*
PICAPOSTE, EL – *WOODPECKER*
RATA, LA – *RAT*
RINOCERONTE, EL – *RHINO*
SERPIENTE, EL – *SNAKE*
TIGRE, EL – *TIGER*
UNICORNIO, EL – *UNICORN*
VENADO, EL – *DEER*
ZORRO, EL – *FOX*

animales del oceáno
ocean animals

BALLENA, LA – *WHALE*
CABALLO MARINO, EL – *SEAHORSE*
DELFÍN, EL – *DOLPHIN*
ERIZO DE MAR, EL – *SAND DOLLAR*
ESTRELLA MARINA, LA – *STARFISH*
LANGOSTA, LA – *LOBSTER*

MORSA, LA – *WALRUS*
PEZ, EL – *FISH*
SIRENA, LA – *MERMAID*
TIBURÓN, EL – *SHARK*
TORTUGA, LA – *TURTLE*

el tiempo
weather

BUEN TIEMPO – NICE WEATHER
CALOR, EL – HEAT
CHARCO, EL – PUDDLE
CICLÓN, EL – TORNADO
FRÍO, EL – COLD
GRANIZO, EL – HAIL
HELADA, LA – FROST
HIELO, EL – ICE
HUMEDAD, LA – HUMIDITY
HURACÁN, EL – HURRICANE

LLOVIZNA, LA – DRIZZLE
LLUVIA, LA – RAIN
NIEBLA, LA – FOG
NIEVE, LA – SNOW
NUBES, LAS – CLOUDS
RELÁMPAGO, EL – LIGHTNING
SOL, EL – SUN
TORMENTA, LA – STORM
TRUENO, EL – THUNDER
VIENTO, EL – WIND

. . . .

VA A ESTAR __. IT'S SUPPOSED TO BE __.

. . . .

BONITO – NICE
CALUROSO – HOT
CON VIENTO – WINDY
DESPEJADO – CLEAR
FRÍO – COLD
GRANIZANDO – HAILING
HÚMEDO – HUMID

LLOVIENDO – RAINING
LLOVIZNANDO – DRIZZLING
NEVANDO – SNOWING
NUBLADO – CLOUDY
RELAMPAGEANDO – LIGHTNING
SOLEADO – SUNNY

términos geográficos
geographic terms

AGUA, EL – WATER
AIRE, EL – AIR
CIELO, EL – SKY
ESTRELLAS, LAS – STARS
FUEGO, EL – FIRE
INUNDACIÓN, LA – FLOOD

LODO, EL – MUD
LUNA, LA – MOON
MAREA, LA – TIDE
SUELO, EL – GROUND
TERREMOTO, EL – EARTHQUAKE
TIERRA, LA – DIRT, EARTH

PALABRAS REFERENTES A LA CASA
HOUSE WORDS

lugares en una casa
places in a house

ESTÁ EN __. IT IS IN THE __.
ESTO ES __. THIS IS __.

. . . .

ABAJO/PLANTA BAJA – DOWNSTAIRS
ADENTRO – INDOORS
AFUERA – OUTDOORS
ARRIBA/PLANTA ALTA – UPSTAIRS
ÁTICO, EL – ATTIC
BALCÓN, EL – BALCONY
BAÑO, EL – BATHROOM
BAR, EL – BAR
BIBLIOTECA, LA – LIBRARY
CERCA, LA – FENCE
CHIMENEA, LA – CHIMNEY/FIREPLACE
COCINA, LA – KITCHEN

COMEDOR, EL – DINING ROOM
CUARTO DE JUEGOS, EL – PLAYROOM
CUARTO DE LOS NIÑOS, EL – CHILDREN'S ROOM
CUARTO DE VISTAS, EL – GUEST ROOM
CUARTO DEL BEBÉ, EL – NURSERY
ENTRADA PARA COCHES, LA – DRIVEWAY
ESTANCIA, LA – FAMILY ROOM
GARAJE, EL – GARAGE
JARDÍN DE ENFRENTE, EL – FRONT YARD

continuará...

JARDÍN, EL – *BACKYARD*
LAVANDERÍA, LA – *LAUNDRY ROOM*
MUEBLES, LOS – *FURNITURE*
OFICINA, LA – *OFFICE*
PASILLO, EL – *HALLWAY*
PISCINA, LA – *POOL*
PORTÓN, EL – *GATE*
PUERTA PRINCIPAL, LA – *FRONT DOOR*
PUERTA TRASERA, LA – *BACK DOOR*
RECÁMARA, LA – *BEDROOM*
SALA, LA – *LIVING ROOM*
SÓTANO, EL – *BASEMENT*
TECHO, EL – *ROOF*
TERRAZA, LA – *PORCH*
VENTANA, LA – *WINDOW*

la cocina
kitchen

BABERO, EL – *BIB*
BASURA, LA – *GARBAGE*
BASURERO, EL – *GARBAGE CAN*
CAFETERA, LA – *COFFEE MAKER*
CALIENTE – *HOT*
CONGELADOR, EL – *FREEZER*
CUBIERTOS, LOS – *SILVERWARE*
CUCHARA, LA – *SPOON*
CUCHILLO, EL – *KNIFE*
GABINETE, EL – *CABINET*
HORNO, EL – *OVEN*
LAVAPLATOS, EL – *DISHWASHER*
LLAVE, LA – *FAUCET*
MESA, LA – *TABLE*
MICROONDAS, EL – *MICROWAVE*
OLLA, LA – *POT*
PAPEL DE ALUMINIO, EL – *ALUMINUM FOIL*
PAPEL DE CERA, EL – *WAX PAPER*
PAPEL DE PLÁSTICO, EL – *PLAST-WRAP*
PARILLA DE GAS, LA – *GAS RANGE*
PLÁSTICO, EL – *SPLASH MAT*
PLATO HONDO, EL – *BOWL*
REFRIGERADOR, EL – *REFRIDGERATOR*
SERVILLETA, LA – *NAPKIN*
SILLA PARA COMER DEL BEBÉ, LA – *HIGHCHAIR*
TAZA, LA – *CUP*
TENEDOR, EL – *FORK*
TOSTADOR, EL – *TOASTER*
VAJILLA, LA – *DISHES*
VASO ENTRENADOR, EL – *SIPPY CUP*
VASO, EL – *GLASS*

el baño
bathroom

BAÑERA, LA – *INFANT TUB*
BAÑO, EL – *BATHROOM*
BANQUITO, EL – *STEP STOOL*
BOTIQUÍN, EL – *MEDICINE CABINET*
CORTINA DE BAÑO, LA – *SHOWER CURTAIN*
EXCUSADO, EL – *TOILET*
LAVABO, EL – *SINK*
LLAVE, LA – *FAUCET*
PAPEL DE BAÑO, EL – *TOILET PAPER*
REGADERA, LA – *SHOWER*
TINA, LA – *BATHTUB*
TOALLA, LA – *TOWEL*
TOALLITA, LA – *WASHCLOTH*

la recámara
bedroom

ALMOHADA, LA – *PILLOWS*
ARMARIO, EL – *ARMOIRE*
BAMBINETO, EL – *BASSINET*
BUREAU, EL – *DRESSER*
CAMA, LA – *BED*
CAMBIADOR, EL – *CHANGING TABLE*
CLOSET, EL – *CLOSET*
COBIJA, LA – *BLANKET*
COLCHA, LA – *BEDSPREAD*
COLCHÓN, EL – *MATTRESS*
CUNA, LA – *CRIB*
DESPERTADOR, EL – *ALARM CLOCK*
EDREDÓN, EL – *QUILT/COMFORTER*
ESPEJO, EL – *MIRROR*
FUNDA, LA – *PILLOWCASE*
LIBRERO, EL – *BOOKSHELF*
LUCESITA, LA – *NIGHT LIGHT*
MECEDORA, LA – *ROCKING CHAIR*
MESITA DE NOCHE, LA – *NIGHTSTAND*
MONITOR, EL – *MONITOR*
PORTACUNA – *PORT-A-CRIB*
SÁBANA, LA – *SHEET*
SÁBANAS DE LA CUNA, LAS – *CRIBSHEETS*

la sala/ el cuarto de juegos
living/play room

CERRADURA, LA – *LOCK*
CORTINA, LA – *CURTAIN*
LÁMPARA, LA – *LAMP*
LLAVE, LA – *KEY*
MESA, LA – *TABLE*
PARED, LA – *WALL*
PERSIANAS, LAS – *SHUTTERS*
PISO, EL – *FLOOR*
PUERTA, LA – *DOOR*

RADIO, EL – *RADIO*
SILLA, LA – *CHAIR*
SOFÁ, EL – *SOFA*
TECHO, EL – *CEILING*
TELÉFONO, EL – *TELEPHONE*
TELEVISIÓN, LA – *TV*
VENTANA, LA – *WINDOW*
VIDEOCASETERA, LA – *VCR*

productos de limpieza
cleaning products

AMONÍACO, EL – *AMMONIA*
ASPIRADORA, LA – *VACUUM*
BASURA, LA – *TRASH*
BOLSA DE BASURA, LA – *TRASH BAG*
CEPILLO, EL – *BRUSH*
CERA PARA EL PISO, LA – *FLOOR POLISH*
CERA PARA LOS MUEBLES, LA – *FURNITURE POLISH*
CUBETA, LA – *BUCKET*
DESINFECTANTE, EL – *DISENFECTANT*
ESCALERA, LA – *LADDER*
ESCOBA, LA – *BROOM*

ESPONJA, LA – *SPONGE*
GUANTE, EL – *GLOVE*
JABÓN, EL – *SOAP*
LIMPIAVIDRIOS, EL – *WINDOW CLEANER*
LÍQUIDO, EL – *LIQUID*
PLUMERO, EL – *FEATHER DUSTER*
RECOGEDOR DE BASURA, EL – *DUSTPAN*
TOALLA, LA – *TOWEL*
TOALLAS DE PAPEL, LAS – *PAPER TOWELS*
TRAPEADOR, EL – *MOP*
TRAPO, EL – *RAG*
VINAGRE, EL – *VINEGAR*

COMIDA
FOOD

carne, aves, pescados y mariscos
meat, poultry, fish & shellfish

ALBÓNDIGA, LA – *MEATBALL*
ALMEJA, LA – *CLAM*
ATÚN, EL – *TUNA*
BISTEC, EL – *STEAK*
CANGREJO, EL – *CRAB*
CARNE DE RES, LA – *BEEF*
CERDO, EL – *PORK*
CORDERO, EL – *LAMB*
GANSO, EL – *GOOSE*
HAMBURGUESA, LA – *HAMBURGER*
JAMÓN, EL – *HAM*

LANGOSTA, LA – *LOBSTER*
PATO, EL – *DUCK*
PAVO, EL – *TURKEY*
PESCADO, EL – *FISH*
POLLO, EL – *CHICKEN*
ROSBIF, EL – *ROAST BEEF*
SALCHICHA, LA – *HOT DOG, SAUSAGE*
SALMÓN, EL – *SALMON*
TOCINO, EL – *BACON*

frutas
fruit

AGUACATE, EL – *AVOCADO*
ARÁNDANOS, LOS – *BLUEBERRIES*
CEREZAS, LAS – *CHERRIES*
CHABACANO, EL – *APRICOT*
CIRUELA PASA, LA – *PRUNE*
CIRUELA, LA – *PLUM*
COCO, EL – *COCONUT*

DÁTILES, LOS – *DATES*
DURAZNO, EL – *PEACH*
FRAMBUESAS, LAS – *RASPBERRIES*
FRESAS, LAS – *STRAWBERRIES*
GRANADA, LA – *POMEGRANATE*
GUAYAVA, LA – *GUAVA*
HIGOS, LOS – *FIGS*

continuará...

KIWI, EL – *KIWI*
LIMA, EL – *LEMON*
LIMÓN, EL – *LIME*
MANDARINA, LA – *MANDARIN*
MANGO, EL – *MANGO*
MANZANA, LA – *APPLE*
MELÓN, EL – *CANTALOUPE*
MELÓN, EL – *MELON*
NARANJA, LA – *ORANGE*
NECATARÍN, EL – *NECTARINE*

PAPAYA, LA – *PAPAYA*
PASAS, LAS – *RAISINS*
PERA, LA – *PEAR*
PIÑA, LA – *PINEAPPLE*
PLÁTANO, EL – *BANANA*
SANDIA, LA – *WATERMELON*
TORONJA, LA – *GRAPEFRUIT*
UVAS, LAS – *GRAPES*
ZARZAMORAS, LAS –
BLACKBERRIES

verduras
vegetables

ACELGA, LA – *CHARD*
ÁJO, EL – *GARLIC*
ALCACHOFA, LA – *ARTICHOKE*
ÁPIO, EL – *CELERY*
BERENJENA, LA – *EGGPLANT*
BERRO, EL – *WATERCRESS*
BETABEL, EL – *BEETS*
BOK CHOY, EL – *BOK CHOY*
BRÓCOLI, EL – *BROCCOLI*
CALABAZA VERDE, LA – *ZUCCHINI*
CALABAZA, LA – *SQUASH*
CAMOTE, EL – *SWEET POTATO/YAM*
CEBOLLA, LA – *ONION*
CEBOLLITAS, LAS – *GREEN ONIONS*
CHICHARROS, LOS – *PEAS*
CHILE MORRÓN, EL – *BELL PEPPER*
CHÍLE, EL – *CHILI PEPPER*
COL, LA – *CABBAGE*
COLES DE BRUSELAS, LAS –
BRUSSEL SPROUTS
COLIFLOR, LA – *CAULIFLOWER*
EJOTES, LOS – *GREEN BEANS*

ELOTE, EL – *CORN*
ESPÁRRAGOS, LOS – *ASPARAGUS*
ESPINACA, LA – *SPINACH*
FRIJOLES, LOS – *BEANS*
HINOJO, EL – *FENNEL*
HONGOS, LOS – *MUSHROOMS*
JICAMA, LA – *JICIMA*
JITOMATE, EL – *TOMATO*
LECHUGA, LA – *LETTUCE*
PAPAS AL HORNO, LAS – *BAKED*
PAPAS COCIDAS, LAS – *BOILED*
PAPAS FRITAS, LAS – *FRIED*
PAPAS, LAS – *POTATOES*
PEPINO, EL – *CUCUMBERS*
PIMIENTO ROJO, EL – *RED PEPPE*
PIMIENTO VERDE, EL – *GREEN*
PEPPER
PUERRO, EL – *LEEK*
PURÉ DE PAPA, EL – *MASHED*
RÁBANO, EL – *RADISHES*
TOMATILLO, EL – *GREEN TOMATO*
ZANAHORIA, LA – *CARROT*

productos lácteos
dairy

BLANCO DEL HUEVO, EL – *WHITE*
CREMA ÁCIDA, LA – *SOUR CREAM*
CREMA, LA – *CREAM*
DESCREMADA – *NONFAT*
ENTERA – *WHOLE*
HELADO/LA NIEVE, EL – *ICE CREAM*
HUEVO DURO, EL – *HARD BOILED*
EGG
HUEVO FRITO, EL – *FRIED EGG*
HUEVO REVUELTO, EL –
SCRAMBLED EGG
HUEVO, EL – *EGG*
LECHE DE SOYA, LA – *SOY MILK*
LECHE, LA – *MILK*
MANTEQUILLA, LA – *BUTTER*
MARGINA, LA – *MARGARINE*
QUESO AMARILLO, EL – *CHEDDAR*

QUESO BLANCO, EL – *JACK*
QUESO COTÁJ, EL – *COTTAGE*
CHEESE
QUESO CREMA, EL – *CREAM*
CHEESE
QUESO DE CABRA, EL – *GOAT*
QUESO PARMESANO, EL –
PARMESAN
QUESO ROQUEFORT, EL – *BLUE*
CHEESE
QUESO TIPO BRIE, EL – *BRIE*
CHEESE
QUESO TIPO FETA, EL – *FETA*
QUESO, EL – *CHEESE*
SEMI-DESCREMADA – *LOWFAT*
YEMA, LA – *YOLK*
YOGHOURT, EL – *YOGURT*

panes, cereales y granos
breads and grains

ARROZ FRITO, EL – *FRIED RICE*
ARROZ INTEGRAL, EL – *BROWN*
RICE

ARROZ SALVAJE, EL – *WILD RICE*
ARROZ, EL – *RICE*
AVENA, LA – *OATMEAL*

CEREAL, EL – *CEREAL*
FIDEOS/LA PASTA, LOS – *PASTA*
GALLETA SALADA, LA – *CRACKER*
HOTCAKES, LOS – *PANCAKES*
PAN BLANCO, EL – *WHITE BREAD*
PAN DE CENTENO, EL – *RYE BREAD*

PAN DE MAÍZ, EL – *CORN BREAD*
PAN FRANCES, EL – *FRENCH TOAST*
PAN INTEGRAL, EL – *WHOLE WHEAT*
PAN TOSTADO, EL – *TOAST*
PAN, EL – *BREAD*
WAFLES, LOS – *WAFFLES*

condimentos
condiments

ACIETE DE OLÍVA, EL – *OLIVE OIL*
CATSUP, LA – *KETCHUP*
CHILE, EL – *HOT PEPPER*
JARÁBE, EL – *SYRUP*
MAYONESA, LA – *MAYONNAISE*
MOSTAZA, LA – *MUSTARD*
PEPINO, EL – *PICKLE*

SALSA DE BARBACÓA, LA –
BARBEQUE SAUCE
SALSA DE SOYA, LA – *SOY SAUCE*
SALSA, LA – *SAUCE*
VINAGRE BALSÁMICO, EL –
BALSAMIC VINEGAR
VINAGRE, EL – *VINEGAR*

preparaciones
preparations

COCINA – *COOK*
COCINA AL VAPOR – *STEAM*
COCINA EN EL ASADOR – *BBQ*
CONGELA – *FREEZE*
CORTA – *CUT*
DESCONGELA – *DEFROST*
FRÍE – *FRY*
HIERVE – *BOIL*
HORNÉA – *BAKE*
LICÚA – *BLEND*
MUELE – *GROUND*
ORGÁNICO – *ORGANIC*

PELA – *PEEL*
PREPARA TIPO KOSHER – *KOSHER*
RALLA – *GRATED*
REBANA – *SLICE*
ROSTIZA/ASA – *ROAST*
SECA – *DRY*
SIN AZÚCAR – *SUGAR-FREE*
SIN CONDIMENTO – *WITHOUT
SEASONING*
SIN GRASA – *FAT-FREE*
SIN SAL – *SALT-FREE*
VEGETARIANO – *VEGETARIAN*

sabores
taste

AMARGO - *BITTER*
COCIDO - *COOKED*
DELICIOSO - *DELICIOUS*
SECO - *DRY*
FRESCO - *FRESH*
HÚMEDO - *MOIST*
CRUDO - *RAW*

MADURO - *RIPE*
SALADO - *SALTY*
AGRIO - *SOUR*
PICANTE - *SPICY*
DULCE - *SWEET*
SABROSO - *TASTY*

ingredientes para hornear
baking ingredients

ACEITE, EL – *OIL*
AZÚCAR, EL – *SUGAR*
BICARBONATO, EL – *BAKING SODA*
CHOCOLATE, EL – *CHOCOLATE*
COCÓA, EL – *COCOA*
HARINA, LA – *FLOUR*
MAIZENA, LA – *CORNSTARCH*

MIEL, LA – *HONEY*
NUECES, LAS – *NUTS*
POLVO DE HORNEAR, EL – *BAKING
POWDER*
SAL, LA – *SALT*
VAINILLA, LA – *VANILLA*

bebidas
beverages

AGUA MINERAL, EL – *MINERAL
WATER*
AGUA, EL – *WATER*
CAFÉ, EL – *COFFEE*

CHOCOLATE CALIENTE, EL – *HOT
CHOCOLATE*
CHOCOLATE FRÍO,
EL – *CHOCOLATE*

continuará...

JUGO DE MANZANA, EL – APPLE JUICE
JUGO DE NARANJA, EL – ORANGE JUICE
JUGO DE UVA, EL – GRAPE JUICE
JUGO, EL – JUICE
LECHE CALIENTE, LA – HOT
LECHE FRÍA, LA – COLD
LECHE, LA – MILK

REFRESCO, EL – SODA
TÉ DE MANZANILLA, EL – CHAMOMILE
TÉ DE MENTA, EL – MINT
TÉ NEGRO, EL – BLACK
TÉ, EL – TEA

hierbas & especies
herbs & spices

ALBAHACA, LA – BASIL
ALCAPARRAS, LAS – CAPERS
CANELA, LA – CINNAMON
CEBOLLÍN, EL – CHIVE
CLAVO, EL – CLOVE
ENELDO, EL – DILL
MENTA, LA – MINT
NUEZ MOSCADO, LA – NUTMEG

ORÉGANO, EL – OREGANO
PEREJIL, EL – PARSELY
PIMIENTA, LA – PEPPER
ROMERO, EL – ROSEMARY
SAL, LA – SALT
SALVIA, LA – SAGE
TOMILLO, EL – THYME

biberones
bottles

AGUA HERVIDA, EL – BOILING WATER
BIBERÓN, EL – BOTTLE
CALIENTE – HOT
CALIENTITO(A) – WARM
CHUPÓN, EL – NIPPLE
FORMULA, LA – FORMULA
FRÍO(A) – COLD

GAS, EL – GAS (BURPS ETC.)
LECHE DE PECHO, LA – BREASTMILK
LECHE, LA – MILK
REFLUJO, EL – REFLUX
SEPILLO PARA BOTELLAS, EL – BOTTLE BRUSH

nueces y semillas
nuts & seeds

AJONJOLÍ, EL – SESAME SEED
ALMENDRA, LA – ALMOND
CACAHUATE, EL – PEANUT
COCO, EL – COCONUT
CREMA DE CACAHUATE, LA – PEANUT BUTTER
MACADAMIA, LA – MACADAMIA
NUEZ DE CASTILLA, LA – WALNUT

NUEZ DE LA INDIA, LA – CASHEW
NUEZ, LA – PECAN
PIÑONES, LOS – PINE NUTS
PISTACHOS, LOS – PISTACHIO
SEMILLA DE GIRASOL, LA – SUNFLOWER SEED
TOFU, EL – TOFU

frijoles
legumes

FRIJOLES BAYOS, LOS – PINTO BEANS
FRIJOLES DE MEDIA LUNA, LOS – LIMA BEANS
FRIJOLES NEGROS, LOS – BLACK BEANS
FRIJOLES REFRITOS, LOS –

REFRIED
FRIJOLES ROJAS, LOS – KIDNEY BEANS
GARBANZOS, LOS – CHICK PEAS
HAICHULAS BLANCAS, LAS – WH BEANS
LENTEJAS, LAS – LENTILS

postres y dulces
sweets & treats

BARQUILLO, EN – ON A CONE
BUDÍN, EL – PUDDING
CHICLE, EL – GUM

CHOCOLATE, EL – CHOCOLATE
DULCES, LOS – CANDY
GALLETA, LA – COOKIE

HELADO, EL – *ICE CREAM*
PASTEL BLANCO, EL – *WHITE CAKE*
PASTEL DE CHOCOLATE, EL – *CHOCOLATE CAKE*
PASTEL DE ZANAHORIA, EL –

CARROT CAKE
PASTEL, EL – *CAKE*
TARTA, LA – *PIE*
VASO, EN – *IN A CUP*

precauciones alimenticias
food safety

AHOGARSE – *CHOKE (TO)*
ALERGIA, LA – *ALLERGY*
ALIMENTOS PERECEDEROS, LOS – *PERISHABLES*
COMIDA, LA – *FOOD*
CONGELAR – *FREEZE (TO)*
ESTERILIZAR – *STERILIZE (TO)*
FECHA DEL VENCIMIENTO, LA –

EXPIRATION DATE
HERVIR – *BOIL (TO)*
LUGARES CALIENTES, LOS – *HOT SPOTS*
MICROBIOS, LOS – *GERMS*
MOHO, EL – *MOLD*
PODRIDO(A) – *ROTTEN*

ACTIVIDADES
ACTIVITIES

afuera de la casa
out of the house

ANDAR EN BICICLETA – *RIDE A BIKE (TO)*
ANDAR EN PATINETA – *RIDE A SCOOTER (TO)*
ANDAR EN PATINETA – *RIDE A SKATEBOARD (TO)*
ARENERO, EL – *SANDBOX*
BAÑO, EL – *BATHROOM*
CARRIOLA, LA – *STROLLER*
CLASE DE ARTE, LA – *ART CLASS*
CLASE DE BAILE, LA – *DANCE CLASS*
CLASE DE MÚSICA, LA – *MUSIC CLASS*
COLUMPIO, EL – *SWING*
DESFILE, EL – *PARADE*
ESCALAR UN ÁRBOL – *CLIMB A*

TREE (TO)
HORA DE LA LECTURA EN LA BIBLIOTECA, LA – *STORY TIME AT THE LIBRARY*
LUNCHERA, LA – *LUNCHBOX*
MOCHILA, LA – *BACKPACK*
MONTAR A CABALLO – *RIDE A HORSE (TO)*
MUSEO DEL NIÑO, EL – *CHILDRENS MUSEUM*
PARQUE, EL – *PARK*
PASTO, EL – *GRASS*
POPÓ DE GATO, LA – *CAT POOP*
POPÓ DE PERRO, LA – *DOG POOP*
REFRIGERIO, EL – *SNACK*
RESBALADIA, LA – *SLIDE*
ZOOLÓGICO, EL – *ZOO*

pasatiempos
hobbies

A ÉL/ELLA LE GUSTA __. *HE/SHE LIKES __.*
ÉL/ELLA ESTÁ APRENDIENDO __. *HE/SHE IS LEARNING __.*

. . . .

ARTE, EL – *ART*
BAILE, EL – *DANCING*
BALLET, EL – *BALLET*
CAMINATA, LA – *HIKING*
CORRER – *JOGGING*
DIBUJO, EL – *DRAWING*
FOTOGRAFÍA, LA – *PHOTOGRAPHY*

LECTURA, LA – *READING*
MÚSICA, LA – *MUSIC*
PASEAR EN BARCO – *BOATING*
PELÍCULAS, LAS – *MOVIES*
PESCA, LA – *FISHING*
PINTURA, LA – *PAINTING*

juguetes & juegos
toys & games

LE GUSTA JUGAR CON __. *HE/SHE LIKES TO PLAY WITH __.*
ÉL/ELLA NECESITA COMPARTIR __. *HE/SHE NEEDS TO SHARE __.*
__ ESTÁ ROTO(A). *__ IS BROKEN.*

· ·

AJEDREZ, EL – *CHESS*
ANIMALES, LOS – *ANIMALS*
AVIÓN, EL – *AIRPLANE*
BALONCESTO, EL – *BASKETBALL*
BARCO, EL – *BOAT*
BÉISBOL, EL – *BASEBALL*
BICICLETA, LA – *BICYCLE*
CAMION DE LOS BOMBEROS, EL – *FIRE TRUCK*
CAMION DE VOLTEO, EL – *DUMP TRUCK*
CAMIÓN, EL – *TRUCK*
CAMION, EL – *TRUCKS*
CANCIÓN, LA – *SONG*
CANICAS, LAS – *MARBLES*
CARICATURAS, LAS – *CARTOONS*
CRAYOLAS, LAS – *CRAYONS*
CUBOS DE MADERA, LOS – *BLOCKS*
CUENTO, EL – *STORY*
CUERDA PARA BRINCAR, LA – *JUMP ROPE*
DISFRAZ, EL – *COSTUME*
ESTÉREO, EL – *STEREO*
FÚTBOL, EL – *FOOTBALL*
GLOBO, EL – *BALLOON*
HISES, LOS – *CHALK*
JUEGO DE DAMAS, EL – *CHECKERS*

JUEGO DE TÉ, EL – *TEA SET*
JUGAR A LA CASITA – *PLAYING HOUSE*
LAPICES DE COLORES, LOS – *COLORED PENCILS*
LIBRO PARA COLOREAR, EL – *COLORING BOOK*
LIBRO, EL – *BOOK*
MONOPOLIO, EL – *MONOPOLY*
MUÑECA, LA – *DOLL*
OSITO DE PELUCHE, EL – *TEDDY BEAR*
PAPALOTE, EL – *KITE*
PATÍNES, LOS – *SKATES*
PATINETA, LA – *SKATEBOARD*
PELOTA, LA – *BALL*
PELUCHE, EL – *STUFFED ANIMAL*
RADIO, LA – *RADIO*
ROMPECABEZAS, EL – *PUZZLE*
RUIDO, EL – *NOISE*
TELEVISIÓN, LA – *TELEVISION*
TITERE, EL – *PUPPET*
TRACTOR, EL – *TRACTOR*
TREN, EL – *TRAIN*
TRICICLO, EL – *TRICYCLE*
VAGÓN, EL – *WAGON*
VIDEOS, LOS – *VIDEOS*

· ·

A ÉL//ELLA LE GUSTA __. *HE/SHE LIKES TO __.*

· ·

APLAUDIR – *CLAP HANDS*
CARRERAS, LAS – *RACE*
CORONA, LA – *CROWN*
DISFRAZARSE – *DRESS UP*
ESCONDIDAS, LAS – *HIDE-AND-GO-SEEK*
FINJIR – *PRETEND*
HACER GALLETAS – *MAKING*

COOKIES
HADA/HADO, EL – *FAIRY*
JUGAR A LAS TRAES – *PLAY CHA...*
MAGIA, LA – *MAGIC*
MONSTRUO, EL – *MONSTER*
REINA, LA – *QUEEN*
REY, EL – *KING*

destinos al aire libre
outdoor destinations

ARROYO, EL – *STREAM*
BOSQUE, EL – *FOREST*
CAMPO, EL – *FIELD*
CERRO, EL – *HILL*
COSTA, LA – *COAST*
CUEVA, LA – *CAVE*
DESIERTO, EL – *DESERT*
LAGO, EL – *LAKE*
LAGUNA, LA – *POND*

MAR, EL – *OCEAN*
MONTAÑA, LA – *MOUNTAIN*
PANTANO, EL – *SWAMP*
PISCINA, LA – *POOL*
PLAYA, LA – *BEACH*
RANCHO, EL – *RANCH*
RÍO, EL – *RIVER*
SELVA, LA – *JUNGLE*
VALLE, EL – *VALLEY*

instrumentos musicales
musical instruments

A ÉL/ELLA LE GUSTA __. *HE/SHE LIKES __.*
ÉL/ELLA ESTÁ APRENDIENDO __. *HE/SHE IS LEARNING __.*
. . . .

CLARINETE, EL – *CLARINET*
GUITARRA, LA – *GUITAR*
ÓRGANO, EL – *ORGAN*
PIANO, EL – *PIANO*
SAXÓFONO, EL – *SAXOPHONE*

TAMBOR, EL – *DRUM*
TROMBÓN, EL – *TROMBONE*
TROMPETA, LA – *TRUMPET*
VIOLÍN, EL – *VIOLIN*

destinos urbanos
urban destinations

VAMOS A __. *WE ARE GOING TO __.*
VIVO CERCA DE __. *I LIVE NEAR THE __.*
. . . .

AEROPUERTO, EL – *AIRPORT*
BANCO, EL – *BANK*
BANQUETA, LA – *SIDEWALK*
BIBLIOTECA, LA – *LIBRARY*
CALLE, LA – *STREET*
CAMINO, EL – *PATH*
CAMPO DE RECREO, EL – *PLAYGROUND*
CENTRO, EL – *DOWNTOWN*
CINE, EL – *MOVIES*
CORREO, EL – *POST OFFICE*
ESCUELA, LA – *SCHOOL*

GASOLINERA, LA – *GAS STATION*
GIMNASIO, EL – *GYMNASIUM*
HOSPITAL, EL – *HOSPITAL*
IGLESIA, LA – *CHURCH*
MUSEO, EL – *MUSEUM*
OFICINA, LA – *OFFICE*
PARQUE, EL – *PARK*
PUEBLO, EL – *TOWN*
PUENTE, EL – *BRIDGE*
RESTAURANTE, EL – *RESTAURANT*
SUPERMERCADO, EL – *MARKET*
TIENDA, LA – *STORE*

la playa & la natación
beach & swimming

ALETAS, LAS – *FLIPPERS*
ARENA, LA – *SAND*
BARCO, EL – *BOAT*
BIKINI, EL – *BIKINI*
CHALECO SALVAVIDAS, EL – *LIFE JACKET*
CHANCLAS, LAS – *FLIP FLOPS*
CORRIENTE, LA – *CURRENT*
CUBETA, LA – *SAND PAIL*
DUNA, LA – *DUNE*
FLOTADORES, LOS – *WATER WINGS*
GAFAS DE BUCEO, LAS – *MASK*
GOGLES, LOS – *GOGGLES*
INSOLACIÓN, LA – *SUNSTROKE*

LENTES OSCUROS, LOS – *DARK GLASSES*
LLANTITA, LA – *SWIMMING RING*
MAR, EL – *SEA*
MAREA ALTA, LA – *HIGH TIDE*
MAREA BAJA, LA – *LOW TIDE*
OLAS, LAS – *WAVES*
PALA, LA – *SHOVEL*
PROTECTOR SOLAR, EL – *SUNSCEEN*
QUEMADURA, LA – *SUNBURN*
SNÓRQUEL, EL – *SNORKEL*
TOALLA, LA – *TOWEL*
TRAJE DE BAÑO, EL – *SWIMSUIT*

jugando en la nieve
snow play

BOLA DE NIEVE, LA – *SNOWBALL*
BUFANDA, LA – *SCARF*
CARÁMBANOS, LOS – *ICICLES*
CHAMARRA, LA – *JACKET*
ESKIS, LOS – *SKIS*
GUANTES, LOS – *GLOVES/MITTENS*
HIELO, EL – *ICE*
MOTONIEVE, EL – *SNOWMOBILE*

MUÑECO DE NIEVE, EL – *SNOWMAN*
NIEVE, LA – *SNOW*
ROPA INTERIOR – *LONG UNDERWEAR*
SNOWBOARD, LA – *SNOWBOARD*
SOMBRERO, EL/CACHUCHA, LA – *HAT*
TRINEO, EL – *SLED*

deportes
sports

A ÉL/ELLA LE GUSTA JUGAR __. *HE/SHE LIKES TO PLAY __.*

BASQUETBOL, EL – *BASKETBALL*
BÉISBOL, EL – *BASEBALL*
BOLICHE, EL – *BOWLING*
BOXEO, EL – *BOXING*
CARRERA, LA – *RUNNING*
FÚTBOL AMERICANO, EL –

FOOTBALL
FÚTBOL, EL – *SOCCER*
GOLF, EL – *GOLF*
TENIS, EL – *TENNIS*
VELEADA, LA – *SAILING*
VÓLIBOL, EL – *VOLLEYBALL*

LA ROPA
CLOTHES

vestiéndose
dressing

ESTO ES SU __ FAVORITO(A). THIS IS HIS/HER FAVORITE__.
POR FAVOR LAVA __. PLEASE WASH THE __.
ESTÁ SUCIO(A). THE __ IS DIRTY __.

EL TRAJE DE BAÑO - *SWIMSUIT*
LA BLUSA - *BLOUSE*
LAS BOTAS - *BOOTS*
EL VESTIDO - *DRESS*
LA CHAMARRA - *JACKET*
EL ABRIGO - *OVERCOAT*
LA PIJAMA - *PAJAMA*
LOS PANTALONES - *PANTS*
EL IMPERMEABLE - *RAINCOAT*
LA CAMISA - *SHIRT*
LOS ZAPATOS - *SHOES*
LOS SHORTS - *SHORTS*

LA FALDA - *SKIRT*
LAS PANTUFLAS - *SLIPPERS*
LOS CALCETINES - *SOCKS*
EL SACO - *SPORTSCOAT*
LAS MEDIAS - *STOCKINGS*
EL TRAJE - *SUIT*
EL SUÉTER - *SWEATER*
LA SUDADERA - *SWEATSHIRT*
LOS TENIS - *TENNIS SHOES*
LA CAMISETA - *T-SHIRT*
LOS CALZONES - *UNDERWEA*

telas
fabrics

ALGODÓN, EL – *COTTON*
CUERO, EL – *LEATHER*
ENCAJE, EL – *LACE*
LANA, LA – *WOOL*
LINO, EL – *LINEN*
LONA, LA – *CANVAS*

MEZCLILLA, LA – *DENIM*
PANA, LA – *CORDUROY*
PIEL, LA – *FUR*
SEDA, EL – *SILK*
TEJIDO, EL – *KNIT*
TERCIOPELO, EL – *VELVET*

pañales
diapers

BOTE DE PAÑALES, EL – *DIAPER PAIL*
CALZÓN DE HULE, EL – *DIAPER COVERS*
CALZONES ENTRENADORES, LOS – *TRAINING PANTS*
CAMBIADOR, EL – *CHANGING TABLE*
PAÑAL DE TELA, EL – *CLOTH DIAPER*

PAÑAL, EL – *DIAPER*
PAÑALERA, LA – *DIAPER BAG*
POMADA PARA ROSADURAS, LA – *DIAPER RASH CREAM*
REPARTIDOR, EL – *DELIVERY PERSON*
SEGUROS, LOS – *PINS*
TALCO, EL – *TALCUM POWDER*
TOALLITAS HUMEDAS, LAS – *WIP*
VELCRO, EL – *VELCRO*

accesorios
accesories

ANILLO, EL – *RING*
ARETES, LOS – *EARRINGS*
BOLSA, LA – *PURSE*
BOLSILLO, EL – *POCKET*
BOTÓN, EL – *BUTTON*
BUFANDA, LA – *SCARF*
CARTERA, LA – *WALLET*
CIERRE, EL – *ZIPPER*
CINTURÓN, EL – *BELT*

COLLAR, EL – *NECKLACE*
CORBATA, LA – *TIE*
DIAMANTES, LOS – *DIAMONDS*
GORRA, LA – *CAP*
GUANTES, LOS – *GLOVES*
ORO, EL – *GOLD*
PERLAS, LAS – *PEARLS*
PULSERA, LA – *BRACELET*
SOMBRERO, EL – *HAT*

colores
colors

AMARILLO – *YELLOW*
ANARANJADO – *ORANGE*
AZUL – *BLUE*
BLANCO – *WHITE*
CLARO – *LIGHT*
DE CUADROS – *CHECKERED*
DE PUNTITOS – *POLKA-DOTTED*

GRIS – *GRAY*
MORADO – *PURPLE*
NEGRO – *BLACK*
OSCURO – *DARK*
ROJO – *RED*
ROSA – *PINK*
VERDE – *GREEN*

tamaños
sizes

CHICO – *SMALL*
DEMASIADO CHICO – *TOO SMALL*
DEMASIADO GRANDE – *TOO BIG*

EXTRA GRANDE – *EXTRA LARGE*
GRANDE – *LARGE*
MEDIANO – *MEDIUM*

arreglo personal
grooming

ACONDICIONADOR, EL – *CONDITIONER*
BAÑO DE BURBUJAS, EL – *BUBBLE BATH*
BROCHE, EL – *BARRET*
CEPILLO, EL – *BRUSH*
CHAMPÚ, EL – *SHAMPOO*
CINTA, LA – *HEADBAND*
CREMA, LA – *LOTION*
ESMALTE DE UÑAS, EL – *NAIL POLISH*
ESPEJO, EL – *MIRROR*

ESPONJA, LA – *SPONGE*
JABÓN, EL – *SOAP*
LISTÓN, EL – *RIBBON*
MAQUILLAJE, EL – *MAKEUP*
PASTA DE DIENTES, LA – *TOOTHPASTE*
PEINE, EL – *COMB*
PERFUME, EL – *PERFUME*
PINTALABIOS, EL – *LIPSTICK*
PINZAS, LAS – *TWEEZERS*
SECADORA PARA EL PELO, LA – *HAIRDRYER*

lavado de ropa
laundry

AGUA CALIENTE – *HOT WATER*
AGUA FRÍO – *COLD WATER*
ALMIDÓN, EL – *STARCH*
APAGADO – *OFF*
BLANQUEADOR, EL/CLORO, EL – *BLEACH/CLOROX*
CICLO PARA ROPA DELICADA, EL – *DELICATE CYCLE*
COLGAR – *HANG*
DETERGENTE, EL – *DETERGENT*
DOBLAR – *FOLD*
EMPEZAR – *START*

ENJUAGAR – *RINSE*
GANCHOS, LOS – *HANGERS*
GIRAR – *SPIN*
LAVADORA, LA – *WASHER*
LAVANDERÍA, LA – *LAUNDROMAT*
LAVAR A MANO – *HAND WASH*
MANCHA, LA – *STAIN*
PARAR – *STOP*
PLANCHA, LA – *IRON*
PRENDIDO – *ON*
PRODUCTOS DE LIMPIEZA –

continuará...

CLEANING PRODUCTS
QUITAMANCHAS, EL – *STAIN REMOVER*
REMOJAR – *SOAK*
ROPA BLANCA, LA – *WHITES*

ROPA DE COLOR, LA – *COLORS*
ROPA SUCIA, LA – *DIRTY LAUNDRY*
SECADORA, LA – *DRYER*
SECAR AL AIRE – *LINE DRY*

SALUD Y SEGURIDAD
HEALTH & SAFETY

heridas
injuries

ACCIDENTE, EL – *ACCIDENT*
AHOGANDO – *CHOKING*
AHOGANDO – *DROWNING*
AMPOLLA, LA – *BLISTER*
CONGELAMIENTO, EL – *FROSTBITE*
CONVULSIÓN, LA – *CONVULSION*
DESHIDRATACIÓN, LA – *DEHYDRATION*
FRACTURA, LA – *FRACTURE*
HEMORRAGIA NASAL, LA – *NOSEBLEED*
HERIDA, LA – *WOUND*
INFLAMACIÓN, LA – *SWELLING*
INSOLACIÓN, LA – *HEATSTROKE*
MORDEDURA DE GATO, LA – *CAT BITE*

MORDEDURA DE PERRO, LA – *DOG BITE*
MORDEDURA DE VIVORA, LA – *SNAKE BITE*
MORDEDURA, LA – *ANIMAL BITE*
MORETÓN, EL – *BRUISE*
PIQUETE, EL – *INSECT BITE*
PIQUETE, EL/MORDEDURA, LA – *BITE*
QUEMADO(A) – *BURNED*
QUEMADURA, LA – *BURN*
ROTO(A) – *BROKEN*
SANGRANDO – *BLEEDING*

síntomas y condiciones médicas
symptoms and medical conditions

ÉL/ELLA TIENE __. *HE/SHE HAS __.*

ACIDEZ, EL – *HEARTBURN*
ALERGIA, LA – *ALLERGY*
ALERGIA, LA – *HAY FEVER*
AMIGDALITIS, EL – *TONSILLITIS*
ATAQUE DEL CORAZÓN, EL – *HEART ATTACK*
ATAQUE, EL – *SEIZURE*
BRONQUITIS, EL – *BRONCHITIS*
CANCER, EL – *CANCER*
DIABETES, EL – *DIABETES*
DIARREA, LA – *DIARREA*
DOLOR DE CABEZA, EL – *HEADACHE*
DOLOR DE ESPALDA, EL – *BACKACHE*
DOLOR DE ESTÓMAGO, EL – *STOMACH ACHE*
DOLOR DE GARGANTA, EL – *SORE THROAT*
ENVENENAMIENTO, EL – *POISONING*
ESCALOFRIOS, LOS – *CHILLS*
ESTRENIMIENTO, EL – *CONSTIPATION*
FIEBRE, EL/CALENTURA, LA – *FEVER*

FURÚNCULO, EL – *BOIL*
GAS, EL – *GAS*
GRIPE, EL – *COLD*
ICTERICIA, LA – *JAUNDICE*
INFECCIÓN, LA – *INFECTION*
INFLAMACIÓN, LA – *SWELLING*
INFLUENZA, LA – *FLU*
KRUP, EL – *CROUP*
MIGRAÑA, LA – *MIGRAINE*
NAUSEA, LA – *NAUSEA*
PAPERAS, LAS – *MUMPS*
PROBLEMAS CARDIACOS, LOS – *HEART PROBLEMS*
QUEMADURA DEL SOL, LA – *SUNBURN*
REFLUJO, EL – *REFLUX*
ROSADURA, LA – *DIAPER RASH*
SALMONELA, LA – *SALMONELLA*
SALPULLIDO, EL – *RASH*
SARAPIÓN, EL – *MEASLES*
TOS, LA – *COUGH*
ULCERA, LA – *ULCER*
VARICELA, LA – *CHICKEN POX*
VIRUELA, LA – *SMALLPOX*
VÓMITO, EL – *VOMIT*

dosis de medicinas
giving medication

ANTES DEL DESAYUNO – *BEFORE BREAKFAST*
CADA CUATRO HORAS – *EVERY FOUR HOURS*
CON COMIDA – *WITH FOOD*
DOS VECES POR DÍA – *TWICE A DAY*

EN LA NOCHE – *AT NIGHT*
ENTRE COMIDAS – *BETWEEN MEALS*
MEDIA CUCHARADITA – *HALF-TEASPOON*
UNA CUCHARADITA – *TEASPOON*

medicinas
medicine cabinet

ANTIHISTAMINA, LA – *ANTIHISTAMINE*
ASPIRINA, LA – *ASPRIN*
CURITA, LA – *BAND AID*
DISENFECTANTE, EL – *DISINFECTANT*
GOTAS PARA LOS OJOS, LAS – *EYE DROPS*
INSULINA, LA – *INSULIN*
JARABE PARA LA TOS, EL – *COUGH SYRUP*
LAXANTE, EL – *LAXATIVE*
MULETAS, LAS – *CRUTCHES*

PASTILLAS PARA LA GARGANTA, LAS – *COUGH DROPS*
POMADA PARA LAS QUEMADURAS, LA – *OINTMENT FOR BURNS*
POMADA, LA – *OINTMENT*
REPELENTE, EL – *INSECT REPELLENT*
SILLA DE RUEDAS, LA – *WHEELCHAIR*
TERMÓMETRO, EL – *THERMOMETER*
VASELINA, LA – *VASELINE*
YESO, EL – *CAST*

partes del cuerpo
parts of the body

BOCA, LA – *MOUTH*
BRAZO, EL – *ARM*
CABEZA, LA – *HEAD*
CADERA, LA – *HIP*
CARA, LA – *FACE*
CEJA, LA – *EYEBROW*
CODO, EL – *ELBOW*
CORAZÓN, EL – *HEART*
COSTILLA, LA – *RIB*
CUELLO, EL – *NECK*
DEDO DEL PIE, EL – *TOE*
DEDO, EL – *FINGER*
DIENTE, EL – *TOOTH*
ESPALDA, LA – *BACK*
ESTÓMAGO, EL – *STOMACH*
HOMBRO, EL – *SHOULDER*
HUESO, EL – *BONE*
LA PIERNA, LA – *LEG*
LABIO, EL – *LIP*

LENGUA, LA – *TONGUE*
MANDÍBULA, LA – *JAW*
MUÑECA, LA – *WRIST*
MUSLOS, LOS – *THIGHS*
NARÍZ, LA – *NOSE*
OJO, EL – *EYE*
OREJA, LA – *EAR*
PANTORRILLA, LA – *CALF*
PÁRPADO, EL – *EYELID*
PECHO, EL – *CHEST*
PENE, EL – *PENIS*
PIE, EL – *FOOT*
PIEL, LA – *SKIN*
POMPA, LA – *BUTTOCK*
RODILLA, LA – *KNEE*
SANGRE, LA – *BLOOD*
TALÓN, EL – *HEEL*
TOBILLO, EL – *ANKLE*
VAGINA, LA – *VAGINA*

artículos de emergencias
emergency items

ALARMA, LA – *ALARM*
CAJA DE FUSIBLES, LA – *FUSE BOX*
CAJA DE PRIMEROS AUXILLOS, LA – *FIRST AID KIT*
EXTINGUIDOR, EL – *FIRE EXTINGUISHER*
MEDIDOR DE GAS, EL – *GAS METER*
VÁLVULA DE AGUA, LA – *WATER VALVE*

contactos en caso de emergencia
people to contact

AMBULANCIA, LA – *AMBULANCE*
CLÍNCIA, LA – *CLINIC*
DEPARTAMENTO DE BOMBEROS,
EL – *FIRE DEPARTMENT*
GRÚA, LA – *TOW TRUCK*

HOSPITAL, EL – *HOSPITAL*
PARAMÉDICO, EL – *PARAMEDIC*
POLICÍA, LA – *POLICE*
VECINO, EL – *NEIGHBOR*

ALGUNOS VERBOS
CONJUGATED VERBS

ser/estar
to be

YO SOY – *I AM*
TÚ ERES – *YOU ARE*
USTED ES – *YOU ARE*
ÉL/ELLA ES – *HE/SHE IS*

NOSOTROS SOMOS – *WE ARE*
USTEDES SON – *YOU ARE*
ELLOS/ELLAS SON – *THEY ARE*

hablar
to speak

YO HABLO – *I SPEAK*
TÚ HABLAS – *YOU SPEAK*
USTED HABLA – *YOU SPEAK*
ÉL/ELLA HABLA – *HE/SHE SPEAKS*

NOSOTROS HABLAMOS – *WE SPEA*
USTEDES HABLAN – *YOU SPEAK*
ELLOS/ELLAS HABLAN – *THEY
SPEAK*

comer
to eat

YO COMO – *I EAT*
TÚ COMES – *YOU EAT*
USTED COME – *YOU EAT*
ÉL/ELLA COME – *HE/SHE EATS*

NOSOTROS COMEMOS – *WE EAT*
USTEDES COMEN – *YOU EAT*
ELLOS/ELLAS COMEN – *THEY EAT*

escribir
to write

YO ESCRIBO – *I WRITE*
TÚ ESCRIBES – *YOU WRITE*
USTED ESCRIBE – *YOU WRITE*
ÉL/ELLA ESCRIBE – *HE/SHE WRITES*
NOSOTROS ESCRIBIMOS – *WE*

WRITE
USTEDES ESCRIBEN – *YOU WRITE*
ELLOS/ELLAS ESCRIBEN – *THEY
WRITE*

necesitar
to need

YO NECESITO – *I NEED*
TÚ NECESITAS – *YOU NEED*
USTED NECESITA – *YOU NEED*
ÉL/ELLA NECESITA – *HE/SHE NEEDS*
NOSOTROS NECESITAMOS – *WE*

NEED
USTEDES NECESITAN – *YOU NEED*
ELLOS/ELLAS NECESITAN – *THEY
NEED*

bilingual babycare

verbos comunes
other common verbs

BARRER – *SWEEP*
BUSCAR – *LOOK FOR*
COMER – *EAT*
COMPRAR – *BUY*
CONTAR – *TELL*
CORRER – *RUN*
CREER – *BELIEVE*
DAR – *GIVE*
DEBER – *MUST*
DECIR – *SAY*
DEJAR – *LET*
DORMIR – *SLEEP*
ENCONTRAR – *FIND*
ESCRIBIR – *WRITE*
ESCUCHAR – *LISTEN*
GUSTAR – *LIKE*
HABLAR – *SPEAK*
HACER – *DO*
IR – *GO*
LAVAR – *WASH*
LEER – *READ*
LIMPIAR – *CLEAN*

MANEJAR – *DRIVE*
MIRAR – *WATCH*
OBTENER – *GET*
OÍR – *HEAR*
OLER – *SMELL*
PENSAR – *THINK*
PODER – *CAN*
PREGUNTAR – *ASK*
RECOMENDAR – *RECOMMEND*
RENUNCIAR – *QUIT*
SABER – *KNOW*
SABOREAR – *TASTE*
SENTIR – *FEEL*
TENER – *HAVE*
TOMAR – *TAKE*
TRABAJAR – *WORK*
VENDER – *SELL*
VENIR – *COME*
VER – *SEE*

A-Z

vocabulario
vocabulary

alfabético: español – inglés ~
alphabetical: Spanish – English

A LA DERECHA	TO THE RIGHT
A LA IZQUIERDA	TO THE LEFT
A LO LARGO DE	ALONG
AAT	
ABAJO DE	UNDER
ABAJO	DOWN
ABAJO/PLANTA BAJA	DOWNSTAIRS
ABEJA, LA	BEE
ABOGADO, EL	LAWYER
ABRAZADERA DENTAL, LA	BRACES (TEETH)
ABRAZAR	CUDDLE/HUG (TO)
ABRELATAS, EL	CAN OPENER
ABRIGO, EL	OVERCOAT
ABRIL	APRIL
ABSCESO, EL	ABSCESS
ABUELA, LA	GRANDMOTHER
ABUELO, EL	GRANDFATHER
ABURRIDO (A)	BORED
ACCESORIOS, LOS	ACCESSORIES
ACCIDENTE, EL	ACCIDENT
ACEITE, EL	OIL
ACELGA, LA	CHARD
ACERCA DE	ABOUT
ACIDEZ, EL	HEARTBURN
ÁCIDO, EL	ACID
ACIETE DE OLÍVA, EL	OLIVE OIL
ACOMPAÑAR	ACCOMPANY (TO)
ACONDICIONADOR, EL	CONDITIONER
ACOSTAR	SLEEP (TO PUT TO)
ACRÍLICO	ACRYLIC
ACTOR, EL	ACTOR
ACTRIZ, LA	ACCTRESS
ACUARIO, EL	AQUARIUM
ADELANTE DE	AHEAD
ADEMÁS	BESIDES
ADENTRO DE	INSIDE
ADENTRO	INDOORS
ADIÓS	GOOD-BYE
ADOLESCENTE, EL	TEENAGER
AEROPUERTO, EL	AIRPORT
AFUERA DE	OUTSIDE
AFUERA	OUTDOORS
AGENCIA, LA	AGENCY
AGITADO (A)	RESTLESS
AGNÓSTICO (A)	AGNOSTIC
AGOSTO	AUGUST
AGRADABLE	PLEASANT
AGRESIVO (A)	AGGRESSIVE
AGRIO(A)	SOUR
AGUA CALIENTE, EL	HOT WATER
AGUA FRÍO	COLD WATER
AGUA HERVIDA, EL	BOILING WATER
AGUA MINERAL, EL	MINERAL WATER
AGUA, EL	WATER
AGUACATE, EL	AVOCADO
AGUILA, EL	EAGLE
AGUJA, LA	NEEDLE

AHIJADO, EL	GODCHILD
AHOGARSE	CHOKE (TO)
AHORA	NOW
AHORITA	RIGHT NOW
AIRE ACONDICIONADO, EL	AIR CONDITIOINING
AIRE, EL	AIR
AJEDREZ, EL	CHESS
ÁJO, EL	GARLIC
AJONJOLÍ, EL	SESAME SEED
AL LADO DE	NEXT TO
ALARMA, LA	ALARM
ALBAHACA, LA	BASIL
ALBÓNDIGA, LA	MEATBALL
ALCACHOFA, LA	ARTICHOKE
ALCAPARRAS, LAS	CAPERS
ALERGIA, LA	ALLERGY
ALERGIA, LA	HAY FEVER
ALETAS, LAS	FLIPPERS
ALGA, EL	ALGAE
ALGODÓN, EL	COTTON
ALGÚN DÍA	SOMEDAY
ALGUNOS(AS)	SOME
ALIMENTO PARA BEBÉ	BABY FOOD
ALIMENTOS PERECEDEROS, LOS	PERISHABLES
ALLÍ	THERE
ALMA, EL	SOUL
ALMEJA, LA	CLAM
ALMENDRA, LA	ALMOND
ALMIDÓN, EL	STARCH
ALMOHADA, LA	PILLOW
ALMUERZO, EL	LUNCH
ALREDEDOR DE	AROUND
ALTAR	ALTAR
ALTO (A)	TALL
AMA DE CASA, LA	HOMEMAKER
AMABLE	FRIENDLY
AMANECER, EL	SUNRISE
AMAPOLA, LA	POPPY
AMARGO(A)	BITTER
AMARILLO(A)	YELLOW
AMBICIOSO	AMBITIOUS
AMBOS(AS)	BOTH
AMBULANCIA, LA	AMBULANCE
AMERICANO, EL	AMERICAN
AMIGDALITIS, EL	TONSILLITIS
AMIGO, EL	FRIEND
AMIGOS, LOS	FRIENDS
AMONÍACO, EL	AMMONIA
AMPOLLA, LA	BLISTER
AÑADIR	ADD (TO)
ANARANJADO(A)	ORANGE (COLOR)
ANCHOA	ANCHOVY
ANESTESIA	ANESTHESIA
ÁNGEL, EL	ANGEL
ÁNGULO, EL	ANGLE
ANILLO, EL	RING
ANIMALES , LOS	ANIMALS

bilingual babycare

ANIMALS SALVAJES, LOS ..... WILD ANIMALES
ANIVERSARIO .... ANNIVERSARY
AÑO, EL.. YEAR
ANOCHE .... LAST NIGHT
ANOCHECER, EL .... DUSK
ANTES DE .... BEFORE
ANTIGÜEDAD, LA..........................ANTIQUE
ANTIHISTAMINA, LA..............ANTIHISTAMINE
ANUNCIO .... ANNOUNCEMENT
APAGADO(A)...OFF
APAGAR...........................TURN OFF (TO)
APARATO, EL...............................APPLIANCE
APARTAMENTO, EL.................. APARTMENT
ÁPIO, EL .... CELERY
APLAUDIR.......................CLAP HANDS (TO)
APLICACIÓN, LA.......................APPLICATION
APRENDER............................... LEARN (TO)
APURARSE.................................HURRY (TO)
AQUÍ... HERE
ARAÑA, LA...................................SPIDER
ARÁNDANOS, LOS ....BLUEBERRIES
ÁRBOL, EL..TREE
ARBUSTO, EL................................BUSH
ARDILLA, LA .... SQUIRREL
ARENA, LA .... SAND
ARENERO, EL .... SANDBOX
ARETES, LOS .... EARRINGS
ARMARIO, EL............................. ARMOIRE
ARQUITECTO, EL .... ARCHITECT
ARREGLAR.........................ARRANGE (TO)
ARREGLARSE............... GROOM (TO)
ARRESTAR ....ARREST (TO)
ARRIBA DE .... ABOVE
ARRIBA .... UP
ARRIBA/PLANTA ALTA.................. UPSTAIRS
ARROYO, EL....................................BROOK
ARROYO, EL....................................STREAM
ARROZ INTEGRAL, EL .... BROWN RICE
ARROZ SALVAJE, EL .... WILD RICE
ARROZ, EL....................................... RICE
ARTE, EL .... ART
ARTISTA, EL................................ARTIST
ASADOR, EL ....BBQ
ASFALTO, EL..............................ASPHALT
ASIENTO DEL COCHE, EL .... CAR SEAT
ASISTENTE, EL.............................ASSISTANT
ASISTIR ....ATTEND (TO)
ASMA, EL...............................ASTHMA
ASOMBROSO .... AMAZING
ASPIRA R .... VACUUM (TO)
ASPIRADORA, LA ....VACUUM
ASPIRINA, LA ....ASPRIN
ATAQUE DEL CORAZÓN, EL.. HEART ATTACK
ATAQUE, EL.......................................SEIZURE
ATEO (A) .... ATHEIST
ÁTICO, EL ....ATTIC
ATLETA, EL.................................ATHLETE
ATÚN, EL .... TUNA

AUNQUE ....ALTHOUGH
AUTO, EL.. AUTO
AUTOBÚS, EL .... BUS
AUTOCARAVANA, EL ....CAMPER
AUTOMÁTICO(A).......................AUTOMATIC
AUTOR, EL..AUTHOR
AVENA, LA .... OATMEAL
AVENIDA, LA .... AVENUE
AVIÓN, EL.. AIRPLANE
AVISPA, LA..................................WASP
AVISPÓN, EL.................................. HORNET
AYER ....YESTERDAY
AYUDAR .... HELP (TO)
AZÚCAR, EL .... SUGAR
AZUL..BLUE
BABERO, EL..BIB
BADMINTON, EL ....BADMINTON
BAHÍA, LA ....BAY
BAILE, EL...................................DANCING
BAJO (A)....................................SHORT
BALCÓN, EL .... BALCONY
BALLENA, LA.................................WHALE
BALLET, EL.................................... BALLET
BAMBINETO, EL......................... BASSINET
BANCA, LA................................ BENCH
BANCO, EL .... BANK
BAÑERA, LA ....INFANT TUB
BAÑO DE BURBUJAS, EL ....BUBBLE BATH
BAÑO, EL...............................BATHROOM
BANQUERO, EL .... BANKER
BANQUETA, LA ....SIDEWALK
BANQUITO, EL........................STEP STOOL
BAR, EL.. BAR
BARANDAL, EL.............................RAILING
BARCO, EL....................................BOAT
BARRER .... SWEEP (TO)
BÁSICO(A).......................................BASIC
BASINICA, LA .... TRAINING POTTY
BASQUETBOL, EL .... BASKETBALL
BASURA, LA .... GARBAGE/TRASH
BASURERO, EL......................GARBAGE CAN
BEBÉ, EL....................................BABY
BEBIDAS ....BEVERAGES
BÉISBOL, EL ....BASEBALL
BERENJENA, LA ....EGGPLANT
BERRO, EL..............................WATERCRESS
BESO, EL .... KISS
BETABEL, EL...................................... BEETS
BIBERÓN, LA..................................BOTTLE
BIBLIA, LA.. BIBLE
BIBLIOTECA, LA................................ LIBRARY
BICARBONATO, EL.................. BAKING SODA
BICHO, EL...BUG
BICICLETA, LA .... BICYCLE
BIEN...WELL
BIENVENIDOS .... WELCOME
BIKINI, EL ....BIKINI
BINOCULARES, LOS....................BINOCULARS

BIÓLOGO, EL	BIOLOGIST
BISTEC, EL	STEAK
BLANCO(A)	WHITE
BLANQUEADOR, EL	BLEACH
BLUSA, LA	BLOUSE
BOCA, LA	MOUTH
BODA, LA	WEDDING
BOK CHOY, EL	BOK CHOY
BOLA DE NIEVE, LA	SNOWBALL
BOLICHE, EL	BOWLING
BOLITAS DE ALGODÓN, LAS	COTTON BALLS
BOLSA DE BASURA, LA	TRASH BAG
BOLSA, LA	BAG/PURSE
BOLSILLO, EL	POCKET
BOMBERO, EL	FIREMAN
BONITO (A)	PRETTY
BORREGO, EL	SHEEP
BOSQUE, EL	FOREST
BOTAS, LAS	BOOTS
BOTE DE PAÑALES, EL	DIAPER PAIL
BOTIQUÍN, EL	MEDICINE CABINET
BOTÓN, EL	BUTTON
BOXEO, EL	BOXING
BRAZO, EL	ARM
BRILLANTE	BRIGHT
BROCHE, EL	BARRETS
BRÓCOLI, EL	BROCCOLI
BRONQUITIS, EL	BRONCHITIS
BUDÍN, EL	PUDDING
BUENA SUERTA	GOOD LUCK
BUENAS NOCHES	GOOD EVENING
BUENAS TARDES	GOOD AFTERNOON
BUENOS DÍAS	GOOD MORNING
BUFANDA, LA	SCARF
BÚHO, EL	OWL
BUREAU , EL	DRESSER
BURRO, EL	DONKEY
BUSCAR LOS	LOOK FOR (TO)
BUZÓN, EL	MAILBOX
CABALLO MARINO, EL	SEAHORSE
CABALLO, EL	HORSE
CABAÑA, LA	CABIN
CABEZA, LA	HEAD
CACAHUATE, EL	PEANUT
CACHORRO, EL	PUPPY
CACTUS, EL	CACTUS
CADA DÍA	EACH DAY
CADA UNO (A)	EACH
CADERA, LA	HIP
CAFÉ, EL	COFFEE
CAFETERA, LA	COFFEE MAKER
CAIMÁN, EL	ALLIGATOR
CAJA DE FUSIBLES, EL	FUSE BOX
CAJA DE PRIMEROS AUXILLOS, LA	FIRST AID KIT
CAJA, LA	BOX (CONTAINER)
CALABAZA VERDE, LA	ZUCCHINI
CALABAZA, LA	SQUASH
CALCETINES, LOS	SOCKS

CALDO, EL	BROTH
CALENTAR	HEAT UP (TO)
CALIENTE	HOT
CALIENTITO (A)	WARM
CALLADO (A)	QUIET
CALLE, LA	STREET
CALLEJÓN	ALLEY
CALOR, EL	HEAT
CALVO (A)	BALD
CALZÓN DE HULE, EL	DIAPER COVERS
CALZONES ENTRENADORES, LOS	PULL UPS
CALZONES, LOS	PANTIES/UNDERWEAR
CAMA, LA	BED
CÁMARA, LA	CAMERA
CAMBIADOR, EL	CHANGING TABLE
CAMBIAR	ALTER (TO)/CHANGE (TO)
CAMELLO, EL	CAMEL
CAMINAR	WALK (TO)
CAMINATA, LA	HIKING
CAMINO, EL	PATH
CAMION DE LOS BOMBEROS, EL	FIRE TRUCK
CAMION DE VOLTEO, EL	DUMP TRUCK
CAMIÓN, EL	TRUCK
CAMISA, LA	SHIRT
CAMISETA, LA	T-SHIRT
CAMOTE, EL	SWEET POTATO/YAM
CAMPAMENTO, EL	CAMPSITE
CAMPO, EL	FIELD
CANAL, EL	CANAL
CANARIO, EL	CANARY
CANCER, EL	CANCER
CANCIÓN, LA	SONG
CANDELERO, EL	CANDLESTICK
CANELA, LA	CINNAMON
CANGREJO, EL	CRAB
CANGURO, EL	KANGAROO
CANICAS, LAS	MARBLES
CANOA, LA	CANOE
CANSADO (A)	TIRED
CANTAR	SING (TO)
CANTIDAD, LA	AMOUNT
CAPILLA, LA	CHAPEL
CAPUCHINO, EL	CAPPUCCINO
CAPULLO, EL	BUD
CARA, LA	FACE
CARACOL, EL	SNAIL
CARÁMBANOS, LOS	ICICLES
CARICATURAS, LAS	CARTOONS
CARINETE, EL	CLARINET
CARNE DE RES, EL	BEEF
CARNICERO, EL	BUTCHER
CARPINTERO, EL	CARPENTER
CARRERA, LA	RACE
CARRIOLA, LA	STROLLER
CARTERA, LA	WALLET
CARTERO, EL	MAIL CARRIER
CASA, LA	HOUSE
CASADO (A)	MARRIED

bilingual babycare

CASARSE	MARRY (TO)
CASCO, EL	HELMET
CASI	ALMOST
CASITA, LA	BUNGALOW
CASTIGAR	PUNISH (TO)
CASTIGO, EL	PUNISHMENT
CASTOR, EL	BEAVER
CATEDRAL, LA	CATHEDRAL
CATÓLICO (A)	CATHOLIC
CATSUP, LA	KETCHUP
CEBOLLA, LA	ONION
CEBOLLÍN, EL	CHIVE
CEBOLLITAS, LAS	GREEN ONIONS
CEBRA, LA	ZEBRA
CEJA, LA	EYEBROW
CELEBRAR	CELEBRATE (TO)
CELOSO (A)	JEALOUS
CENA, LA	DINNER
CENICERO, EL	ASHTRAY
CENIZA, LA	ASH
CENTÍMETRO, EL	CENTIMETER
CENTRO, EL	DOWNTOWN
CEPILLO DE DIENTES, EL	TOOTHBRUSH
CEPILLO, EL	BRUSH
CERA PARA LOS MUEBLES, LA	FURNITURE POLISH
CERA PARA PISO, LA	FLOOR POLISH
CERCA DE	NEAR
CERCA, LA	FENCE
CERDO, EL	PORK
CEREAL, EL	CEREAL
CEREBRO, EL	BRAIN
CEREZAS, LAS	CHERRIES
CERRADURA, LA	LOCK
CERRO, EL	HILL
CERVESA, LA	BEER
CHABACANO, EL	APRICOT
CHALECO SALVAVIDAS, EL	LIFE JACKET
CHAMPÚ, EL	SHAMPOO
CHANCLAS, LAS	FLIP FLOPS
CHANGO, EL	MONKEY
CHARCO, EL	PUDDLE
CHEF, EL	CHEF
CHEQUERA, LA	CHECKBOOK
CHICHARROS, LOS	PEAS
CHICLE, EL	GUM
CHICO(A)	SMALL
CHILE MORRÓN, EL	BELL PEPPER
CHILE, EL	CHILI PEPPER/HOT PEPPER
CHIMENEA, LA	CHIMNEY/FIREPLACE
CHISTOSO (A)	FUNNY
CHIVO, EL	GOAT
CHMARRA, LA	JACKET
CHOCOLATE CALIENTE, EL	HOT CHOCOLATE
CHOCOLATE, EL	CHOCOLATE
CHUPÓN, EL	NIPPLE
CHUPÓN, EL	PACIFIER
CICLO PARA ROPA	DELICATE CYCLE
CICLÓN, EL	TORNADO
CIELO, EL	HEAVEN/SKY
CIERRE, EL	ZIPPER
CINE, EL	MOVIES
CINTA, LA	HEADBAND/TAPE
CINTURÓN, EL	BELT
CIRCO, EL	CIRCUS
CIRUELA PASA, LA	PRUNE
CIRUELA, LA	PLUM
CITA DE NEGOCIOS, LA	BUSINESS MEETING
CITA, LA	APPOINTMENT
CIUDAD, LA	CITY
CLARO (A)	FAIR
CLARO(A)	LIGHT (COLOR)
CLASE DE ARTE, LA	ART CLASS
CLASE DE BAILE, LA	DANCE CLASS
CLASE DE MÚSICA, LA	MUSIC CLASS
CLASE DE TAP, LA	TAP DANCING CLASS
CLAVO, EL	CLOVE/NAIL
CLÍNCIA, LA	CLINIC
CLOSET, EL	CLOSET
COBIJA, LA	BLANKET
COCHE, EL	CAR
COCHINO, EL	PIG
COCIDO EN EL HORNO	BAKED
COCIDO	COOKED
COCINA R AL VAPOR	STEAM (TO)
COCINA, LA	KITCHEN
COCINAR	COOK(TO)
COCO, EL	COCONUT
COCÓA , EL	COCOA
COCODRILO, EL	CROCODILE
CÓDIGO DE ÁREA, EL	AREA CODE
CODO, EL	ELBOW
COL, LA	CABBAGE
COLCHA, LA	BEDSPREAD
COLCHÓN, EL	MATTRESS
COLES DE BRUSELAS, LAS	BRUSSEL SPROUTS
COLGAR	HANG (TO)
COLIFLOR, LA	CAULIFLOWER
COLLAR, EL	NECKLACE
COLONIA/VECINDAD, LA	NEIGHBORHOOD
COLORES	COLORS
COLUMPIO, EL	SWING
COMEDOR, EL	DINING ROOM
COMER	EAT (TO)
COMESTIBLES, LOS	GROCERIES
COMETA, LA	KITE
COMEZÓN, LA	ITCH
COMIDA(S), LA(S)	MEAL(S)
COMIDA, LA	FOOD
COMO	AS
CÓMO	HOW
CÓMODO	COMFORTABLE
COMPARTIR	SHARE (TO)
COMPENSACIÓN, LA	COMPENSATION
COMPORTARSE	BEHAVE (TO)
COMPRAR	BUY (TO)
CON VIENTO	WINDY

CON	WITH
CONDADO, EL	COUNTY
CONDOMINIO, EL	CONDO.
CONEJO, EL	RABBIT
CONGELADOR, EL	FREEZER
CONGELAMIENTO, EL	FROSTBITE
CONGELAR	FREEZE (TO)
CONOCIDO , EL	ACQUAINTANCE
CONTABLE, EL	BOOKKEEPER
CONTAGIOSO (A)	CONTAGIOUS
CONTAR	TELL (TO)
CONTENTO(A)/FELÍZ	HAPPY
CONTRA	AGAINST
CONTRATAR	HIRE (TO)
CONTRATO, EL	CONTRACT
CONVULSIÓN, LA	CONVULSION
CORAZÓN, EL	HEART
CORBATA, LA	TIE
CORDERO, EL	LAMB
CORONA, LA	CROWN
CORREA, LA	LEASH
CORREA, LA	SAFETY STRAP
CORREO, EL	MAIL/POST OFFICE
CORRER	JOG(TO)/RUN (TO)
CORRIENTE, LA	CURRENT
CORTAR	CUT (TO)
CORTÉS	POLITE
CORTINA DE BAÑO, LA	SHOWER CURTAIN
CORTINA, LA	CURTAIN
COSA, LA	THING
COSTA, LA	COAST
COSTILLA, LA	RIB
COYOTE, EL	COYOTE
CRAYOLAS, LAS	CRAYONS
CREATIVO (A)	CREATIVE
CREER	BELIEVE (TO)
CREMA ÁCIDA, LA	SOUR CREAM
CREMA DE CACAHUATE, LA	PEANUT BUTTER
CREMA PARA BEBÉS, LA	BABY CREAM
CREMA, LA	CREAM/LOTION
CRIADA, LA	MAID
CRISTIANO (A)	CHRISTIAN
CRUDO(A)	RAW
CRUZ, LA	CROSS
CUADRA, LA	BLOCK (CITY)
CUALQUERA PARTE	ANYWHERE
CUALQUIER (A)	ANY
CUALQUIERA COSA	ANYTHING
CUALQUIERA PERSONA	ANYONE
CUÁNDO	WHEN
CUARTO DE JUEGOS, EL	PLAYROOM
CUARTO DE LOS NIÑOS, EL	CHILDREN'S ROOM
CUARTO DE VISTAS, EL	GUEST ROOM
CUARTO DEL BEBÉ, EL	NURSERY(CHILDREN)
CUARTO, EL	QUARTER
CUBETA, LA	BUCKET
CUBETA, LA	SAND PAIL
CUBIERTOS, LOS	SILVERWARE
CUBOS DE MADERA, LOS	BLOCKS
CUCHARA, LA	SPOON
CUCHARADITA, LA	TEASPOON
CUCHILLO, EL	KNIFE
CUELLO, EL	NECK
CUENTA, LA	BILL
CUENTO, EL	STORY
CUERDA PARA BRINCAR, LA	JUMP ROPE
CUERO, EL	LEATHER
CUERVO, EL	CROW
CUEVA, LA	CAVE
CUIDADO	CAREFUL
CUIDAR NIÑOS	BABYSIT (TO)
CULPA, LA	BLAME
CUMPLEAÑOS, EL	BIRTHDAY
CUNA, LA	CRIB
CUÑADA,LA	SISTER-IN-LAW
CUÑADO, EL	BROTHER-IN-LAW
CURITA, LA	BAND-AID
DAR	GIVE (TO)
DÁTILES, LOS	DATES
DE MAL HUMOR	GRUMPY
DE CUADROS	CHECKERED
DE NADA	YOU'RE WELCOME
DE PUNTITOS	POLKA-DOTTED
DE	FROM
DEBER	MUST
DECIR	SAY (TO)
DEDO DEL PIE, EL	TOE
DEDO, EL	FINGER
DEJAR	LET (TO)
DELANTAL	APRON
DELFÍN, EL	DOLPHIN
DELICIOSO(A)	DELICIOUS
DENTISTA, EL	DENTIST
DEPARTAMENTO DE BOMBEROS, EL	FIRE DEPA
DEPORTES, LOS	SPORTS
DEPRIMIDA (A)	DEPRESSED
DERECHO	STRAIGHT AHEAD
DERRAMAR	SPILL (TO)
DESAYUNO, EL	BREAKFAST
DESCARGER	UNLOAD (TO)
DESCONGELAR	DEFROST (TO)
DESEAR	WISH (TO)
DESECHADOR, EL	GARGBAGE DISPOSAL
DESEMPLOVAR	DUST (TO)
DESFILE, EL	PARADE
DESHIDRATACIÓN, LA	DEHYDRATION
DESIERTO, EL	DESERT
DESINFECTANTE, EL	DISENFECTANT
DESPEDIR	FIRE (TO)
DESPEJADO(A)	CLEAR
DESPERTADOR, EL	ALARM CLOCK
DESPERTAR	WAKE UP (TO)
DESPIERTO (A)	AWAKE
DESPUES DE	AFTER/AFTERWARDS
DETERGENTE, EL	DETERGENT
DETRÁS DE	BEHIND

DIABETES, EL	DIABETES
DIABLO, EL	DEVIL
DIAMANTES, EL	DIAMOND
DIARIO	DAILY
DIARREA, LA	DIARREA
DIAS FESTIVOS, LOS	HOLIDAYS
DIBUJAR	DRAW
DIBUJO, EL	DRAWING
DICIEMBRE	DECEMBER
DIENTE DE LEÓN, EL	DANDELION
DIENTE, EL	TOOTH
DIFÍCIL	DIFFICULT
DINERO, EL	MONEY
DINOSAURIO, EL	DINOSAUR
DIOS	GOD
DIRECCIÓN, LA	ADDRESS
DISENFECTANTE, EL	DISINFECTANT
DISFRAZ, EL	COSTUME
DISFRAZARSE	DRESS UP (TO)
DISPONIBLE	AVAILABLE
DIVERTIDO	AMUSING
DIVERTIRSE	FUN (TO HAVE)
DIVORCIADO (A)	DIVORCED
DOBLAR	BEND (TO)/FOLD (TO)
DOBLE, EL	DOUBLE
DOCTOR, EL	DOCTOR
DOLOR DE CABEZA, EL	HEADACHE
DOLOR DE ESPALDA, EL	BACKACHE
DOLOR DE ESTÓMAGO, EL	STOMACH ACHE
DOLOR DE GARGANTA, EL	SORE THROAT
DOMINGO, EL	SUNDAY
DORMIDO (A)	ASLEEP
DORMIRSE	SLEEP (TO)
DOS VECES	TWICE
DULCE	SWEET
DULCE, EL	CANDY
DUNA, LA	DUNE
DURAZNO, EL	PEACH
E.U.A.	U.S.A.
EDAD, LA	AGE
EDIFICIO, EL	BUILDING
EDREDÓN, EL	COMFORTER/QUILT
EDUCADO (A)	WELL MANNERED
EJÉRCITO, EL	ARMY
EJERICICIOS AEROBICÓS	AEROBICS
EJOTES, LOS	GREEN BEANS
EL (MASC.) LA (FEM)	THE
EL ANIMAL	ANIMAL
EL MORETÓN	BRUISE
ÉL	HE
ELEFANTE, EL	ELEPHANT
ELLA	SHE
ELLAS	THEY (FEM.)
ELLOS	THEY (MASC.)
ELOTE, EL	CORN
EMBARAZADA	PREGNANT
EMOCIONADO (A)	EXCITED
EMPEZAR	BEGIN (TO)

EMPEZAR	START (TO)
EMPLEADO. EL	EMPLOYEE
EMPRENDEDOR, EL	ENTREPRENEUR
EMPRESARIO, EL	BUSINESSMAN
EN BARQUILLO	ON A CONE
EN MEDIO	MIDDLE
ENCAJE, EL	LACE
ENCARGO, EL	ERRAND
ENCIMA DE	ON TOP OF
ENCONTRAR	FIND (TO)
ENELDO, EL	DILL
ENERO	JANUARY
ENFERMERA, LA	NURSE
ENFERMO (A)	SICK
ENJUAGAR	RINSE
ENOJADA	ANGRY
ENROLLAR	ROLL (TO)
ENTONCES	THEN
ENTRADA PARA COCHES, LA	DRIVEWAY
ENTRE	BETWEEN
ENTREVISTA, LA	INTERVIEW
ENVENENAMIENTO, EL	POISONING
ERIZO DE MAR, EL	SAND DOLLAR
ESCALAR UN ÁRBOL	CLIMB A TREE
ESCALAR	CLIMB (TO)
ESCALERA, LA	LADDER
ESCALOFRIOS, LOS	CHILLS
ESCARABAJO, EL	BEETLE/ROLY-POLY
ESCOBA, LA	BROOM
ESCONDER	HIDE (TO)
ESCONDIDILLAS, LAS	HIDE-AND-GO-SEEK
ESCORPIÓN, EL	SCORPION
ESCOUTS , LAS	GIRL SCOUTS
ESCOUTS, LOS	BOY SCOUTS
ESCRIBIR	WRITE (TO)
ESCRITOR, EL	WRITER
ESCUCHAR	LISTEN (TO)
ESCUELA, LA	SCHOOL
ESKIS, LOS	SKIS
ESMALTE DE UÑAS, EL	NAIL POLISH
ESPALDA, LA	BACK
ESPÁRRAGOS, LOS	ASPARAGUS
ESPEJO, EL	MIRROR
ESPERAR	WAIT (TO)
ESPINACA, LA	SPINACH
ESPONJA, LA	SPONGE
ESPOSA, LA	WIFE
ESPOSO	HUSBAND
ESQUINA, LA	CORNER
ESTADO, EL	STATE
ESTADOS UNIDOS, LOS	UNITED STATES OF AMERICA
ESTAMPA, LA	STICKER
ESTANCIA, LA	FAMILY ROOM
ESTAR	BE (TO)
ESTE	EAST
ÉSTE/ÉSTA	THIS ONE
ESTÉREO, EL	STEREO
ESTERILÍZAR	STERILIZE (TO)

ESTÓMAGO, EL	STOMACH
ESTORNUDO, EL	SNEEZE
ESTOS/ESTAS	THESE
ESTRELLA MARINA, LA	STARFISH
ESTRELLA, LA	STAR
ESTRENIMIENTO, EL	CONSTIPATION
EVITAR	AVOID (TO)
EXCUSADO, EL	TOILET
EXTINGUIDOR, EL	FIRE EXTINGUISHER
EXTRA GRANDE	EXTRA LARGE
FÁCIL	EASY
FALDA, LA	SKIRT
FAMILIA, LA	FAMILY
FAMOSO (A)	FAMOUS
FEBRERO	FEBRUARY
FECHA DEL VENCIMIENTO, LA	EXPIRATION DATE
FELICIDADES	CONGRATULATIONS
FELIZ CUMPLEAÑOS	HAPPY BIRTHDAY
FEO (A)	UGLY
FIDEO, EL	NOODLE
FIEBRE/ CALENTURA, LA	FEVER
FIESTA, LA	PARTY
FIN DE SEMANA, EL	WEEKEND
FINJIR	PRETEND (TO)
FLACO (A)	THIN
FLORE, LA	FLOWER
FLOTADORES, LOS	WATER WINGS
FORMULA, LA	FORMULA
FOTOGRAFÍA, LA	PHOTOGRAPHY
FRACTURA, LA	FRACTURE
FRAMBUESAS, LAS	RASPBERRIES
FRESAS, LAS	STRAWBERRIES
FRESCO(A)	FRESH
FRÍER	FRY (TO)
FRIJOLES BAYOS, LOS	PINTO BEANS
FRIJOLES DE MEDIA LUNA, LOS	LIMA BEANS
FRIJOLES NEGROS, LOS	BLACK BEANS
FRIJOLES REFRITOS	REFRIED BEANS
FRIJOLES, LOS / HABICHUELAS, LOS	BEANS
FRIJOLES, LOS	LEGUMES
FRÍO (A)	COLD
FRONTERA, LA	BORDER
FRUTA, LA	FRUIT
FUEGO, EL	FIRE
FUERTE	STRONG
FUNDA, LA	PILLOWCASE
FURÚNCULO, EL	BOIL (SKIN)
FÚTBOL AMERICANO, EL	FOOTBALL
FÚTBOL, EL	SOCCER
GABINETE, EL	CABINET
GAFAS DE BUCEO, LAS	MASK
GALLETA SALADA, LA	CRACKER
GALLETA, LA	COOKIE
GANCHOS, LOS	HANGERS
GANGA, LA	BARGAIN
GANSO, EL	GOOSE
GARAJE, EL	GARAGE
GARBANZOS, LOS	CHICK PEAS
GAS, EL	GAS (BURPS)
GASOLINERA, LA	GAS STATION
GATEAR	CRAWL (TO)
GATITO, EL	KITTEN
GATO, EL	CAT
GEMELOS	TWINS
GERANIO, EL	GERANIUM
GERENTE, EL	MANAGER
GIMNASIO, EL	GYMNASIUM
GIRAR	SPIN (TO)
GIRASOL, EL	SUNFLOWER
GLOBO, EL	BALLOON
GOGLES, LOS	GOGGLES
GOLF, EL	GOLF
GOLPEAR	HIT (TO)
GOMA, LA	ERASER
GORDO (A)	FAT
GORRA, LA	CAP
GOTAS PARA OJOS, LAS	EYE DROPS
GOTEAR	LEAK (TO)
GRACIAS	THANK YOU
GRAMO, EL	GRAM
GRANADA, LA	POMEGRANATE
GRANDE	BIG/LARGE
GRANIZO, EL	HAIL
GRANJERO, EL	FARMER
GRAVA, LA	GRAVEL
GRILLO, EL	CRICKET
GRIPE, EL	COLD (SICK)
GRIS	GRAY
GRITAR	YELL (TO)
GRÚA, LA	TOW TRUCK
GUANTE, EL	GLOVE
GUANTES, LOS	GLOVES/MITTENS
GUAPO (A)	GOOD LOOKING
GUARDAR	KEEP (TO)
GUAYAVA, LA	GUAVA
GUITARRA, LA	GUITAR
GUSANO, EL	WORM
GUSTAR	LIKE (TO)
HABLAR	SPEAK (TO)
HACER GALLETAS	MAKING COOKIES
HACER	DO (TO)/MAKE (TO)
HACHA, EL	AX
HADA, EL	FAIRY
HAICHULAS BLANCAS, LAS	WHITE BEANS
HALCÓN, EL	HAWK
HALLOWEEN, EL	HALLOWEEN
HAMACA, LA	HAMMOCK
HAMBURGUESA, LA	HAMBURGER
HÁMSTER, EL	HAMSTER
HARINA, LA	FLOUR
HASTA	UNTIL
HEBILLA, LA	BUCKLE
HELADA, LA	FROST
HELADO/EL, NIEVE, LA	ICE CREAM
HELECHO, EL	FERN
HEMORRAGIA NASAL, LA	NOSEBLEED

bilingual babycare

HERIDA	INJURY
HERIDA, LA	WOUND
HERIR	HURT (TO)
HERMANA, LA	SISTER
HERMANO, EL	BROTHER
HERVIR	BOIL (TO)
HIEDRA, LA	IVY
HIELO, EL	ICE
HIGOS, LOS	FIGS
HIJA, LA	DAUGHTER
HIJASTRA, LA	STEPDAUGHTER
HIJASTRO,EL	STEPSON
HIJO, EL	SON
HINOJO, EL	FENNEL
HIPOPOTAMO, EL	HIPPO
HISES, LOS	CHALK
HOJA DE LAUREL, LA	BAY LEAF
HOJA, LA	LEAF
HOLA	HELLO
HOMBRE, EL	MAN
HOMBRO, EL	SHOULDER
HONGOS, LOS	MUSHROOMS
HORAS, LAS	HOURS
HORMIGA, LA	ANT
HORNÉAR	BAKE (TO)
HORNO, EL	OVEN
HOSPITAL, EL	HOSPITAL
HOTCAKES, LOS	PANCAKES
HOY EN LA NOCHE	TONIGHT
HOY	TODAY
HUESO, EL	BONE
HUEVO, EL	EGG
HUMEDAD, LA	HUMIDITY
HÚMEDO(A)	HUMID/MOIST
HURACÁN, EL	HURRICANE
ICTERICIA, LA	JAUNDICE
IGLESIA, LA	CHURCH
IMPERMEABLE, EL	RAINCOAT
IMPRESIONANTE	AWESOME
IMPUESTOS, LOS	TAXES
INFECCIÓN, LA	INFECTION
INFECTADO (A)	INFECTED
INFIERNO, EL	HELL
INFLAMACIÓN, LA	SWELLING
INFLAMADO (A)	SWOLLEN
INFLUENZA, LA	FLU
INSIGNIA, LA	BADGE
INSOLACIÓN, LA	HEATSTROKE/SUNSTROKE
INSULINA, LA	INSULIN
INTELIGENTE	INTELLIGENT
INTERESADO (A)	INTERESTED
INUNDACIÓN, LA	FLOOD
INVIERNO, EL	WINTER
IRGO (TO)	
JABÓN, EL	SOAP
JAMÓN, EL	HAM
JARÁBE, EL	SYRUP
JARDÍN DE ENFRENTE, EL	FRONT YARD
JARDÍN, EL	BACKYARD/GARDEN
JARDINERO, EL	GARDENER
JEFE, EL	BOSS
JICAMA, LA	JICIMA
JIRAFA, LA	GIRAFFE
JITOMATE, EL	TOMATO
JÓVEN	YOUNG
JÓVEN, EL	YOUNG PERSON
JOYERÍA, LAS	JEWELRY
JUDÍO (A)	JEWISH
JUEGO DE DAMAS, EL	CHECKERS
JUEGO DE TÉ, EL	TEA SET
JUEGOS DEL PARQUE, LOS	PLAYGROUND
JUEVES, EL	THURSDAY
JUGAR A LA CASITA	PLAYING HOUSE
JUGAR A LAS TRAES	PLAY CHASE
JUGAR	PLAY (TO)
JUGO DE CAJITA, EL	JUICE BOX
JUGO DE MANZANA, EL	APPLE JUICE
JUGO DE NARANJA, EL	ORANGE JUICE
JUGO DE UVA, EL	GRAPE JUICE
JUGO, EL	JUICE
JUGUETE, LA	TOY
JULIO	JULY
JUNIO	JUNE
JUNTOS(AS)	TOGETHER
KILO, EL	KILO
KIWI, EL	KIWI
KRUP, EL	CROUP
LABIO, EL	LIP
LADRILLO, EL	BRICK
LAGARTO, EL	LIZARD
LAGO, EL	LAKE
LAGUNA, LA	POND
LÁMPARA, LA	LAMP
LANA, LA	WOOL
LANGOSTA, LA	LOBSTER
LÁPICES, LOS	PENCILS
LARGO(A)	LONG
LATA, LA	CAN
LAVABO, EL	SINK
LAVADORA, LA	WASHER
LAVANDA, LA	LAVENDER
LAVANDERÍA, LA	LAUNDRY ROOM
LAVAPLATOS, EL	DISHWASHER
LAVAR A MANO	HAND WASH (TO)
LAVAR	WASH (TO)
LAXANTE, EL	LAXATIVE
LECHE DE SOYA, LA	SOY MILK
LECHE MATERNA, LA	BREASTMILK
LECHE, LA	MILK
LECHUGA, LA	LETTUCE
LECTURA, LA	READING
LEER	READ (TO)
LENGUA, LA	TONGUE
LENTEJAS, LAS	LENTILS
LENTES DE SOL, LOS	SUNGLASSES
LENTES OSCUROS, LOS	DARK GLASSES

LENTO (A)	SLOW
LEÓN, EL	LION
LEVANTAR	LIFT (TO)
LIBÉLULA, LA	DRAGONFLY
LIBRA, LA	POUND
LIBRERO, EL	BOOKSHELF
LIBRO, EL	BOOK
LICENCIA DE MANEJAR, LA	DRIVER'S LICENCE
LICENCIA, LA	LICENSE
LICÚAR	BLEND, TO
LILA, LA	LILAC
LIMA, EL	LEMON
LIMÓN, EL	LIME
LIMPIAR	CLEAN (TO)
LIMPIEZA DE CASA, LA	HOUSE CLEANING
LIMPIO (A)	CLEAN
LINO, EL	LINEN
LIQUADORA, LA	BLENDER
LÍQUIDO, EL	LIQUID
LISTÓN, EL	RIBBON
LITRO, EL	LITER
LLANTITA, LA	SWIMMING RING
LLAVE, LA	FAUCET/KEY
LLEGAR	ARRIVE (TO)
LLENO(A)	FULL
LLORAR	CRY (TO)
LLOVIZNA, LA	DRIZZLE
LLUVIA, LA	RAIN
LO DEMÁS	REST OF
LOBO, EL	WOLF
LODO, EL	MUD
LODOSO (A)	MUDDY
LONA, LA	CANVAS
LUCES, LAS	LIGHTS
LUCESITA, LA	NIGHT LIGHT
LUEGO	LATER
LUGAR NATAL, EL	BIRTHPLACE
LUNA, LA	MOON
LUNCHERA, LA	LUNCHBOX
LUNES, EL	MONDAY
MACADAMIA, LA	MACADAMIA
MADRASTRA,LA	STEPMOTHER
MADRE, LA	MOTHER
MADURO (A)	MATURE/RIPE
MAESTRO, EL	TEACHER
MAGIA, LA	MAGIC
MAIZENA, LA	CORNSTARCH
MALA HEIRBA, LA	WEED (PLANT)
MALDITO (A)	MEAN
MALETÍN, EL	BRIEFCASE
MALO (A)	BAD
MAÑANA	TOMORROW
MAÑANA, LA	MORNING
MANCHA, LA	STAIN
MANDARINA, LA	MANDARIN
MANDÍBULA, LA	JAW
MANEJAR	DRIVE (TO)
MANGO, EL	MANGO
MANTEQUILLA, LA	BUTTER
MANZANA, LA	APPLE
MAPACHE, EL	RACCOON
MAQUILLAJE, EL	MAKEUP
MAR, EL	OCEAN/SEA
MAREA ALTA, LA	HIGH TIDE
MAREA BAJA, LA	LOW TIDE
MAREA, LA	TIDE
MARGARINA , LA	MARGARINE
MARGARITA, LA	DAISY
MARIPOSA, LA	BUTTERFLY
MARIQUITA, LA	LADYBUG
MARTES, EL	TUESDAY
MARZO	MARCH
MÁS O MENOS	MORE OR LESS
MÁS	MORE
MASCOTA, LA	PET
MAYO	MAY
MAYONESA, LA	MAYONNAISE
MAYOR	OLDER
MECANICO, EL	MECHANIC
MECEDORA, LA	ROCKING CHAIR
MEDIA NOCHE, LA	MIDNIGHT
MEDIANO(A)	MEDIUM
MEDIAS, LAS	STOCKINGS
MEDIDAS, LAS	MEASUREMENTS
MEDIDOR DE GAS, EL	GAS METER
MEDIODÍA, EL	NOON
MELÓN, EL	CANTALOUPE/MELON
MENSAJE, EL	MESSAGE
MENTA, LA	MINT
MENTIR	LIE (TO)
MES PASADO, EL	LAST MONTH
MES, EL	MONTH
MESA, LA	TABLE
MESITA DE NOCHE, LA	NIGHTSTAND
METRO, EL	METER
MEZCLILLA, LA	DENIM
MICROBIOS, LOS	GERMS
MICROONDAS, EL	MICROWAVE
MIEL, LA	HONEY
MIENTRAS	DURING
MIERCOLES, EL	WEDNESDAY
MIGRAÑA, LA	MIGRAINE
MIL MILLONES	BILLION
MILÍMETRO, EL	MILLIMETER
MILLA, LA	MILE
MIMADO (A)	SPOILED
MIRAR	WATCH (TO)
MISA, LA	MASS
MISMO (A), EL(LA)	SAME
MITAD, LA	HALF
MOCHILA, LA	BACKPACK
MOHO, EL	MILDEW/MOLD
MOJADO (A)	WET
MOLESTO (A)	ANNOYED
MONITOR, EL	MONITOR
MONO(A)	CUTE

bilingual babycare

MONOPOLIO, EL	MONOPOLY
MONSTRUO, EL	MONSTER
MONTAÑA, LA	MOUNTAIN
MORADO(A)	PURPLE
MORDEDURA DE GATO, LA	CAT BITE
MORDEDURA DE PERRO, LA	DOG BITE
MORDEDURA DE SERPIENTE, LA	SNAKE BITE
MORDEDURA, LA	ANIMAL BITE/BITE
MORDER	BITE (TO)
MORMÓN (A)	MORMON
MORSA, LA	WALRUS
MOSCA, LA	FLY
MOSQUITO, EL	MOSQUITO
MOSTAZA, LA	MUSTARD
MOTONIEVE, EL	SNOWMOBILE
MOVER	MOVE (TO)
MUCHACHA, LA	YOUNG GIRL
MUCHACHO, EL	YOUNG BOY
MUCHO	A LOT (MORE)
MUCHOS(AS)	MANY
MUDARSE	RELOCATE (TO)
MUEBLES, LOS	FURNITURE
MUJER, LA	WOMAN
MULETAS, LAS	CRUTCHES
MUÑECA, LA	DOLL/WRIST
MUÑECO DE NIEVE, EL	SNOWMAN
MUSEO DEL NIÑO, EL	CHILDRENS MUSEUM
MUSEO, EL	MUSEUM
MÚSICA, LA	MUSIC
MÚSICO, EL	MUSICIAN
MUSLOS, LOS	THIGHS
MUSULMÁN (A)	MUSLEM
MUY	VERY
NACIMIENTO, EL	BIRTH
NACIONALIDAD, LA	NATIONALITY
NADA	NOTHING
NADIE	NO ONE
NARANJA, LA	ORANGE (FRUIT)
NARÍZ, LA	NOSE
NATACIÓN, LA	SWIMMING
NATURALEZA, LA	NATURE
NAUSEA, LA	NAUSEA
NAVIDAD, LA	CHRISTMAS
NECATARÍN, EL	NECTARINE
NECESITAR	NEED (TO)
NEGRO(A)	BLACK
NERVIOSO (A)	NERVOUS
NIDO, EL	NEST
NIEBLA, LA	FOG
NIETA, LA	GRANDDAUGHTER
NIETO, EL	GRANDSON
NIEVE, LA	SNOW
NIÑA, LA	LITTLE GIRL
NIÑERA, LA	BABYSITTER
NIÑERA, LA	NANNY
NINGUNO (A)	NONE
NIÑO, EL	CHILD/LITTLE BOY
NIÑOS, LOS	CHILDREN

NO	NO
NOCHE, LA	EVENING/NIGHT
NOMBRE, EL	NAME
NORTE	NORTH
NOSOTROS	WE
NOVIO (A), EL (LA)	FIANCÉE
NOVIA, LA	BRIDE/GIRLFRIEND
NOVIEMBRE	NOVEMBER
NOVIO, EL	BOYFRIEND
NUBES, LAS	CLOUDS
NUBLADO(A)	CLOUDY
NUECES, LAS	NUTS
NUERA, LA	DAUGHTER-IN-LAW
NUEVO (A)	NEW
NUEZ DE CASTILLA, LA	WALNUT
NUEZ DE INDIA, LA	CASHEW
NUEZ MOSCADO, LA	NUTMEG
NUEZ, LA	PECAN
NÚMERO, EL	NUMBER
NUNCA	NEVER
O	OR
OBEDECER	OBEY (TO)
OBTENER	GET (TO)
OCCURENTE	IMAGINATIVE
OCTUBRE	OCTOBER
OCUPADO (A)	BUSY
OESTE	WEST
OFICINA, LA	OFFICE
OÍR	HEAR (TO)
OJO, EL	EYE
OLAS, LAS	WAVES
OLER	SMELL (TO)
OLLA, LA	POT (COOKING)
OLOER, EL	ODOR
OLVIDAR	FORGET (TO)
ONZA, LA	OUNCE
ORÉGANO, EL	OREGANO
OREJA, LA	EAR
ORGÁNICO(A)	ORGANIC
ÓRGANO, EL	ORGAN
ORINA, LA	URINE
ORO, EL	GOLD
ORUGA, LA	CATEPILLAR
OSCURO(A)	DARK
OSITO DE PELUCHE, EL	TEDDY BEAR
OSO, EL	BEAR
OTOÑO, EL	AUTUMN/FALL
OTRO (A)	ANOTHER
OTRA VEZ	AGAIN
PACIENTE	PATIENT
PADRASTRO, EL	STEPFATHER
PADRE, EL	FATHER
PAGAR	PAY (TO)
PAÍS, EL	COUNTRY
PÁJARO, EL	BIRD
PALA, LA	SHOVEL
PALO, EL	STICK
PAN BLANCO, EL	WHITE BREAD

ESPAÑOL vocabulario

PAN FRANCES, EL	FRENCH TOAST
PAN TOSTADO, EL	TOAST
PAN, EL	BREAD
PANA, LA	CORDUROY
PANADERO, EL	BAKER
PAÑAL DE TELA, EL	CLOTH DIAPER
PAÑAL, EL	DIAPER
PAÑALERA, LA	DIAPER BAG
PANTALONES, LOS	PANTS
PANTANO, EL	SWAMP
PANTORRILLA, LA	CALF
PANTUFLAS, LAS	SLIPPERS
PAPAS, LAS	POTATOES
PAPÁS/PADRES, LOS	PARENTS
PAPAYA, LA	PAPAYA
PAPEL DE ALUMINIO, EL	ALUMINUM FOIL
PAPEL DE BAÑO, EL	TOILET PAPER
PAPEL DE CERA, EL	WAX PAPER
PAPEL DE PLÁSTICO, EL	PLASTIC WRAP
PAPEL, EL	PAPER
PAPERAS, LAS	MUMPS
PARA	FOR
PARADA DEL AUTOBÚS, LA	BUS STOP
PARAMÉDICO, EL	PARAMEDIC
PARAR	STOP (TO)
PARDO/ CAFÉ	BROWN
PARED, LA	WALL
PARIENTES, LOS	RELATIVES
PARILLA DE GAS, LA	GAS RANGE
PÁRPADO, EL	EYELID
PARQUE, EL	PARK
PARTERA, LA	MIDWIFE
PASAPORTE, EL	PASSPORT
PASAS, LAS	RAISINS
PASCUA, LA	EASTER
PASEAR EN BARCO	BOATING
PASILLO, EL	HALLWAY
PASTA DE DIENTES, LA	TOOTHPASTE
PASTA, LA	PASTA
PASTEL BLANCO, EL	WHITE CAKE
PASTEL DE CHOCOLATE, EL	CHOCOLATE CAKE
PASTEL DE ZANAHORIA, EL	CARROT CAKE
PASTEL, EL	CAKE
PASTO, EL	GRASS/LAWN
PATEAR	KICK (TO)
PATÍNES, LOS	SKATES
PATINETA, LA	SCOOTER/ SKATEBOARD
PATINETA, LA	SKATEBOARD
PATIO, EL	PATIO
PATO, EL	DUCK
PAVO, EL	TURKEY
PECHO, EL	CHEST
PEDIATRA, EL	PEDIATRICIAN
PEDIR	ASK FOR
PEGAMENTO, EL	GLUE
PEINE, EL	COMB
PELA , LA	PEEL
PELEAR	FIGHT (TO)
PELÍCULA, LA	MOVIE
PELIGROSO(A)	DANGEROUS
PELIRROJO (A)	RED HEAD
PELOTA, LA	BALL
PELUCHE, EL	STUFFED ANIMAL
PELUQUERÍA, LA	BARBER SHOP
PENE, EL	PENIS
PENSAR	THINK, (TO)
PEPINO, EL	CUCUMBERS/PICKLE
PERA, LA	PEAR
PERDIDO(A)	LOST
PEREJIL, EL	PARSELY
PEREZOSO(A)	LAZY
PERFUME, EL	PERFUME
PERÍCO, EL	PARROT
PERIODISTA, EL	JOURNALIST
PERLAS, LAS	PEARLS
PERNO, EL	BOLT
PERO	BUT
PEROCUPARSE	WORRY (TO)
PERRO, EL	DOG
PERSIANAS, LAS	SHUTTERS/BLINDS
PERSONA MAYOR, LA	OLDER PERSON
PERSONA, UNA	PERSON
PERSONAS, LA	PEOPLE
PESADILLA, LA	NIGHTMARE
PESAR	WEIGH ,(TO)
PESCA, LA	FISHING
PESCADO, EL	FISH
PETUNIA, LA	PETUNIA
PIANO, EL	PIANO
PICANTE	SPICY
PICAPOSTE, EL	WOODPECKER
PICNIC, EL	PICNIC
PIE, EL	FOOT
PIEDRA, LA	ROCK
PIEL, LA	FUR
PIEL, LA	SKIN
PIERNA, LA	LEG
PIJAMA, LA	PAJAMA
PILA, LA	BATTERY
PIMIENTA, LA	PEPPER
PIMIENTO ROJO, EL	RED PEPPER
PIMIENTO VERDE, EL	GREEN PEPPER
PIÑA, LA	PINEAPPLE
PIÑONES, LOS	PINE NUTS
PINTALABIOS, EL	LIPSTICK
PINTAR	PAINT (TO)
PINTURA, LA	PAINTING
PINZAS , LAS	TWEEZERS
PIQUETE, EL	STING/INSECT BITE
PISCINA, LA	POOL
PISO, EL	FLOOR
PISTACHOS, LOS	PISTACHIO
PIZZARÓN, EL	BLACKBOARD
PLANCHA, LA	IRON
PLANEAR	PLAN (TO)
PLANTA, LA	PLANT

bilingual babycare

PLÁSTICO, EL	SPLASH MAT
PLASTILINA, LA	CLAY/PLAY DOH
PLÁTANO, EL	BANANA
PLATO HONDO, EL	BOWL
PLAYA, LA	BEACH
PLOMERO, EL	PLUMBER
PLUMAS, LAS	PENS
PLUMERO, EL	FEATHER DUSTER
PLUMONES, LOS	MARKERS
POBRE	POOR
POCO, UN	A LITTLE
PODER	CAN (BE ABLE)
PODRIDO (A)	ROTTEN
POLICÍA, EL	POLICEMAN
POLICÍA, LA	POLICE
POLILLA, LA	MOTH
POLLO, EL	CHICKEN
POLVO DE HORNEAR, EL	BAKING POWDER
POMADA, LA	OINTMENT
POMPA, LA	BUTTOCK
POPÓ DE GATO, LA	CAT POOP
POPÓ DE PERRO, LA	DOG POOP
POPÓ, LA	POOP
POQUITO, UN	A TINY BIT
POR EJEMPLO	FOR EXAMPLE
POR FAVOR	PLEASE
POR HORA	HOURLY
POR QUÉ?	WHY
PORQUE	BECAUSE
PORTERO, EL	DOORMAN
PORTÓN, EL	GATE
PRECIOSO(A)	BEAUTIFUL
PREGUNTA LA	QUESTION
PREGUNTAR	ASK (TO)
PREMATURO(A)	PREMATURE
PREMIO, EL	REWARD
PRENDER	TURN ON (TO)
PRENDIDO(A)	ON
PREOCUPADO (A)	WORRIED
PRESIDENTE, EL	PRESIDENT
PRESIONADO (A)	PRESSURED
PRIMA. LA	COUSIN (FEMALE)
PRIMAVERA, LA	SPRING
PRIMERO (A)	FIRST
PRIMO, EL	COUSIN (MALE)
PRINCIPIANTE, EL	BEGINNER
PROBLEMAS CARDIACOS, LOS	HEART PROBLEMS
PROFESIÓN, LA	PROFESSION
PROFESIONAL	FREELANCER
PRONOMBRES, LOS	PRONOUNS
PRONTO	SOON
PROTECTOR SOLAR, EL	SUNSCEEN
PROTESTANTE, EL	PROTESTANT
PRÓXIMA VEZ, LA	NEXT TIME
PRÓXIMO (A), EL(LA)	NEXT ONE
PRÓXIMO MES, EL	NEXT MONTH
PSICÓLOGO, EL	PSYCHOLOGIST
PUEBLO, EL	TOWN

PUENTE, EL	BRIDGE
PUERRO, EL	LEEK
PUERTA PRINCIPAL, LA	FRONT DOOR
PUERTA TRASERA, LA	BACK DOOR
PUERTA, LA	DOOR
PUESTA DEL SOL, LA	SUNSET
PULGA, LA	FLEA
PULGADA, LA	INCH
PULIR	POLISH (TO)
PULSERA, LA	BRACELET
PUNTUAL	PUNCTUAL
QUÉ	WHAT
QUEBRAR / ROMPER	BREAK (TO)
QUEDARSE DORMIDO (A)	FALL ASLEEP (TO)
QUEMADO (A)	BURNED
QUEMADURA , LA	SUNBURN/BURN
QUERER	WANT (TO)
QUESO AMARILLO, EL	CHEDDAR
QUESO COTÁJ, EL	COTTAGE CHEESE
QUESO CREMA, EL	CREAM CHEESE
QUESO PARMESANO, EL	PARMESAN
QUESO ROQUEFORT, EL	BLUE CHEESE
QUESO TIPO BRIE, EL	BRIE CHEESE
QUESO TIPO FETA, EL	FETA
QUESO, EL	CHEESE
QUIÉN	WHO
QUIETO (A)	CALM
QUINTILLIZOS	QUINTUPLETS
QUITAMANCHAS, EL	STAIN REMOVER
QUIZÁS	MAYBE
RÁBANO , EL	RADISHES
RADIO, EL	RADIO
RAÍZ, LA	ROOT
RALLA	GRATE (TO)
RAMA, LA	BRANCH
RANCHO, EL	RANCH
RÁPIDO (A)	FAST
RARO (A)	STRANGE
RASGUÑO, EL	SCRATCH
RATA, LA	RAT
RATO, UN	AWHILE
RATÓN, EL	MOUSE
REBANAR	SLICE (TO)
RECÁMARA, LA	BEDROOM
RECETA, LA	PRESCRIPTION
RECICLAR	RECYCLE (TO)
RECOGEDOR DE BASURA, EL	DUSTPAN
RECOMENDAR	RECOMMEND (TO)
REEMPLAZAR	REPLACE (TO)
REFLUJO, EL	REFLUX
REFRESCO, EL	SODA
REFRIGERADOR, EL	REFRIDGERATOR
REFRIGÉRAR	REFRIDGERATE (TO)
REFRIGERIO, EL	SNACK
REGADERA, LA	SHOWER
REGADOR, EL	SPRINKLER
REGALO, EL	PRESENT
REINA, LA	QUEEN

REÍRSE	LAUGH (TO)
RELÁMPAGO, EL	LIGHTNING
RELIGION, LA	RELIGION
REMOJAR	SOAK
RENUNCIAR	QUIT (TO)
REPARTIDOR, EL	DELIVERY PERSON
REPELENTE , EL	INSECT REPELLENT
REPETIR	BURP (TO)
RESBALADIA, LA	SLIDE
RESBALOSO (A)	SLIPPERY
RESIDENTE LEGAL, EL	LEGAL RESIDENT
RESPIRAR	BREATHE (TO)
RESPUESTA, LA	ANSWER
RESTAURANTE, EL	RESTAURANT
REY, EL	KING
RICO (A)	RICH
RINOCERONTE, EL	RHINO
RÍO, EL	RIVER
RODILLA, LA	KNEE
ROJO(A)	RED
ROMERO, EL	ROSEMARY
ROMPECABEZAS, EL	PUZZLE
ROPA BLANCA, LA	WHITES (CLOTHES)
ROPA INTERIOR, LA	LONG UNDERWEAR
ROPA SUCIA, LA	DIRTY LAUNDRY
ROPA, LA	CLOTHES
ROSA	PINK
ROSA, LA	ROSE
ROSADURA, LA	DIAPER RASH
ROSBIF, EL	ROAST BEEF
ROSTIZAR/ASAR	ROAST (TO)
ROTO (A)	BROKEN
RUBIO (A)	BLOND
RUIDO, EL	NOISE
SABADO, EL	SATURDAY
SÁBANA, LA	SHEET
SÁBANAS DE CUNA, LAS	CRIBSHEETS
SABER	KNOW (TO)
SABOREAR	TASTE (TO)
SABROSO(A)	TASTY
SACERDOTE, EL	PRIEST
SACO, EL	SPORTSCOAT
SAL, LA	SALT
SALA, LA	LIVING ROOM
SALADO(A)	SALTY
SALARIO, EL	SALARY
SALCHICHA, LA	HOT DOG/SAUSAGE
SALMÓN, EL	SALMON
SALMONELA, LA	SALMONELLA
SALÓN DE BELLEZA, EL	BEAUTY SALON
SALPICA	SPLASH, (TO)
SALPULLIDO, EL	RASH
SALSA DE BARBACÓA, LA	BBQ SAUCE
SALSA DE SOYA, LA	SOY SAUCE
SALSA, LA	SAUCE
SALTAMONTES, EL	GRASSHOPPER
SALUD	BLESS YOU (AFTER A SNEEZE)
SALVIA, LA	SAGE
SANDIA, LA	WATERMELON
SANGRE, LA	BLOOD
SANTO, EL	SAINT
SAPO, EL	FROG
SARAPIÓN, EL	MEASLES
SASTRE, EL	TAILOR
SAUVE	SOFT
SAXÓFONO, EL	SAXOPHONE
SECADOR PARA EL PELO	HAIR DRYER
SECADORA, LA	DRYER
SECAR AL AIRE	LINE DRY
SECO (A)	DRY
SEDA, LA	SILK
SEGURIDAD, LA	SAFETY
SEGURO DE AUTO, EL	AUTO INSURANCE
SEGUROS, LOS	PINS
SELVA, LA	JUNGLE
SEMANA PASADA, LA	LAST WEEK
SEMANA, LA	WEEK
SEMILLA DE GIRASOL, LA	SUNFLOWER SEED
SEMILLA, LA	SEED
SENO, EL	BREAST
SEÑORITA, LA	SINGLE WOMAN
SENTIR	FEEL (TO)
SEPILLO PARA BOTELLAS, EL	BOTTLE BRUSH
SEPTIEMBRE	SEPTEMBER
SER	TO BE
SERPIENTE, EL	SNAKE
SERVICIO A DOMICILIO, EL	DELIVERY SERVICE
SERVILLETA, LA	NAPKIN
SHORTS, LOS	SHORTS
SI	IF/YES
SIEMPRE	ALWAYS
SIESTA, LA	NAP
SILLA DE RUEDAS, LA	WHEELCHAIR
SILLA PARA COMERDEL BEBÉ, LA	HIGHCHAIR
SILLA, LA	CHAIR
SIMPÁTICO (A)	NICE
SIN AZÚCAR	SUGAR-FREE
SIN GRASA	FAT-FREE
SIN SAL	SALT-FREE
SIN	WITHOUT
SINAGOGA, LA	SYNAGOGUE
SIRENA, LA	MERMAID
SNÓRQUEL, EL	SNORKEL
SNOWBOARD, LA	SNOWBOARD
SOBRE, EL	ENVELOPE
SOBRINA, LA	NIECE
SOBRINO, EL	NEPHEW
SOFÁ, EL	SOFA
SOL, EL	SUN
SOLEADO(A)	SUNNY
SOLO	ALONE
SÓLO/SOLAMENTE	ONLY
SOLTERO (A)	SINGLE
SOMBRA, LA	SHADE
SOMBRERO, EL	HAT
SORPRENDIDO (A)	SURPRISED

SOSTÉN, EL	BRASSIERE
SÓTANO, EL	BASEMENT
SU	THEIR
SUCIO (A)	DIRTY
SUDADERA, LA	SWEATSHIRT
SUEGRA, LA	MOTHER – IN – LAW
SUEGRO, EL	FATHER-IN-LAW
SUELO, EL	GROUND
SUEÑO, EL	DREAM
SUÉTER, EL	SWEATER
SUFICIENTE	ENOUGH
SUPERMERCADO, EL	MARKET
SUR	SOUTH
TALCO, EL	TALCUM POWDER
TALÓN, EL	HEEL
TAMAÑOS, LAS	SIZES
TAMBOR, EL	DRUM
TARDE	LATE
TARDE, LA	AFTERNOON
TARTA, LA	PIE
TAZA, LA	CUP
TÉ DE MANZANILLA, EL	CHAMOMILE
TÉ, EL	TEA
TECHO, EL	CEILING
TECHO, EL	ROOF
TEJIDO, EL	KNIT
TELA, LA	FABRIC
TELÉFONO, EL	TELEPHONE
TELEVISIÓN, LA	TELEVISION/TV
TEMPORADAS DEL AÑO, LAS	SEASONS
TEMPRANO	EARLY
TENDER LA CAMA	MAKE THE BED
TENEDOR, EL	FORK
TENER	HAVE (TO)
TENIS, EL	TENNIS
TENIS, LOS	TENNIS SHOES
TERCIOPELO, EL	VELVET
TERMINAR	FINISH
TERMÓMETRO, EL	THERMOMETER
TERRAZA, LA	PORCH
TERREMOTO, EL	EARTHQUAKE
TÍA, LA	AUNT
TIBURÓN, EL	SHARK
TIEMPO COMPLETO	FULL TIME
TIEMPO, EL	TIME
TIEMPO, EL	WEATHER
TIENDA, LA	STORE
TIERRA, LA	DIRT/EARTH
TIGRE, EL	TIGER
TIJERAS, LAS	SCISSORS
TÍMIDO (A)	SHY
TINA, LA	BATHTUB
TÍNTORERIA, LA	DRY CLEANERS
TÍO, EL	UNCLE
TIPO KOSHER	KOSHER
TIRADERO, EL	MESS
TIRAR	THROW AWAY (TO)
TITERE, EL	PUPPET
TOALLA, LA	TOWEL
TOALLAS DE PAPEL, LAS	PAPER TOWELS
TOALLITA, LA	WASHCLOTH
TOALLITAS DESECHABLES EN EL EXUSADO, LAS	FLUSHABLE WIPES
TOALLITAS HÚMEDAS, LAS	WIPES
TOBILLO, EL	ANKLE
TOCINO, EL	BACON
TODO EL MUNDO	EVERYBODY
TODOS	ALL/EVERYTHING
TOFU, EL	TOFU
TOMAR	TAKE (TO)
TOMATILLO, EL	GREEN TOMATOES
TOMILLO, EL	THYME
TONTO (A)	DUMB
TORMENTA, LA	STORM
TORONJA, LA	GRAPEFRUIT
TORTUGA, LA	TURTLE
TOS, LA	COUGH
TOSTADOR, EL	TOASTER
TRABAJAR	WORK (TO)
TRABAJO, EL	WORK
TRACTOR, EL	TRACTOR
TRAER	BRING (TO)
TRAJE DE BAÑO, EL	BATHING SUIT
TRAJE DE BAÑO, EL	SWIMSUIT
TRAJE, EL	SUIT
TRANSPORTE, EL	TRANSPORTATION
TRAPEADOR, EL	MOP
TRAPEAR	MOP (TO)
TRAPO, EL	RAG
TREN, EL	TRAIN
TRICICLO, EL	TRICYCLE
TRILLIZOS	TRIPLETS
TRINEO, EL	SLED
TRISTE	SAD
TROMBÓN, EL	TROMBONE
TROMPETA, LA	TRUMPET
TRUENO, EL	THUNDER
TÚ	YOU (FAMILIAR)
TULIPÁN, EL	TULIP
ULCERA, LA	ULCER
ÚLTIMO (A), EL(LA)	LAST
UN, UNA	A, AN
UNICORNIO, EL	UNICORN
USTED	YOU (FORMAL)
USTEDES	YOU (PL.)
UVAS, LAS	GRAPES
VACA, LA	COW
VACACIÓN, LA	VACATION
VACIAR	EMPTY (TO)
VAGINA, LA	VAGINA
VAGÓN, EL	WAGON
VAINILLA, LA	VANILLA
VAJILLA, LA	DISHES
VALIENTE	BRAVE
VALLE, EL	VALLEY
VÁLVULA DE AGUA, LA	WATER VALVE

bilingual babycare

Notes

YOUR RECOMMENDATIONS MAKE THE LILAGUIDE BETTER!
please share your notes with us at www.lilaguide.com

Notes